D0511024

The advent of feminism has given rise to a whole literature exploring the lives and attitudes of women. But why, asks Anna Ford, has so little been written by and about the other fifty per cent of the population?

For three years Ms Ford travelled around the country, meeting men from all walks of life, from cabinet ministers and bishops to murderers and dustmen, and inviting them to talk about themselves. Their conversations – ranging from work to women, from families to fantasies – are remarkably candid and revealing, and what they have to say makes controversial and compelling reading which will evoke astonishment and recognition in both men and women.

MEN
A Documentary

Anna Ford

CORGI BOOKS

MEN

A CORGI BOOK   0 552 12727 2

Originally published in Great Britain by George Weidenfeld
& Nicolson Limited

PRINTING HISTORY

Weidenfeld & Nicolson edition published 1985
Corgi edition published 1986

This book is set in 11/12 pt Cheltenham

Corgi Books are published by Transworld Publishers Ltd.,
61 – 63 Uxbridge Road, Ealing, London W5 5SA, in Australia
by Transworld Publishers (Aust.) Pty. Ltd., 26 Harley
Crescent, Condell Park, NSW 2200, and in New Zealand by
Transworld Publishers (N.Z.) Ltd., Cnr. Moselle and
Waipareira Avenues, Henderson, Auckland.

Made and printed in Great Britain by
Hunt Barnard Printing Ltd., Aylesbury, Bucks.

Contents

ACKNOWLEDGEMENTS   vi

1   WHY MEN?   7

2   MEN AS SONS   14

3   MEN AS HUSBANDS   35

4   WIVES   61

5   MEN AS FATHERS   76

6   MEN AS LOVERS AND CUCKOLDS   102

7   DIVORCED MEN   121

8   MAN VERSUS WOMAN   131

9   SEX   151

10   HOMOSEXUALITY   189

11   WORK   206

12   UNEMPLOYMENT, REDUNDANCY AND RETIREMENT   233

13   MEN AND THEIR FEELINGS   249

14   AGEING AND APPEARANCE   272

15   TRADITIONAL MAN   282

16   MAN AND MODERN WOMAN   292

17   CHANGE – THE NEW MEN?   310

18   CONCLUSION   322

INDEXES   330

Acknowledgements

I should like to thank Richard Hoggart for a most helpful exploratory conversation in the early days of my research, Sue Ayton who cheerfully transcribed hundreds of hours of tapes overcoming the difficulties of regional dialect and recordings often made in less than perfect conditions. Emma Dally for invaluable help with research and transcription; Victoria Glendinning who read parts of the manuscripts and gave continual encouragement, my husband Mark for his unflagging support and confidence, and Victoria Petrie-Hay of Weidenfeld and Nicolson for her immediate enthusiasm and support.

I should also like to thank the large number of organizations all over the country: Trade Unions, Professional Associations, Clubs, Local Authorities, Government Departments, Private Firms and Public Industries who helped put me in touch with the men I wanted to interview.

Most of all I should like to thank all the men who agreed to be interviewed, and then gave me as much time as I needed. For their honesty, interest, encouragement, and bravery in agreeing to take part in such a project, and to reveal so much about themselves.

A.F.

Chapter One

WHY MEN?

During the last three years, I have travelled up and down the country revisiting places familiar to me, and staying in towns and countryside that I had never seen, asking men to talk about themselves.

The idea for a book about men began to take shape some years ago, prompted by a number of interests and experiences. Why had so much been written about the lives and attitudes of women and so little about the world of men, and why, more important, was there so little real first-hand information from men themselves? It seemed that few accounts of this kind existed, and although some information could be gleaned from novels, poetry, autobiography and social history, these were not usually by or about ordinary men, those with whom millions of women share their lives at home and at work. I was interested to find out more about Englishmen without their layers of camouflage, partly because I've always been more curious about people than about anything else, and have preferred to observe rather than to belong. I would also rather listen to people talk about themselves than talk about myself; and I wanted, as a woman, to find out more about the world of men.

I grew up in the late 1940s, the second child in a family of five, the only sister among four brothers. We were brought up in country vicarages, mostly in remote districts of Cumberland. At that time, and in the fifties, it was expected that men would have careers and that girls would, on the whole, marry and stay at home. I knew few women who worked and virtually none who had an interesting job, let alone careers, apart from teachers. My mother had been a successful professional actress in the West End before marrying at the age of twenty-three, but then she had followed tradition, given up her work, had children and gone wherever her husband's career took him.

It had seemed to me from an early age that men were somehow more important than women. Fathers were looked after, their needs and comforts thought about and provided for; in return they saw to their families' needs and made most of the major decisions. Rarely in my childhood did I see a man doing housework or preparing a family meal, although he might help with the drying up.

My curiosity about other people's lives led me to study social anthropology at Manchester University in the early sixties, and later to become a journalist. Anthropology taught me a great deal about the difference between what people say they do and what they actually do. I also learnt something from the department's much refined sport of gossip. Later I took a post-graduate course in Adult Education and taught the social sciences at O- and A-level in a college in Belfast. I taught in Northern Ireland for four years until 1974, two of them spent as Staff Tutor in Social Science for the Open University, where part of my job entailed visiting Long Kesh each week to tutor students who were interned there; it was my first experience of talking to men behind bars.

I then took a short contract job as a researcher on local programmes for Granada Television in Manchester. I had little intention of staying in television or making it my career – but I did, later moving to London to work for the BBC on a current affairs programme called *Man Alive*. Through my television work at the BBC and ITN and, for a short spell, on TV-AM I met an extremely broad cross-section of our society and observed a number of widely reported political and professional situations from close at hand and behind the scenes. I was as intrigued as ever by what made people, but in particular men, tick.

As I had worked on television current affairs programmes for some years, my address book was full of the names of politicians, trade union officials, charity organizers, doctors, teachers, scientists, actors, sportsmen, diplomats, coalminers, bomb-disposal experts, farmers and circus artists, to mention but a few. It was to these people, and to my friends and acquaintances, that I turned when I wanted to interview a wide variety of English males. One hundred and twenty men were interviewed at length on tape, and many others found time to talk about experiences of particular significance to them. Their ages ranged from eighteen to ninety-four and they covered all socio-economic classes, professional and non-professional, skilled and unskilled, long-term unemployed and newly redundant, rich and poor, left-wing and right-wing, famous and obscure, powerful and powerless, and were drawn from all over England.

Of those approached only four declined to see me: Denis Thatcher and the Archbishop of Canterbury; Sir Freddie Laker, who was writing his autobiography, and Oliver Reed, who may not have got my letter as he didn't reply.

All the interviews were deliberately open-ended. There was no formal questionnaire demanding that each man talk about exactly the same things, just as there was no theory or thesis about men waiting to be proved. The idea was to encourage men to talk about the things that they wanted, for whatever reason, to talk

9

about. They could concentrate on only one aspect of their lives if they so preferred, or they could range widely. They were told their conversation would be recorded and used as direct quotations in a book with a documentary form. They were encouraged to talk with as little inhibition as possible, and I hope felt secure that they were not being judged as they opened up. It was easy to arrange a meeting-place and it was left to the men as far as possible to suggest somewhere where they would feel comfortable. It was most often at their work-place or in a bar near by, rarely at home. Some of them found it difficult to tell their wives about the interview in case they might later be recognized. In order to allow these men to speak frankly, without fear of identification, all names and locations and, in most cases, the surrounding circumstances have been changed in order to preserve the anonymity of the interviewees. Some were interviewed on several different occasions, and most on average for several hours; therefore much has had to be edited out. The meaning of what was said has not been changed deliberately or, it is hoped, in error, by the necessary editing. I hope I have caught the flavour, the essence, the passion and the individuality of their prejudices and opinions so that each unique personal tone of voice can be heard with all its warmth, its quirkiness and vehemence. Some have been quoted at much greater length than others because I felt their stories were unusually interesting and gave great insight into particular aspects of the male world.

Apart from the men I interviewed at length using a tape-recorder, I talked to many more in odd moments. I talked with them as I worked with them, mostly in television studios or filming; as I sat beside them on committees and in planning meetings, and as I ate beside them in canteens, railway buffets, bars, charity lunches, dinner parties and at supper with friends. I fell into

10

conversation in hotel lobbies, in taxis, trains, queues, shops and aeroplanes; I answered back when I was shouted at from building sites, and interrupted the peace of those on holiday in Italy, France, the Caribbean, and in England. With some exceptions, all the men interviewed have been English and living permanently in England. To venture into the Celtic fringe to talk to Scotsmen, Irishmen and Welshmen, with their broad cultural and historical differences, would make the drawing of even tentative conclusions almost impossible.

In all this I had the advantage of being known because of having presented the nightly news from ITN. I had enough curiosity value for people to answer the letters I sent them, and not put the phone down when I asked for an interview. I wanted to know about them, and they wanted to know a bit about me. In the early days of these interviews, I was told by a number of people, mostly men, not to believe what anyone told me because they wouldn't tell the truth. Men, they said, will boast to you, exaggerate their lives to make them interesting, never show their weaknesses or failures – in fact, not give away what they really feel about anything. Part of me expected this to be true. I was continually surprised by the candour with which men were eventually willing to talk. There did not finally seem to be any taboo areas of conversation. They answered the most intimate questions about their marriage, or sexual preference and fantasies, and even pinpointed the one thing in their life of which they were most ashamed. Yet I was surprised how many men said they had never had so frank a conversation with anyone before, and that they found themselves, for the first time, talking about things they had hardly been conscious of.

There was often what I can only express as a sense of relief as they settled back to examine their lives and feelings. Even the presence of a tape-recorder ceased to be inhibiting, and at the end of three hours many said they had enjoyed themselves. Some men said that putting their thoughts into words had been so useful to them that they would like to keep talking. All were generous with their time. Conversations were frequently on subjects that women think about daily and discuss with their friends but many of the men interviewed said they know no one they could talk to in an unthreatening way about such matters, which they regretted. The interviews were transcribed and the material for the book organized on the basis of what seemed most important to these men. Others might have spoken of different experiences or stressed the importance of each subject in another way. Some subjects, like sport, are given less coverage because although they may be an abiding male passion, not much that was new or revealing was said by the interviewees. Many clearly enjoyed the release of aggression, the sense of belonging to the pack, the pleasure of competition, of winning, of success, of doing something well – a change from humdrum work – but beyond that even the professionals seemed at a loss to describe in anything other than the simplest terms what sport meant to them. My own feeling was that the pleasures *were* simple, and just as described, but so much of this had been said before.

It has been suggested to me that I began this book as an attack on men; I can only say that I hope I approached the subject with an open mind. I wanted to hear what men would tell me. Despite being a woman in a patriarchal society, I do not dislike men, and in the conclusion I explain exactly what I now feel about their world, having been admitted behind the barricades.

So what do I like about men and why do I enjoy their company? The things I particularly like about men are

12

their differentness, their simplicity, their cleverness, their ability to amuse and re-tell life better than it is, their sense of fun, their intelligence, their dependence on women, their boyishness – even childishness – their ability to devote themselves single-mindedly to their interests, their charm, their insecurity, their character and, above all, when they reveal it, their gentleness and vulnerability. In fact, some of my best friends are men.

But what would I find behind the familiar music-hall stereotypes of the man in the bowler hat, or the tough no-nonsense northerner? Would what they said most often be likely to be what they had thought about least? Would I be admitted to the innermost lives and thoughts of men who are so often caught in those group conspiracies against women? Would I find common sets of assumptions which cut across classes and ages? Would there be a sharp division in attitudes between young and old? Of course, it is arguable that there are as many meanings as there are people, but what I hoped would happen was that the hidden meanings common to men, which often lie behind their words, would begin to emerge.

Chapter Two

MEN AS SONS

When men talked about their parents, they often showed a greater intensity of feeling, whatever the shade of love or hate, than at any other time in the interviews. I was startled by the passions revealed and the vigorous descriptions given, sometimes recalled more than sixty years later. They rarely expressed an equal sense of affection for both parents and some men, quite late in life, still blamed one or other parent for having irrevocably damaged their lives. I came across a great deal of unresolved anger, particularly against mothers, who were often spoken of with fear and loathing, as though they still had power of moral judgement over their sons. If they had rejected her they felt guilty; if they had allowed her to dominate, they felt bitter.

Jo aged forty-nine, a Liverpudlian, was constantly fighting depression for the very good reason that he had been made redundant several times in his life and was still unemployed, but all his anger was directed against his mother who had always belittled him in preference to his elder brother.

Her whole attitude towards me as a child was different. She almost seemed to resent me. My mother was always praising him – he could do no wrong. She seemed to get very short-tempered with me and ran me down a lot. I was unhappy then and I hate her now for what she did to me. When my mother died I didn't go to her funeral.

Other men felt their parents had demanded too much of them and were always disappointed. Mick, a forty-year-old who works in the film industry, said he had only just begun to feel the pleasure of self-confidence and found the honesty to face his own shortcomings. All his early life he had lived up to some grand expectation that his mother had of him, which had led him into a life of subterfuge and uncomfortable dishonesty.

If you were to meet my mother you would think, that charming wonderful woman. Fancy having her as a mother, you'd be able to tell her everything. Because she chats, people from the town we lived in, my friends who are still around, go and chat to her, tell her their problems. I couldn't tell her anything like that, there was no communication. I thought at the time I was protecting her but it wasn't that at all. I was protecting myself. I didn't want her criticism, I didn't want the response that she would give: 'You're disappointing me', 'You're another disappointment', 'You've done something else.' I lived with a girl when I was at university in the sixties, and I never dared admit it to my mother. I'd behave completely differently now. I was a pretty conventional young man, and that's a lot to do with her. My parents were divorced, my father was an alcoholic, something else I didn't admit at the time. I hid it till I was thirty. I just used to pretend that I came from a nice happy background.

Arthur, a retired rural dean of seventy, said he had always hoped that he would find out that he had been adopted, though he had never enquired. Because he had found his mother so intolerable he could not bear the idea of being her son.

I never liked Mother. I once told her I could murder her. I remember saying that with deep passion. She used to read my private letters which weren't all that important, but I thought it unforgivable.

Ian, a dentist aged thirty-three, found it hard to be

demonstrative with his own children because his mother's coolness had affected him.

I really don't know why my mother had children; we seemed to be an awful nuisance to her. She spent as little time with us as possible. I don't remember her cuddling me, or listening to anything I had to say.

Mike, a company executive of fifty-one with four children, had similar problems. His greatest regret was his inability to have any physical relationships with his own children; he had never cuddled them or even put his arm round them, and now it seemed almost too late to start. He had been brought up by an imposing grandmother, although his parents had been alive: his mother and father separated when he was very young.

Neither of them were very cuddly people. In my home, physical contact, touching, physical gestures were not part of life at all.

The desire for affection, for attention from parents, the feeling of rejection when it is not forthcoming, the guilt and the lasting pain, are not Freudian fantasies but all too real to some men. As Colin, an advertising copywriter aged forty-six, said:

My mother died when I was fifteen. My father married again very quickly. But I still feel guilty about my mother; there she was and none of us really took any notice of her, none of us thought about *her* much. She worked non-stop for the pleasure of looking after us. I know mothers are like that but I'd hate it to happen to my wife. My wife often talks about us having children but, honestly, I'm rather nervous. Deep down, I think there's an awful feeling that it was us children that really killed my mother.

Harry, a silversmith, has had various successes in his life, but now, at fifty-four and married three times, he wonders what went wrong.

The first woman in my life was called Mrs Stone. It was a name that suited her amazingly well. She looked after me and my sister when I was very little. My mother was away working some of the time to help the family finances. Mrs Stone was naturally hard-hearted and made us eat everything. I remember my sister hiding slimy bacon fat in her knickers to drop it on the way to school. Although I'm sympathetic to Women's Lib intellectually, on an emotional plane I'm not absolutely happy about it because I think my mother abandoned me when I probably needed her most. I remember being scolded by Mrs Stone for leaving an enormous brown turd under the garden shed. Why wasn't my mother there, and would she have been really cross?

It has always seemed to me that women ruled. Not of course the important outside political world of business, power and politics; but the intimate things, the things of the family, behaviour, what is right and wrong. My father was away for the war and several years afterwards. I grew up in a household almost entirely of women. My mother had a great friend, a woman chemist, who lived with us and probably got my sister and I to go to college. The men who came into our ken at this time seemed to go along with what the women said, either for an easy life or perhaps from a sense of guilt. My father came back from the war and into battle with my mother. On the whole he seemed to be the silent partner. I remember he left a patch of oil from his hair on the wallpaper behind the sofa – he worked in a garage then; he had a passion for cars and was happiest under any old bonnet. Anyway, my mother used to round on him for this stain on her household. He dumbly went out to his workshop, an ex-army officer with decorations for bravery in the field, chastised, whistling grimly through his teeth. He's been dead for ten years and I miss him. I suppose you need your mother to love you; but you need a father around so you can gain his respect.

Toby, a twenty-three-year-old management trainee at a large London store, was sympathetic to the demands of modern feminists because of his mother's behaviour and his father's treatment of her:

17

My mum's quite humble. She's strange, Mum. She never thinks of herself; she always thinks of the children, she always thinks of other people. If somebody has a baby, even if she doesn't know them she'll send them a present. Even though she's got very very little money, she'd spend her last £2, or whatever, on a present for somebody else's baby she doesn't even know. She's that type of person. When my dad used to take her to restaurants, she would just pick the cheapest thing on the menu. If somebody bought her a diamond ring or some really beautiful clothes, she'd never wear them because she wouldn't want to seem too dressed up.

My mother left home when I was fourteen. There was a day when Dad said, 'Right, out!'

That night was terrible. I remember it very vividly. I was asleep upstairs and I heard all the shouting, so I came downstairs and said, 'What's going on?'

Dad said, 'Your mum's leaving *now*.'

Mum had met this guy just before she left, but my father had already been going out with somebody else, so it was him that started it all off. And when she did the same thing, he didn't like it. It seems very unfair. I blame my dad for all this more than anybody. It was more that my dad was away a lot of the time. In fact, my dad went out with two people before my mother left. With one, he actually left home and stayed. After that, I don't know how Dad can turn round and say, 'Look –'. I just couldn't believe it.

It was the worst thing in my life, when my mother and father weren't getting on well and they were at home. Not when my mother left. I felt helpless in a way because I was too young to do anything about it. At thirteen, fourteen, you're too young to say, 'Look, Dad, don't you dare say anything else!' or 'Mum and Dad, what in the hell do you think you're doing fighting?' I didn't feel so sad for myself but for my sister, because I could see the effect it was having on her. She used to go upstairs and cry because she didn't understand what was going on. That went on for about a year.

After my mum had gone we all realized things were far better the way they were. We saw our mum regularly and also had peace and quiet at home.

Now Toby totally accepts, and is surprised that others don't, that women have to lead independent lives, and finds it hard to comprehend that they used to be constantly treated as less important than men. He found it sad that his mother had always downgraded herself. Arthur, the rural dean who admitted he had wished to kill his mother, said he got on well with his father – although he only got to know him just before he died.

He was a gentle, intelligent man who used to hide behind the paper and his work. He was very tolerant. I felt quite protective towards him. I remember coming home from school one day when I was thirteen and telling him he must not read *All Quiet on the Western Front* because, I thought, what will he do if he comes to that awful line, 'letting out a mighty fart'? I thought if he reads the word 'fart', it will be the end, he won't be able to stand it. He was so proper, bless his heart. And he was so delighted that his son had tried to save him from a fate worse than death.

But most men felt much more antagonistic and defiant. Edward, a forty-eight-year-old bank manager, knew that he had been virtually at war with his father in his teens:

I don't think a woman can understand that. I've squared up to my father. We've never had a fight and we've never had violence between us. But when boys are in their teens and chemically are becoming very aggressive and very self-assertive, they think their father knows nothing.

Paul, a teacher in his thirties, who described his father as 'an authoritarian old bully', remembers the actual day when he knew he had won this battle with his father, so that henceforward their relationship was on quite a different footing, but fears he sees too much of his father in himself.

I was about to go to college; I must have been eighteen and still living at home. I'd made some remark to my father that he wanted an apology for. He blew his top and insisted I apologize, but I didn't think I was in the wrong. A year before I'd have done it and slunk out. I just looked at him and walked out of the house. I knew from that moment that I'd cracked it. He's never behaved like that to me again. . . . I'd say I felt it as a mixture of freedom and pity. I was actually sorry for the old bugger – I suppose I didn't like to see him beaten. . . . I was the last of three sons and I was leaving home. My father was a school teacher and he was very old-fashioned. The thing that irritated me a lot was how he used to shout at us children: 'I will not have you behaving in that way in *my* house,' It made me wonder where the rest of us lived. He also tried to send us to our rooms when we were quite old. He just always had to be in control. The awful thing is I can see myself in him, now, when I'm teaching. I say something sharp to a kid and I think, Hell, I sounded just like Father.

Security officer Dennis, aged fifty-nine, who admits he is extremely strict with his own children and has only recently managed to share any family decisions with his wife, blames the Victorian nature of his own upbringing.

My mother was very submissive, very. And providing she supplied my father with an evening meal, life was all right. If she didn't have one, there would be trouble. He never struck her but he kept her short of money. He and his brother would go out and spend money on drink, but if *she* wanted more money he wouldn't give it to her. Then she'd say, 'Well, you went out and had some drink.'

He'd reply, 'I work for it, you work here. I earned it, I will spend it how I think.'

My mother never worked outside the house, no. He wouldn't let her and I think she then accepted that that was her fate. Her sisters were the same, her mother was the same: she accepted it.

He never praised me in front of other people, he would put me down. When I got married he gave me a second-hand TV set. He resented me and I resented him because he was a bully. I tell him that.

But a London dustman, thirty-five-year-old Kevin, had a sneaking admiration for parental firmness.

My father was strict with us. He wouldn't think twice about giving me a belt. He'd belt me for bunking off school. He caught me smoking once, and he gave me a belt for that. Hasn't stopped me smoking, though.

If I had any children, I think I'd bring them up the same way that my parents brought us up. It never done us any harm.

Men who knew that their fathers were having affairs saw only their mothers' points of view. Not one thought his father had good reason for the affair, even with hindsight, which led some to develop feelings of intense dislike for their fathers, which they carried into adult life. Steven, an RAF officer in his mid-forties, said:

My mother was divorced by my father before I was born. He's dead now – he died last year. I do resent the fact that he left us. My mother wasn't bitter about my father in a malicious nasty way, but I suppose it must have filtered through to make me resent my father. He called round once, about three years ago. It was the first time I'd ever seen him. I didn't quite sling him out of the house but I left him standing on the doorstep.

I don't feel I've been a very good father. The kids seem to be all right, but I'm not sure if they just put up with me or what. I just feel I know so little about being a father, because I've never had any instructions, if you like.

Barry, a young musician of twenty-five, thought his parents had a perfect marriage until his mother discovered his father was having an affair. He now thinks women are too submissive and doubts if he will ever trust anyone enough to consider marriage:

My father had been having an affair for five years; my mother literally went into the car and found a letter. I seriously don't think she'll ever get over it completely, although she's now living with someone else. I was away at school and it was like jumping chapters for me. I remember that time vividly. You become very impressionable at that age – eleven or twelve. One holiday everything was normal, the next holiday something was wrong, but no one was really saying anything.

My father kept saying,'Oh, your mother's not very happy, she's just not very well.' I remember we had a holiday in Hove and my mother was just crying all the time, and then she left early. She just got on the train and went. There was just this total alienation between my parents and I didn't know why. I was sympathetic to my mother because she was the one that was overtly suffering, and after the split up I went through a time of disliking my father. I was a real bastard. I made him suffer badly. I used him purely as a means of finance for six years. He tried to spoil me, tried to buy me, and his new wife tried to buy me. I hate his wife and she knows that I hate her. I mean I'm just so horrible to her, yet all the time she's nice to me. I hate her more for that. If she turned round and said, 'Fuck off' or 'Go to hell', I'd respect that, but, no, she sort of whinges up to me. It's certainly affected my view of marriage – I won't get married. You can never trust anyone sufficiently. My mother trusted my father totally. I don't think she was wrong to do that but she was certainly naive. My father used to do a lot of travelling and it transpired that through the travelling he would go off with this other woman. He would always say, 'Oh, don't worry, I'll phone you.' I think my father realizes he made a mistake. He lost my mother and got what he was looking for and now he realizes it's not what he wanted anyway.

My mother is always gentle, always listens. She's someone who will always stand by me whatever I do, however cruel I am. She'll always stand by me, she'll always love me. There's nothing that she wouldn't do for me.

I'm not sure how all this has affected my view of women. It's very difficult. You see, if I say that I think women are submissive, I think to a certain extent it's true.

Some working-class men talked with pride of their strict upbringing; they felt that what had been good for them and had guided them in life was equally good for their children. Others obviously also thought that what had been good enough for their mothers was also good enough for their wives and hinted as much, although they did not say so directly. Their mothers had been at home all day long so they tended to assume that they must have been happy with their lot. Some of them talked a little uneasily about their wives being rather different.

Ron, at forty-eight, is the senior foreman in a large factory.

My father was the old-fashioned sort; what he said went. He was strict. I could never have a motorbike, for instance, when I was sixteen. I was going to leave home because I couldn't have one. Until I was twenty-one the couple of times I asked him, he just said, 'No.' I feel the same about my son. I would hate him to go round on a motorbike.

My father's a motor engineer. He works for British Rail. My mother's only ever worked for a very limited period, during the war, just on assembly. I don't think my father ever liked her working. She's the old-fashioned type that stops at home. . . .

My mother's a very homely person. She comes from up north, so there's always a good table. That's why I'm the size I am, because she thinks more about putting things on the table and keeping the house comfortable than anything. That's her job and she's quite happy to do it.

She's very loyal and really very nice. If I had clashes with my father as a youngster, she used to act as a buffer. My father would never hit us, though my mother would. She had a stick on the table if we were misbehaving. She only ever whacked us in a temper – never in cold blood. I had a normal happy childhood. Before I was married my mother had done everything for me.

My wife's not really like my mother, no. She's a little bit independent, and she's quite well educated, a lot better educated than I am. When my wife was ill I used to feel a little bit sorry for myself but, I mean, I could go to my mother's.

In this way wives were expected to fulfil the role of absent mothers in marriage. Jack, a forty-three-year-old Cumbrian farmer, has seven brothers and sisters, and saw his mother's role, that of cook and general factotum, as essential to the proper running of the farm. It was an important job that she was proud to do. He says the pattern of farm life has not changed much in forty years; in harvest time, the men may still get fed before the women, and would never think to help in the house.

Well, come lambing or harvest time, I need all the help I can get. We can't stop for food some days – eat on the hoof and have a good tea when we get in. I never helped in the house when I were a boy, wouldn't have thought to. As the girls grew up, they had their jobs to do and helped Mam. We just came in to eat and went out again. Yes, we did get the best of everything, that was the way.

Everyone thought the world of my mother; she wasn't a big woman but she was very strong. I don't remember her ever being ill. She were up at five or six of a morning. She looked after the dairy, separated the milk, made butter and cream, looked after t'chickens and t'calves and any weak lambs. She'd help with harvest if she could, she liked coming out to the fields. Well, I'd say she *was* happy. I've never stopped to think, really. We all relied on her a lot. She had a hard life, but happy, I should think.

Men from poor backgrounds were full of admiration for the way their mothers had managed under difficult conditions. Walter is a fifty-four-year-old train driver from the north-east.

I was nine when the war started; my dad was on the reserve in the army so he went off straightaway on Friday the 1st of September 1939. I was the man of the family then. My mother got a job as a full-time postwoman, and she was there from the start of the war up to five or six years ago, delivering post. Conditions have improved now, but they weren't too good then. They used to have split shifts – they started at five in the morning, which meant getting up at four and walking there. She worked till about ten, then used to go home until about one in the afternoon, then come back again. It was from five in the morning until five at night. And she did that and

24

looked after three children as well. She used to take in washing twice a week. I used to go up the middle-class end of town with a little trolley and a basket and collect the washing that she did for threepence. And then she used to buy apples and make toffee-apples and sell them. She had a very hard life.

The ghosts of the wars still haunt remarkably many families, but when the war finished Walter's father returned and new adjustments had to be made all round.

I was fifteen when my father came back from the war, I suppose to a large extent we were strangers by then. He and my mother didn't get on well; it was a difficult period. It was a difficult relationship before the war and then six years is a long time. My father had, in fact, been in the front line all the time – he went to Africa and he went through Italy. But my mother didn't want to know. So he used to talk to me when he'd had a couple of drinks. He's cried, he's broke down and cried to me, to get if off his chest. He had had some nasty experiences. He was the only survivor, for some reason – all the others got killed. A number of times that happened. He was thirty-nine then. He often used to say he wished he'd never come back. He wished he'd died with his comrades.

Steven, the RAF officer mentioned earlier, was brought up entirely by women until his mother remarried, but this didn't make him any more at ease with them.

When I was young I was totally embarrassed by females. Perhaps all the overpowering women being in control made me feel like that – I've never really analysed it.

I could only remember women as characters in my life – aunts, grandmothers – and no men really except for a renegade uncle, the black sheep of the family, who always seemed to be running away from something. By the time I was twenty, I was still blushing at the thought of mentioning a girl's name or asking a girl out.

So not having had a close male figure to model himself on, and feeling ill at ease with women, he joined the

RAF and found the comradeship and male stereotypes and even the father-figure he had lacked.

I loved every minute of it. I suddenly felt totally more at ease with a group of chaps than I was talking to a girl. It was very disciplined at college, we had a super chap there, a flight sergeant, who struck the fear of God into everybody, but also had our utmost respect. I suppose that was part of the indoctrination that went on.

In the case of Ronald, a thirty-two-year-old VAT inspector, a happy boarding-school atmosphere had made up for family deficiencies:

I get on well with my parents but you wouldn't ever call us close. Neither my mother nor my father are very demonstrative, and affection towards both myself and my sister was probably more in a material sense than any physical sense. I missed them at times. . . . I feel more affection sometimes from my father than I do from my mother. I think she must have cuddled me, but you were always aware that it was like a stiff arm, not a real giving. I've thought about the effect that has had on me sometimes. My wife and I are very much that way – lots of cuddles. Now my sister is very good at making sort of superficial relationships with people, she has a lot of very good friends. But she's twenty-five now – this is going to sound awful – and she's never had a proper boyfriend. She hasn't been able to form a link, and she was the one that stayed at home and didn't go to boarding school. She was the one surrounded by that atmosphere between my parents all her life.

Nanny, like the RAF or boarding school, often helped to enhance narrow, dreary or cold childhoods. Many men spoke of nanny's influence as a surrogate mother and how they still referred subconsciously to nanny's strictures on behaviour. Because these men saw so much of their nanny as children, and lived almost exclusively in the nursery, their early memories of their parents were sometimes rather hazy. Much has been written about that aspect of English childhood; here I will quote a retired diplomat, Harold, aged ninety-four.

I was born in 1890 – quite a long time ago. In a way I remember my early years better than I remember more recent times. I think one's impressions were so much nearer the ground, as it were, and you got much more indelible impressions of life as a child. I loved life in the nursery. We had a very jolly and cuddly nanny. She was rather strict but full of interesting things to say. My parents were not as close to us then, but I can remember being fond of them both. My father wasn't an ogre, as many fathers were in those days, but of course, as children we didn't see a great deal of him. He was a lawyer with a busy practice and a bit of a dreamer. My mother was charming and gentle. I certainly don't remember either of them cuddling us as children, Good Heavens, no. We were taken downstairs each day – if required – between four and five and allowed to play in my mother's drawing room. But silently: we were not allowed to make a noise. My mother died when I was a boy and I minded bitterly. My mother at that age meant a great deal more to me than my father had.

Many men I spoke to mentioned the tedium of ageing parents. Even when as children they had been fond of them, there were many irritating things about them as they grew older. One of the worst things was coping with parents who would not accept that their children were now adults themselves. Mothers worried about their sons' mortgage commitments and lifestyle, and were often overtly critical of the way the grandchildren were being brought up. Although many men still said they respected their parents, they admitted that it was an advantage to have a house that was simply too small to be shared with them. It was a common belief that the presence of one or other parent put an unbearable strain on a marriage. At forty-nine Leslie is a successful advertising executive with a large house on the outskirts of London. He said:

Oddly enough my wife could cope if my mother came to live with us, but I should have to leave home after about twenty-four hours. She is the most irritating woman imaginable, and thinks every trivial thing she says is interesting. In every conversation she relates everything to herself. If I told you the most fascinating story about Paris, she would say, 'Oh, yes, I went to Paris once.' I'm lucky enough to be able to pay for her to go to a home, and I'm afraid that's what'll happen.

Walter, from a poor working-class district in the north, is irritated by his mother's narrowness as she grows older and gets out and about less – though he can see that she had the brain to become better educated. It is not surprising perhaps that, without a husband and three children to look after, her intelligence 'showed itself less and less as time went on'. What is odd is that, with the benefit of some education himself, and after some thought, he cannot see why she was held back.

I'm not particularly close to my mother. I give her what she's entitled to as a mother, but I didn't choose her and she didn't choose me. I thank her for what she did for me but, as soon as I established my life away from the nest, that was it. What irritates me about her is the level of conversation and her interests. When I'm concerned with wider principles and the wider world, she confines herself into a smaller area. I avoid her. She talks of trivialities, domestic trivialities, and she'll treat me as though I'm still a seven-year-old or an eight-year-old.

It's always been my contention that girls are more intelligent than boys, but something stifles, snuffs them out at some point in time. I don't know what causes this. When my mother was at school, she was kept on, she was used as cheap labour as a teacher, so she had quite an amount of intelligence and education. It just showed itself less and less as time went on.

Parents who openly expressed preferences between their children created lifelong jealousies. The Liverpudlian Jo, quoted first in this chapter, said he had felt that his mother had always loved his elder brother more than him:

My brother would always have things that were new. He was taken to the shops and allowed to choose them. I always had his hand-me-downs, things I didn't like, but I had no choice. He got new things when he didn't need them; I didn't get the things I needed. It wasn't just the material things – her whole attitude to me as a child was different.

I could hear the rancour in this man's voice even now after thirty-five years. Others felt that they had not been wanted, that they were an unfortunate afterthought, altogether a mistake, whereas a much loved brother was not so regarded. Parental attitudes towards sisters could colour a man's way of looking at women for life. Jack, the Cumbrian farmer, was well aware that his sisters were expected to do women's work about the place, like their mother, while he was off with his brothers to learn men's work, for that was the nature of their lives. But in some families men were discouraged from being independent and were kept in a curious state of proud subjection.

The Jewish mother who treats her husband as another child, no matter how powerful he might be in the outside world, and who forces her children to even greater dependence and feelings of guilt, is an extreme example of what happens when strong and powerful women of any faith are given no outlet in the world at large and so spend all their time dominating their children's lives. There is no way of pleasing such a mother. Jeremy, aged twenty-nine, an estate agent, is a classic example of this.

I was born in a comfortable Jewish suburb. My father works in the rag trade and has done very well for himself. . . .

I get on with my parents up to a point. In a sense, I think I'm

29

largely responsible for that. I think I could have made it a lot more difficult than it is. In fact, when I was an adolescent I did make life difficult. That period's still going on as far as they're concerned in some ways. They're not strict Orthodox Jews, but they're mainstream bourgeois – in the classic French sense of bourgeois – straight-down-the-road, highly conformist, and they keep a kosher household. As a child I used to think that kosher was the same for everyone, but soon found that we were not absolutely kosher like the people who live next door who were utlra-Orthodox. Nor did we accept what the Reform Synagogue do where they don't seem to be so worried about being kosher. It just seemed that we determined what was right for us.

My father's a bizarre man in many ways. He's got a very lively individual sense of humour, and is very practical and wheeler-dealerish about the way he treats money. He was keen on sports. And all of that was quite exciting to a kid, because you could grow up and get your cricket and your football, and it would all be encouraged and yet it fell within those neatly defined boundaries of still remaining Jewish. It didn't conflict with it because achievement, in those fields, was still about being Jewish as well. *We* can achieve in those fields; *we* can be good at cricket – which is actually something that I think is excellent. . . . At the same time, there were some very sharp limitations placed on me by my father about things I could do and couldn't do. For example, I've never quite forgiven them for [my] not being able to take part in school productions because it conflicted with the Sabbath. One of the rules was that Friday night was sacrosanct; Saturday, sacrosanct. Going to things on those days, therefore, was out. I certainly resented it bitterly then; I really objected to that but I never ran away from it. . . .

My parents were certainly not well-educated in the sense that they never went to college – but they did have challenges in their youth, there's no doubt about it. They broke out of certain strict Polish Jewish ideas–I suppose Yiddish conceptions – yet at the same time, held on to the bulk of them. And I think the war did a lot to bring them back into line, out of any sort of threat of unorthodoxy. My father was a businessman at a very early age and he saw that as a way of surviving. His values grew out of his everyday life and practice.

Part of my parents' vision is so tightly sealed that as a child I looked out amazed at the rest of the world and asked, what are they really like – bacon, non-kosher food, non-Jewish values, the whole language of *goyim*, otherness, things that are not of us, things that have nothing to do with us? And I knew that for me to break out would be to have everything break down. . . . It would be a betrayal of their traditions; it would be a betrayal of their community. They regard themselves as standard-bearers. Other people may not follow it as well as we do, but we intend to stick to this, they say, and we can't see why you shouldn't either.

My first girlfriend was Jewish, but a Reformed Jew. Her parents invited me out. It was probably one of the first times I had not had kosher food. I didn't die – I didn't expect to die! And when I came home, I thought, Okay, I'm going to test the water. Of course, the reaction was completely wild, completely over the top. My father refused to tell my mother on the grounds that it would upset her too much. He was absolutely in a rage – door slamming, and saying 'I've a good mind not to let you see the girl again.' He never actually did use that as a sanction because I think he knew that it wouldn't happen. Even today, I probably envisage the problems of family life in my head as being worse than they would be if I was actually to talk them out. To friends who thought for a long time that I was giving in too much to my family, and not fighting enough, I used to say, 'No, you don't understand what it would mean to them.' And, of course, they would be heartbroken, but in a sense they're heartbroken anyway. I think that's the position we've probably arrived at now. If I married out, I think they would cut me off – but not necessarily materially. I think they would be heartbroken. I don't think there's a satisfactory solution.

I am an atheist. From the age of sixteen onwards, I decided that I was either going to be an Orthodox rabbi or a revolutionary. And in fact I became a revolutionary. Not because I was a dogmatist; it's just that you've either got to take what you're doing seriously or not do it at all. On that principle, I shifted very far to the left. I went through a rapid self-education process, trying to come up with all the answers to all the problems in the world.

My brother became a Zionist and used it as an escape from my parents because it was the only way he could get out. He wasn't prepared to fight on any of the more serious issues. I think my parents are aware of that and have never quite forgiven him for it. I suspect in a way they feel they've lost him. I had such a poor view of myself because I was never good enough as a kid to do the things they wanted me to do. . . . I could never satisfy them. And it just got worse because it then collided with the fact that I wanted to do other things than what they wanted. I wasn't going to be a businessman, I wasn't going to enter the business, I wasn't going to be a Jewish man, I wasn't going to have a family. . . . Destroying their innermost hopes left a huge sense of guilt, which I've still got. And that's always been the most terrible shackle on my relationship to women, I think, as well. In a practical sense, I wonder if they'll cut me off. But much deeper, emotionally, than that, in order to have a relationship with someone, even if they didn't know about it, I've got to somehow cope with this tightrope that I'm walking. At college, people were astonished. They said, 'How can you still be like that? Why didn't you deal with all that when you were younger, like the rest of us?'

The biggest questions of my life, emotionally, are what I would like *not* to have. I would love to have had a childhood in which I wasn't repressed; I wish I didn't have such a low opinion of myself and didn't lack self-confidence. It all gets me down and it's a very intricate relationship between that and guilt and sexual feelings; they're all bound together in this tight little nucleus.

Many social and cultural traditions are handed down to the next generation through the family . . . which assures society's continuity, but also means that patterns are slow to change. For the most part, many of the grandparents of those talking in this chapter were themselves the product of a much sterner, older ethos when fathers were out at work all day, sharing with the mother neither responsibility nor affection for the children. The father dominated because he was the bread-winner and, more often than not, the family's sole means of support. Social services were meagre. The mother was often a prisoner of child-bearing, struggling bravely, old before her time, sharing a house and a bed, but not a life, with a distant – and frequently disloyal – husband. The offspring of such marriages had softened the tradition by the time they became parents but they were still inclined to be disciplinarians, not given to cuddling and human contact, often indifferent and occasionally neglectful. The men had affairs, while the women were still sometimes drudges who had given up their work to look after the family; the father still dominated and the mother still ran the house without benefit of machinery.

Not all memories of childhood were as harsh as those of the Jewish estate agent, but all had taken a good hard look at how their parents had treated them and recognized what they had not cared for. They were unlikely to repeat exactly the same mistake with their own off-spring, but few had looked at the overall family pattern and thought it could do with a major overhaul.

One or two were drily aware that they had not made many changes to the old patterns of parental behaviour and had the honesty to admit it. They did not think the way they had been reared had been all that bad, found it hard to display affection, and knew that they were set in a similiar mould to their own parents. Even those who were most antagonistic to the way they had been brought up did not express any desire for radical change: most wished to correct specific wrongs which they felt they had suffered and to soften the outline, but overall the impression is one of caution. Many had been part of the enormous social changes forced on families by increasing social mobility and in particular by major rehousing programmes, where the old extended family pattern has disappeared. Running through all the conversations is a feeling that the older generation were tougher, harsher, more uncompromising than they need have been; that parents should be kinder, more affectionate, more sympathetic and gentler with their children. Later I look at how these men cope with being parents in their turn, but first, men as husbands.

Chapter Three

MEN AS HUSBANDS

Despite misgivings about what they might have heard and seen in their own parental homes, despite the divorce figures, when they grow up most adults want to get married. The assumption that those who desire a female companion will fall in love and marry is socially a strong one. A few informants had nightmares and phobias about being in a trap, but for the most part they went ahead with greater or lesser enthusiasm. Many reasons were put forward for deciding to get married, but several stood out clearly: because they had made their girlfriend pregnant, because they had fallen in love, because they wanted a regular sex-life, because they wanted children, or because they were unhappy living on their own and craved companionship.

Robin, a forty-eight-year-old insurance salesman, felt forced into marriage.

I was twenty-five when I first got married, and she was pregnant. It was the thing to do in those days. My father said, 'If she's good enough to sleep with, she's good enough to marry', and you just didn't leave a girl with a baby because it was very, very bad form. I did have doubts about it. I regret it from her point of view and I regret it from my own. I think she had reservations too: we weren't the right sort of type to get married, we didn't really gel.

He lived to regret it. After years of painful quarrels, the marriage broke up. He had been pressured into it by an earlier generation, but Bob, a fifty-eight-year-old prison officer, tells an extraordinary story of how he was ensnared by the woman herself.

I was born in 1926. My father was an ex-army officer – a disillusioned one – who turned poultry farmer. Largely because of ill health, I didn't go to school until I was eight. I was desperately shy and for a long time they thought I was going to be a dwarf; I just didn't grow. I was a skinny, miserable little fella. In 1938 I was sent to boarding school where I was terribly unhappy. I was bullied and made fun of. There were two schoolmistresses and one master who used to take the mike out of me something terrible. They poked fun at me. I started thinking I ought to throw myself over a cliff, and I retreated into myself because I was so small. In the end, my parents realized that all was not well and they sent me to another school in Devon. That was as different as could be and I stayed very happily there until 1944. . . .

I joined the Parachute Regiment because it was the nearest I could get to being in the air force and I'd failed the entrance exams.

I had a girlfriend by this time. I'd met her in Scotland when I was doing my training up there. The thing had been progressing favourably but then we had a hell of a row. She'd come down for the weekend . . . to stay in this seedy little hotel in Bayswater on her own – I wasn't with her – and it was a bloody awful place, from what she described. Somehow the thing got out of hand and we had a damn good row and she went back to Scotland.

If it wasn't within days, it was within weeks, but I was standing at a bus stop having been to the cinema. There was a woman in the queue who got into conversation with me, and we travelled back on the bus together. She was chattering away and said she worked in the army telephone exchange. We arranged to meet the next Sunday afternoon.

I suppose I was in need of comforting, but one thing led to another, and then I began to live with her. She was vastly older than I was. I was not quite twenty-one and she claimed to be thirty-two. I wasn't bothered. This went on for six months when, without any warning, she said, 'I'm going to have a baby. You're the father.'

I didn't know what to do. I believed her, of course. . . . I must have been a very naive twenty-one-year-old; people in those days were. I didn't know very much. I'd been a virgin; she was the first woman I'd ever had. I'd been keeping myself, you see, for the girl in Scotland. Anyway, I didn't have any money, I couldn't buy her off. And she didn't invite me to. I didn't want to marry her at all but I'd been accepted for the officers' training school and I knew that I couldn't do that with a paternity order round my neck. It left me with only one alternative. I married her in Woking Registry Office in 1948. I can remember weeping bitterly with her in a field outside, the evening before we were married.

We'd been married about a month when she said she wasn't pregnant any more. I got a message from the company commander saying that my wife was ill and I'd better go home. When I got home she was sitting there quite cheerfully smoking a cigarette. 'What's wrong with you?' I asked.

'It's gone,' she said.

'What do you mean?' I said. 'What's gone?'

'The baby. It's gone down the lav.'

Well, I think I said, 'Christ, you could've brought it on three weeks earlier.'

Anyway, that was that. I don't think she was ever pregnant. She'd married me. I was trapped. Hooked. If ever a bloke was hooked, I was then. There had been things I liked about her. She was a wholesome woman and she was fun. She was well-dressed, well-groomed and scrupulously clean. . . . After I'd been to the officers' training school I got commissioned and was posted to Carlisle. A colleague of mine had a posting in West Africa and I asked him if he would change with me. He was delighted; he'd got a girlfriend in North Wales. I told my wife that I was going to West Africa and I was going without her. . . . She was furious. Livid. . . .

I was out in West Africa for eighteen months and I used to write to her to keep her quiet. Then, later, I came back to take a draft of troops out to Malaya. On my embarkation leave I tried to find out a few bits and pieces about my wife. I found her in the milliner's shop where she was working and I told her quite unceremoniously that I wanted to talk to her. We wandered up to the park.

'Look,' I said to her, 'I want to know how old you are. I want to know who your father was and what he did; whether you're divorced or not; and where you lived.'

When she said she wouldn't tell me, I said I'd someone who would. I started walking away and she shouted at me to come back. As I walked on more and more quickly, she started shouting louder at me. Eventually I was running as hard as I could through the park with her just shrieking her head off in hysterics and running after me. Suddenly, there was this silence as the shrieking stopped. I looked round. She must have caught her toe in a paving stone because she'd gone down as if she'd been pole-axed. I ducked in behind a tree and looked. Courting couples came up to see what all this noise was about, and windows and doors were opening. Anyway, a crowd of people gathered round and I went off to a telephone kiosk to phone the police, in case she said I'd attacked her or knocked her down. There was no knowing what she might have said.

I went to the police station and met this fellow who said, 'We know your wife. She and another woman ran a place during the war which was closed down.' He said it was the sort of place that people went into single and came out in pairs. 'I've a feeling she's committed bigamy by marrying you,' he said. Well, it would have been wonderful for me if she had.

The policeman fixed up a meeting between her, her solicitor and me in a café the following morning. Before she turned up, the solicitor asked, 'Why, in God's name, did you marry her?'

'The baby,' I told him.

'Christ!' he said. 'That was no baby. Do you know how old she is? She's in her fifties.'

By then that news didn't surprise me all that much.

My wife turned up and we had a cup of coffee and a long chat. The solicitor said to her, 'Look, let the boy go. He's never going to have anything to do with you. You're just

38

making a complete mess of his life. He's young enough to find someone of his own age.'

'No,' she said. 'I'll never let him go. He married me, and that's that.'

She cleared off in tears and her solicitor said he'd work on her and try to get her to change her mind. But he said, 'I don't think she will. The best thing you can do is apply for a divorce yourself in time.'

Some time later I did try to get a divorce. I was still in the army and I met the girl I first fell in love with in Scotland. We met again quite by chance. We spent a couple of leaves together, and we were going to make a go of it. The old brigade major said, 'Look, I know a firm of solicitors who should be able to get you a divorce. It'll cost you,' he said, 'but at least have a go.'

So I got them working on it but they didn't get very far because her own solicitor couldn't get the same story out of her twice. She refused, in the end, to go ahead with divorce. We gave her grounds but she wouldn't bite. The law has changed since then and I could divorce her now if I wanted. But there's the financial side of it, and that's much much more significant than the law itself. If I divorce her, I would have to pay alimony and she could claim a half of whatever I have. I just hope and pray and keep my fingers crossed that the idea of divorcing me will never enter her head. I don't think it will now, but it would be so much worse if she agreed now than it would have been ten, fifteen years ago. Now I pay her £3 a week. She's still alive even though she was born in 1898 – I found that out later. A court order was made against me in 1961 when I was pretty well poverty-stricken and grubbing along at home. Then some years ago, out of the blue, I got this letter from the DHSS saying that my wife had applied for supplementary benefit and they didn't feel justified in meeting this request in view of the fact that she was married to me and only getting £13 a month. I had to fill out this wretched form with all my income and outgoings – it was a squalid, dreadful business – and I was invited at the same time to meet one of these fellas in the local office. I did that and we discussed the business for about an hour. I don't think he liked me very much. To be thoroughly snobbish, I spent sixteen and a half years in the army sneering at the civil service, and quite frankly, what I've seen and heard of them since, I don't think I'm going to change my mind very much about civil servants. He obviously thought it was disgraceful that someone earning what I do should pay his wife £13 a month. And there was probably a great deal of justification in it. I mean, if you just read about it in the newspaper, it wouldn't look very good.

If I heard that my wife had died, I think I'd probably feel more for Puff, my cat that died yesterday, than for her. I've had nothing whatsoever to do with her for thirty years. I suppose I would feel some sense of relief but she hasn't affected my life in any way, apart from the fact that I haven't been able to marry anyone else. But for a while it was a social slur, being trapped like that – at least, I regarded it as such.

I don't think any of this has made me bitter about women. It doesn't seem to. I've had five girlfriends and I've been fond of all of them. I've been in love with them all, I think. Of course, I could have done without that disastrous marriage. I didn't really get over it for years and years. But then, when I could have divorced her, I had no desire to. People say to me, 'You're a wily bugger. As long as you're married to her, you can't marry anyone else.' There's probably something in that. I don't think I'm particularly mercenary, but I do think of this from the financial point of view.

Alec, a septuagenarian funeral director, had most definitely not been conned into marriage.

I fell madly in love with my wife at first sight, and stayed in love with her for half a century. I was too shy to approach her at first. I don't know why it worked . . . our backgrounds were quite different . . . she hadn't had any of the advantages of life at all. . . . We never had bad times. Ours was a marriage made in Heaven. I know this sounds as though I'm stretching it, but of all the women that I've met, I can't imagine myself ever having been married to anybody else at all. . . . Undoubtedly attitudes to marriage today are different from when we married. When I married my wife I don't think there was ever the slightest thought of divorce. 'Till death us do part' meant just that. Whereas nowadays quite a lot of people are saying they're married until they get fed up with each other.

Another romantically inclined interviewee was forty-eight-year-old Ron, the factory foreman who talked about his strict old-fashioned parents in the previous chapter:

I was twenty-four when I got married. We got married because we fell in love, really. . . . I hadn't been in love before. I think I must have been a little immature in those days, not to have thought about marriage or wanted to think about it. . . . I was quite happy at home, I was having a good time . . . but looking back there was no point in taking on that responsibility so early. I just met somebody I enjoyed going out with, we had lots of good times together, we'd been on holiday together. . . . I really enjoyed that, so I thought, well, this is the girl for me.

I'm a bit of a kid myself. I just thought it would be nice to have a little semi-detached, and have my own patch, and have somebody to worry about me and look after me.

That wonderful notion of being looked after appealed to many men. John, a management consultant aged forty-five, could not believe his luck.

The best thing that's ever happened to me was meeting my wife. No question. My hastily cobbled philosophy of trial and error led me halfway up the aisle two or three times, with engagements talked about, threatened. Then I married. It's so convenient. My God, it's lovely to have some gorgeous bird who's always there and always caring, and always just lovely to be with. It's the most laid-back life on earth.

These men, who wished to be relieved of their single state, would suddenly decide it was time to get married and look around for candidates. A retired MP, seventy-two-year-old Bernard, said:

41

There were two girls I might have married, both at Oxford with me. One was brunette, one was blonde: I married the blonde. I think I made the right decision.

Those who married because they wanted children talked much more of their pleasure in their sons and daughters than of the relationship they had with their wives. A sixty-one-year-old barrister, Malcolm, explained:

I enjoyed having sons, someone to hand the family name on to. I've enjoyed launching them into the world, they're all three successful in their own ways. . . . When they were little I felt very close to them; I think it's one of those times that a man can afford to relax and show his natural affections. We had a lot of fun.

Underlying this may well be the feeling that a man can be a child again with his own children, whereas in the rest of his world he is measured and judged for his performance at every level. A man can enjoy the pleasure of entertaining, teaching and pleasing his children, simply by his presence; here at least are people who are impressed by his skills and uncritical of him as a man. And if men talked of leaving home it was almost without exception their children who held them back. They did not wish to lose this special relationship which they might not ever have with anyone else.

There were a few men from a variety of backgrounds and generations who believed that loyalty and faithfulness within marriage were very important. In none of the cases interviewed, however, was this because of religious beliefs in the sanctity of marriage, but rather, they said, because they had absolute values in this as in other areas of their lives. To these men, marrriage was for life: the marriage vows were seen not as restrictions but as promises which they prided themselves on keeping. These few men were certainly what might be described as good citizens – they liked their work, had risen to responsible positions, were well thought of by colleagues, seemed more than usually tolerant of their children's modern lifestyles, had given much time and effort to bringing up these children, and seemed very much at ease with themselves. They also all described themselves as 'rather conservative'.

Some men said the recipe for a good marriage was having a comfortable and beautiful home that was a pleasure to return to at the end of the day, combined with a wife who had remained their best friend through thick and thin. Husbands were full of praise for wives who had the home-making instinct, though Ben, a book-maker of sixty-four, whose wife didn't work, said he never knew quite what he was coming home to because his wife moved the furniture round and changed the décor so often. Home is rarely the centre of a man's world, as it is for many women. Many however see it as their bolthole from the pressures of the world, and want it to remain undisturbed by argument or criticism: a place to be left alone in, uncritically free to be as you are and do as you like.

Giles, a forty-four-year-old insurance broker, has a tiny flat in London and a house by the sea. Although he and his wife have both had affairs, they are still the best of friends and share the same leisure interests. He said he couldn't imagine any circumstances that would make him leave home, and as he spoke he gave the impression that, for him, home was even more important than family life.

We've been married for over twenty years and the girl I'm living with is totally different to the girl I married, clearly. We've both grown up together, and we're great friends. It's nice to have a really good friend at home who you can cuddle up with in front of the fire, sit and watch television with, talk to, play cards with or entertain with. I think home is very,

very important. Strangely enough though, the home – the house – is not particularly important to her, but it is to me. I like symmetry, order and beautiful things. I'm much more materialistic than she is. I think my family life is adequate. There's always something going on, but I like my life in London very much. I think what stimulates me is money and business, whereas what stimulates my wife is the children and sailing. I have a flat in London so that I can live a separate life, and I won't go back home if I'm in London after half-past six.

The men who said they were most happily married were the ones who thought of their wives as close friends and were able to confide most of their troubles to them. This view was most often expressed by middle-class, professional men for whom the division between home and job was often welcome: they wanted to be able to return home and leave all thought of work and its frustrations at the office. But if things were going wrong and there was a crisis, they found their wives the main props to whom they turned for comfort and advice. A wife could sympathize over the stupidities of some of the people he worked with, although she'd probably never met them, and listen to the particular frustrations of the day even though she was often rather in the dark about the job itself.

For men whose work was often carried on from home – clergymen, community workers, teachers, and this fifty-five-year-old trade union branch secretary – their wives were a reliable and valuable back-up on many occasions. Alf said:

My wife is the sort of person I can share everything with. I'm involved in the railways, that's my main employment, and then in the trade union. I've been a trade union branch secretary for years, when you become a father confessor to all your members with their problems. I'm not always at home, so my wife picks up the telephone and gets the story and gives the sympathy. Then she tells me, and she knows just about as much about their ways now, and trade unions, as what I do, simply through contacts and talking in the home.

Other men were well aware that their wives had always taken second place to their work, often because of the nature of the job. Men who were away in the forces, and could not always have their wives close by, talked of the strains on their marriage, but others, like Ken, a fifty-three-year-old senior fireman, had known from the start that work took first place:

I must admit, she's come second-best to the job. She occasionally says that to me. She knows that if there's something to do with the job, whatever we was going to do it'll be pushed off. I try to avoid it, especially now, towards the end of my career. I try to give her more attention, but it doesn't work. It's just there. And I think I've been very, very selfish at times. But in the end, she will admit, well, she won't let anybody kick the Brigade. It's given us a good living. She hasn't worked for fifteen years.

Some men enjoyed the division of life between work and home because it allowed them to be two different people: at work men exhibited qualities that their wives might not recognize.

Many of the men interviewed who had married very young now regretted it in one way or another. They often said that, if they had known what kind of men they were going to become, they would have waited to find someone more suitable. The problem was sometimes the inability of the wife to keep pace with them, as Nick, a police sergeant of thirty-nine from Manchester, experienced.

I have one regret about marriage. It's not so much that I'm married, but that I married at the age I did. I was twenty-one, I'm now thirty-nine. Looking at myself now and my needs, I think I would have married somebody different. We came

45

from the same area. It was a sort of childhood thing. I think that put the mockers on it right from the beginning. Just because we had the background in common doesn't mean we had a lot of other things in common. . . . It sounds big-headed in a way, but my education is better than what my wife's is. That places pressures on the marriage, because I have interests that I've kept from school; I read books, I'm interested in history and ornithology. And there are interests I've developed since then, which we don't share.

In fact, some men felt they'd been pushed into marriage too early by eager girlfriends, and had suffered the consequences of having no home of their own, and starting married life with the in-laws. These men, all working-class, had married in their early twenties when their wives were still in their teens. They were all in favour now of their children living together before marriage. They rather sadly thought the best years of their lives had been in their late teens.

Many thought the choice of partner was such a hit-and-miss affair that, after some years of marriage, they weren't surprised that so few couples they knew had managed to make a success of it. For most of them there was an enormous gap between the dream of a wife and house of their own, and the reality of the demands and constraints of marriage, and wives with whom they couldn't communicate and who failed to understand their needs.

Mike, the company executive, felt, like so many, that no one had ever told him what being married would entail.

I think the biggest problem with marriage is, first of all, that it is not something you train for, nobody tells you what it's going to be like. We get married, we don't know what it means, what we've got to do, or how we should relate. . . . You have to learn that relating to a wife, or husband, is quite different from relating to a parent or somebody else. I think a

46

husband and wife should genuinely become a couple; it's possible but it's very difficult. I think we make it almost impossible in our society. We rarely give young couples an opportunity to talk with successfully married people. But even if we did, it's so very difficult to get a married couple to talk openly about the *real* things that have made it a success. And I think the real thing that makes them successful is being absolutely open about their *feelings*, and recognizing there is nothing *right or wrong* about feelings, they just are.

The resentment that wives felt for husbands' outside interests was often mentioned: sport, hobbies, in fact anything apart from work that seemed to be taking them away from wife and children. Husbands found it hard to strike the right balance if their wives had no real interests of their own outside the home, but didn't share their husbands' interest either. Probation officer Patrick, aged thirty-eight, a keen climber and athlete, managed on the whole to do what he wanted but had to put up with resentment at home, which he felt other men with more home-based interests might not suffer.

I do make decisions without consulting my wife, yes. . . . I'm a fairly selfish individual and I think she realized that from the start when we first got married. So she knows that if I'm going off climbing, then I'll go. She likes to be consulted, although she knows it makes no difference. The pressure on me is knowing that I can only push it so far. . . . I feel guilty sometimes about being away from home so much and not being the model husband. I still go climbing – I'm planning a trip to the Himalayas in a couple of years, though it's a slow process dropping all the hints to get my wife used to the idea before I finally tell her I'm going. I don't run much – I don't get enough training, I don't have enough time, and it causes so much hassle. My wife gets very cheesed off if I start putting on running gear. She doesn't say anything but she really gets fed up. The difficulty now is that if I run anything under ten miles it's of no consequence, which means that I have to be out for maybe an hour and a half. I think it's unfair that I do it really.

For many men this was the major marital battle-ground. Many men who enjoyed supporting a team of some kind had to put up with the 'Saturday cold shoulder' they got from their wives. Women reacted to sport in different ways, but for many it was seen to be a way in which men could avoid their responsibilities, and opt out of things that needed to be done at home.

But as long as men and women organize their marriages in the traditional fashion where the woman feels she's 'stuck at home all week with the children' and the man feels that at least at the weekend he's entitled to 'a little time to himself' this pattern of fear, resentment and misunderstanding is bound to continue.

A man such as Patrick found it hard that his wife had started married life by wanting to stay at home and look after the children, then gradually found she had a less interesting life than her husband, and so wanted *him* to give up some of *his* interests. Husbands' suggestions that wives should take up a hobby themselves were often scorned. But perhaps they had not discussed a fairer division of time off from household chores and responsibility for children. Wives often hoped that husbands would take control at weekends, leaving them free, but this seldom happened if the husbands were keen on sports or had hobbies and outside interests. Other men resented their wives' complaints about the boredom of home life and lack of initiative in doing anything positive about it. Husbands were often made to feel guilty about their own pleasure in their work compared to their wives' life of drudgery.

Many a husband complained that, although his wife seemed only too happy to get married at the time, no sooner had they left the church than the hints started as to what improvements he could make in himself. Such a view was neatly put by Sydney, a retired lecturer from Yorkshire, aged seventy-two.

Basically women are very unfair; they don't know where to stop. They meet a man and they fall in love with him, and he has one or two qualities, like all human beings have, that are not so hot, and then women will say, 'Ah well, when we get married I'll soon put a stop to that.' I mean, the very qualities she fell in love with she wants to stop him having, and I think that's wrong.

Marriage may seem the solution to those who do not enjoy being bachelors, but it does place constraints on them that are often felt to be unnatural. Most of the men interviewed didn't see themselves as naturally monogamous: it was the reason most often mentioned for men to feel at odds with marriage.

Andrew, a forty-five-year-old GP from East Anglia, said he had married his wife, a nurse, because he had been genuinely in love with her. She is younger than him and they have been happily married for twenty-two years, but he questions what that means for a man, and illustrates the delicate balancing act required between pleasure, conscience and expedience.

I've not been divorced or separated; in fact, we're very happily married. But happily married means what? I don't know. I don't feel that monogamy is a natural state for men; it's a hurtful question for most people. I don't know about women, but I think most men have the feeling they wish to prove their virility in some strange way. How many times you have to do it to prove it, God knows. . . . I don't think it's a biological urge to procreate, so much as ego and conquest, the challenge, the race. You've only got to look at the figures for separation and divorce. . . . I often think that for men, and it's true for me, the most fruitful relationships they have with women are the ones they make long after they got married . . . your horizons are much broader, and you meet people of a similar intellect. You gain a great deal from those relationships, but they're the ones society doesn't enable you to fulfil very easily. I do have women friends and I find it very difficult because if they're attractive I want to have a physical relationship too. . . . I find

49

it very hard to separate the two. . . . I think the fear is always that of losing something you value. If you've got something you value in marriage, you have to think a little carefully of the consequences of being found out. But yes. I have had affairs, though I'd hate my wife to find out.

Hugh, thirty-five, a country solicitor, also felt that the major constraint for him was a sexual one.

Marriage does seem to be an unnatural state for men, and I find that more so as I get older. I think men are more promiscuous than women generally, meaning that sex is more important. The crucial factor to the woman, it seems to me, is the feeling and the closeness and the relationship other than sex. The mental togetherness.

The fact that wives seemed less interested in sex after they had got married was a common complaint from husbands. Wilf is a thirty-six-year-old caretaker whose wife works part-time. He felt that the marriage ceremony itself gave him the feeling of being tied down.

I felt we didn't need the formal thing of going through a ceremony. I'm convinced that if we hadn't gone through with that we'd be happier. I think I feel in the background there's always this tie, and in certain respects it stops you working at it perhaps, because there you are, you've got it.

We had a far better sex relationship before we got married and were living together. Living together was not the right word, because I still had a room in a friend's house and I slept there when it was convenient. I felt that my wife's sex drive dropped after marriage . . . long before we had a baby. She was just less inclined . . . it was almost an obligatory duty . . . though the novelty was still there for a time. Often, before we were married, if we had the opportunity we'd take it, even if it was just a quick one. As soon as you're married the opportunity is always there, so you don't.

My wife and I have rather different sexual tastes . . . she won't co-operate with my ideas. I'm definitely the underwear man, and various other little kinks I've got . . . some are a bit stronger than others. Anal sex is something I enjoy and that's accommodated, perhaps even enjoyed, by her on occasions. But if you stood my wife sideways she'd go straight up and down. I bought her sexy underwear but none of it suits her. She doesn't find me physically attractive ever since I've started putting on weight. The tragic thing is that I feel no inclination to lose weight because of it. I feel happier at this weight anyway.

One company chairman of seventy-two, who had been married four times, thought that was too many, but he put it down to the fact that, like many men, he didn't like being hemmed in. Intensely responsible and extremely successful in his job, he cared less for personal responsibilities.

On the whole I've been lucky in my wives and my wives have been unlucky in me, although they're always very nice to me. I got three of them to divorce me. I'm very involved in my work and the responsibility required there on the whole hasn't gone against the grain. If one's got position and leadership, then one has responsibility too, but men don't always care to pay so much attention to that. I think my life would be incomplete without my family attachments, but I view women as just as important, if not more important, to me than my work, and more important than a wife and family.

Many men thought that faithfulness in marriage was the ideal state, but the temptations were often too hard to resist and anyway 'people never are', as one young army officer put it. A handful of men said they had remained faithful throughout marriage, and of the men interviewed they were largely the ones who had never slept with anyone other than their wife. These husbands included young and old alike, and the information was given not with pride but with a sense of what can only be described as contentment with their lot.

Chris, a twenty-five-year-old bank clerk from South Shields, was one of a number of young married men who had what seemed to be a clear plan of action, financially, at work and in his marriage. He had no particular wish to have children, had been married for two years and known his wife for seven.

I first slept with someone when I was eighteen – it was the girl who is now my wife. She's the only person I've slept with. I have never really looked at anybody else. I think we're both rather conservative; we both tend to frown upon experimental things, and we haven't found the first two years difficult at all. There are no flaws that either of us see in each other; nobody's perfect but we get on very well. We don't have an awful lot in common, but that might be a good thing. . . . We do have quarrels . . . and they're usually about something totally trivial. We never have any major arguments.

Some men said that they had never been so clearly aware of how much they depended on their wives until they became ill. Ron's wife had a haemorrhage which resulted in some brain damage:

She just collapsed in the kitchen. She's forty-seven. She's at home now, but she goes to the rehabilitation centre every morning. It's knocked us all for six, really. It's changed her in that she can't concentrate any more. She can't even cook a meal. . . .

It's very upsetting for my daughter, because they are very close. My wife was always there when she came home from school – they'd have a little chat. I can't do that. I keep saying to her, this is the beauty of education – you can cope with it, you're an intelligent girl and you know that you're not going to go through life and have everything very easy for you. The boy seems to be all right. He misses her. But we're coping all right. You have to cope with it. I can't just say that's it, and get my mother round.

I've had to take on most things at home. I have to plan the menus, and I do the shopping. Luckily we have one of these twin tubs, but I still can't iron. My neighbours have been very good, or my sister will come and help. . . . I don't run out of a lot of things, but it's just planning the running of a home. I knew there was a lot of work involved, but I never realized how much.

When men were asked to say what annoyed them most about their wives, many gave an illustration of some mildly irritating habit, like picking her toenails while watching television, wearing curlers at home when she could afford to go to the hairdresser, asking him to do jobs around the house as soon as he had returned from work, or (and this was a frequent complaint) insisting on listing the trivialities of her day as soon as he returned from work. Hugh, the solicitor mentioned earlier who felt that marriage was an unnatural state for men, was precise on this point.

The thing that irritates me most about my wife is that when I come back from work – I might have had a drink at the office – and get home, I want to read the paper and watch the seven o'clock news. She immediately wants to tell me what she's been doing all day. We've just moved to a new house and there's an enormous amount to be done and organized, and she's very good and capable at doing it. I'm rather glad because it doesn't bother me. I mean, I take an interest but only up to a point. I don't listen to what she's saying, I just say yes or no. But she has a sense of humour.

A number of working-class men whose wives had part-time jobs or who did not work at all complained that their wives never let up on the housework. William, aged thirty-three, a van driver whose wife works part-time was a typical example.

My wife's thirst for work irritates me. She works three days a week. She's got the house to run – she's good at that. I've got no complaints about that. But she goes almost to the other extreme: she puts too much into it. I remember last time we tried to go on holiday. There I was waiting to go, and there she was still scrubbing the floors. And up to an hour before we

53

were going to the theatre on Saturday, she was washing windows and washing curtains, hanging curtains. Maybe it's an unfair criticism. I suppose I'd criticize her if she wasn't house-proud. She's one of these people who don't like sitting around and doing nothing.

Repetitive, aggravating behaviour infuriated husbands, particularly when a wife was a prisoner of her own obsessions, becoming anti-social and introverted. Fred, a dustman of forty, felt goaded almost beyond endurance by his wife's pride in her home.

My wife's a bit of a worrier, whether it's because she don't do a full-time job or what, I don't know. It's the children mainly. And I'm not one for gardening and we've got a lovely big garden, and it looks like a jungle sometimes. She says, 'What will people think when they walk past and see the grass overgrown?' Well, I couldn't give a monkey's what they think. It's what the house is like inside that I worry about, not the outside. As I say, she keeps it clean, though sometimes I think she does it a bit too much. She's always changing rooms about and doing spring cleaning . . . you try to watch something on the telly and she'll get the hoover out. . . .

'For Christ's sake, put it away till this has ended.'

'Oh, I've got to do the hoovering, I must do the hoovering.'

That's what I mean, she's got to make sure everything is clean. She's very homely, my wife, not one for going out a lot. It's a job to get her to go out on a Saturday night for a drink. She says she'd rather have a drink indoors and watch the telly.

The list of things that irritated men about their wives continued with 'She won't do the washing up before she goes to bed . . . she leaves it and I keep telling her'(fireman); 'My wife is always telling me what I think when I don't – it's the lowest form of conversation, I don't know why she does it'(musician); 'My wife doesn't like me going out with my mates, and she nags me if I sit around at home and I'm not doing anything. When I get home from work I'm entitled to sit down for a bit, she's always wanting things done in the house'(factory worker); and 'My wife gets very concerned about money. As far as I'm concerned quite unnecessarily so. I think at times she gets almost paranoid about it'(policeman). And worrying about money was a common marital problem. The wives who worried most seemed to be the ones who didn't work, but wives also nagged their husbands about how they spent their money.

But some men, like fifty-nine-year-old security officer Dennis, laid down the law quite firmly from the first day of married life.

My wife is like my mother. Yes. She said at first, my wife, that in her family it was the woman who's the boss and looked after the money. We had a clash about that. I'd seen her father going out with the boys with his ten-shilling note. I said, 'Look dear, I'm afraid I'm not going to do this. I am going to be the boss, or else we call it off.' She accepted that and, touch wood, we've had a wonderfully happy marriage. My wife's never told me that she isn't happy.

Many men said they were aware that they didn't do enough around the house, but their wives had an efficient method of housework, so they somewhat guiltily left the bulk of it to them. If both were working, as is very common today, a lot of men on shift work were more likely to share the shopping and cooking on the days that they got home first. Quite an unexpectedly high number of younger working-class men enjoyed cooking and would have been happy to do it most of the time if asked. Comparatively few men did any heavy cleaning or cleaned the lavatory at home, though washing clothes either at home or in the launderette seemed quite a common task. On the whole, men didn't mind wielding the hoover, but many drew the line at ironing. There were a number of older working-class men who clung to the traditional roles. Fifty-five-year-old Jack, a buyer in a factory, has a north-country wife who was brought up to 'look after her man', and he said:

My wife's very homely – she comes from the north-east, where the husband has to be looked after first. When my wife puts something on the table, of course best cut of meat or the largest portion goes to myself.

But even for Jack times have had to change a little, and he's now concerned about how his behaviour has affected his sons:

I still live a little in the past where the women are in the home. My wife happens to work and earn money as well, which is handy. But I do believe that I haven't really adapted to the present generation where husband and wife play an equal part. I do the washing up ever so well now, but I didn't always, not ever. . . . I do it all now and I'm very pleased to do it, really. I always remember my father saying he either washed or wiped every Christmas Day without fail, and that was it. I really come along in that same mould. I have to encourage my eldest son to do it as well because he's like me – my young one's more like his mother. I see my oldest son as a carbon copy of myself, and I'm not pleased.

Some men complained that when they did help in the house their wife seemed not to notice, or had not thanked them for doing what they considered to be her work.

A number of young men, mostly though not exclusively middle class, were making great efforts to move their lifestyle away from the traditional patterns of role playing in marriage. Clive, a policeman of twenty-six, was endeavouring to be more helpful.

I'm selfish in that I go to work, and I don't do as much at home as I would expect . . . my wife works. We've got a little boy that we had in July but up until then she was earning good money and expected me to make a contribution to the housework. But I never do, I just don't do enough. It's not that I don't want to, it's just that if I come in in the evening, it will not occur to me to do the ironing – it just does not enter my brain.

I can do it, and when hints are dropped then I do it. It's not so bad now because I work nine to five, and have the weekends off, but when I was doing shift work and had days off in the week I would wake up and the first thing that would enter my head would be which golf course shall I use. That would be it. It would not occur to me to do anything in the house.

I think it's probably my upbringing when my mother had devoted her life to my father ... she was his servant. There was no two ways about it. He was born in 1919 and was typical of that generation. He is the man, he earns the money. He does not belittle her or anything like that, but they have quite distinct roles. I think she accepts it. My mother and father cannot understand the relationship that I have with my wife. They think that I should be the masterful boss, and lay the law down, whereas our marriage is much more democratic. In fact, I leave the decisions to her, unless I think it's absolutely ridiculous. Decisions about furnishings and holidays and things like that. . . . I know whatever she wants will suit me fine. You're a long time dead and I like to smile. I don't like starting an argument and the easiest way out of it is to agree.

Most of the men interviewed seemed to have had little experience of talking about how emotional problems, sexual problems or profound differences of opinion were dealt with in marriage. They gave the impression, and sometimes actually said, that they wanted life at home to go as smoothly and easily as possible. They didn't want questions fired at them, nor too heavy a burden of emotional demands. They did not like their wives 'wanting to have things out', which usually meant they were being criticized in some way. They felt frightened by women's expressions of feeling and their need to respond to it. Even though so many of them readily admitted that their behaviour in marriage was often selfish, they didn't want this behaviour remarked upon or reformed. Many men did not want the consequences of their actions pointed out, nor did they want to be disturbed by the thought that they had some responsibility for other people's feelings, or should consider them deeply. There seemed to be little evidence of much fruitful communication between husbands and wives over their differences about important issues, except in anger at a crisis point. If such talks did take place they were rarely, according to these men, initiated by husbands. Men disliked their wives getting angry or aggressive and yet, aware of the near violence of their wives' feelings, could not find the right way to deal with them. Men often wondered what it was they had done wrong and explained their wives' emotional state in terms of pre-menstrual tension, tiredness or nerves.

Men were also bewildered by what it was their wives were trying to tell them, Graham, an economist of thirty-eight, was typical.

My wife goes very quiet sometimes and I know something's wrong. If I ask her, she won't always say. I think very often she feels that I'm reserving things from her. 'Why don't you talk to me? What are you thinking now?' I try to be sensitive to what's happening, but my attitude to it can vary. I don't always want to comfort her in a verbal way, but I'll usually try to convey by stroking, cuddling, that I'm still here, that I do care.

Men are not usually brought up to allow the emotional needs of others to interfere with what they do. Looking after an ill relative or taking care of the children can impose demands on the average man that he has not bargained for, and which he would readily admit interfere with his top priorities – himself and his work.

Traditional men are disturbed by women who are no

longer satisfied with accepting a vicarious life – wives who choose their own friends, have independent interests and who are not always there to play the traditional role of wife and mother. Not many men complained that their wives had 'outgrown them', as husbands frequently said they had outgrown their wives, but there were some complaints of their wives' extra-curricular activities. Douglas, a thirty-seven-year-old fireman, said:

My wife had two friends who started doing part-time courses with the Open University. Neil(our only son) was seventeen and virtually off our hands. I don't know about these courses but she was out at the study centre, watching television at all odd hours, writing essays, that sort of thing. She was spending more and more time with her two friends studying at their houses. I saw less and less of her. I thought I'd have a go myself, but I dropped out after a few months – I lost interest, I suppose. She's kept it up. I know my job left her lonely very often, but I don't feel we have a proper home any more. I don't know what'll happen – we've certainly been growing apart. I've told her she's wasting her time because there won't be any jobs if she gets her exams. I think she's trying to prove something.

We read our children fairy stories which end 'and then they got married and lived happily ever after'. Our society assumes that marriage, love and sex are inextricably entwined and this ideal is encouraged and reinforced by parental pressure, family lore, moral education and religion. The mass media, advertising and popular culture add a sugar-coating of romance to the whole concept and suggest total commitment of one person to another forever. Reality is rather different. A man meets a girl when he is in his twenties or thirties and for one reason or another, more often than not just because he feels it is time to get married, he decides to go ahead. Many admit that no one ever talked to them about the realities of marriage, least of all their own parents. Nor had anyone helped them to discern what kind of person they were, what needs or expectations they had or what might make them happy with one partner rather than another. Some are looking for personal security, a niche in society, for a home of their own; others want children, warmth, comfort, love or regular sex: all crave happiness. But whatever the reasons that impel them into marriage, a gap remains between the ideal in their minds and the practical everyday irritations of living cheek by jowl with another person: this gap between the romantic ideal and reality can lead to disappointment, disillusionment, nagging and bitterness. It can cause either party to seek solace elsewhere or to divorce. But before looking at these aspects, here are some portraits of wives by husbands.

Chapter Four

WIVES

How a man visualizes the woman he has married can be most revealing, so some men were asked to describe their wives in detail. A few found it too difficult to do on the spur of the moment but were happy to submit their thoughts to me in writing, after they had had time to think.

PATRICK
Probation Officer

My wife is very sharp, very perceptive. She looks feminine, but she's tough. She knows me like the back of her hand. The only time I was really coming close to having an affair was when I fell in love with a young Asian girl whom I had interviewed for a job. I say I fell in love with her, but curiously enough I never actually spoke to her about it, and never had an affair with her as such, other than meetings. And yet, all the doors were open. I didn't because of fear, really, fear that I was treading into waters that were really dangerous. Yet I was transfixed with this girl, and I would actually try and engineer situations so I'd see her. Then one evening, I might have been talking about her, or something, and my wife suddenly said, 'Look, I don't know if you're having an affair with that girl or not. The only thing I will say is, don't come crying on my shoulder and telling me about her.'

That absolutely shook me rigid, the fact that it had become

so obvious. I suppose I mentioned the girl's name a lot. So my wife thought, 'I can tell that those two are having an affair.' With a little intuition, she can tell. She's a pretty shrewd girl – she's a Scorpio, and Scorpios are. That absolutely terrified me to the point of thinking, God, I can see the whole marriage being threatened, and then I was forced to make some kind of decision.

RON
Factory Foreman

My wife used to have a habit that irritated me. She used to empty tealeaves down the sink. My mother used to do it, too. And I said to her in the end, 'Here,' I said, 'I'm bustin' to go to the toilet. I can't go 'cause the bloody sink's full of tealeaves.'

'You dirty devil!' she said.

And do you know, she's never done it since. Course, we have teabags now, but in them days there were no teabags.

I have two or three little habits that my wife doesn't like. I'm sorry, but wherever I was, if I wanted to break wind, I broke wind. And that annoyed her. 'You dirty devil!' she said.

I said, 'What are you talking about? It's not dirty. The Queen does that but she keeps hers quiet. But I can't.' But since then, she's the same as me now. She's realized that it is natural and you can't cover it up.

TIM
Postman

I don't kiss my wife very often now but I don't have to, because I've only got to look at my missus and she knows I still love her.

WILLIAM
Van Driver

I have this habit of putting my point of view before my wife puts hers. It irritates her. I've tried to stop but I can't. If I cuddle my wife in front of people she doesn't like it. She doesn't like affection being shown outside the house. She doesn't like me drinking either. The only thing that irritates me about her is her petty conversaion. In the evenings, she'll tell me about Mrs Jones and her baby, or somebody's got something or bought something, and I'm not interested. And I'll go read the paper and ignore her. The other thing that irritates me is her tidiness. I'll put something down, and I'll want it later on. She'll put it away. Even after twenty-nine years she still does it, but I wouldn't change her for a million pounds.

WALTER
Train Driver

I don't argue with my wife. She's very volatile and I don't argue, which gets her very upset. Her way is to get stuck in and sort it out physically. I often get the impression that my wife would like me to get stuck in and give her a good hiding. She's not one you can reason with normally. I can't examine a situation and give her an analysis because that would enrage her even more. I keep cool, calm and collected and she gets more and more annoyed. She gets annoyed about all sorts of things – like I don't take her out enough. We've got two children, you know, and I'm quite busy. And there's the financial side of it, because when I take her out it does cost quite a lot because she says, 'You don't take me out very often so you're not going to sell me short.' Which means that I can't afford to take her out very often.

We've been married ten years. I've worked at it.[Laughs] As long as I keep working at it, it'll go on. I'm often tempted to say I'd rather be single, but then there's a lot of constraints on me.

HUGH
Solicitor

If we row, it's about me coming home late, or going to watch rugger. My wife hasn't really got a natural life of her own. She hasn't developed very much, although she's an intelligent woman. I'm more gregarious than she is – she doesn't mind staying in, if I'm there, and watching the telly, which I don't like.

TOM
Miner

I've been married twenty-three years. I don't think I ever regret it. I mean, if I hadn't married the one I have now, I would've married somebody else, but I don't think I ever regret it.

BILL
Furniture Removal Man

My marriage hasn't been successful; that's made me unhappy, obviously. It's not totally as I would have expected it to be. It's not completely satisfactory at the moment on the sexual side of the partnership. It's entirely satisfactory in every other direction – we're great friends, great companions – but there is that one thing that is regrettable to me, and I'm sure it is to my wife, too. We just don't feel that way with each other any more. I'm sure we both have the built-in desire, but not with each other. That's the real problem. But it's something that we've learned to live with, we've learned to accommodate, given what's happened in the past. It is difficult, and I don't know what the answer to it is, but there's no way now that I would ever contemplate leaving my wife or splitting the marriage. I think after thirty-four years of marriage, albeit rocky at times, and even though there's something missing that I want and I'm sure she wants, I can't bring myself to stop it. I could be selfish and say, 'Right, I've still got the desires, in a man, for a physical relationship', but it would make me guilty in leaving my wife. She's shared my life; she's built what we have together. It's not a lot but it means a lot to us.

NEIL
Naval Officer

My second wife does mind me being away from home. We haven't been married two years yet, and I've never been away for more than two months at a time. About the longest time you might be away nowadays in the navy is seven months. So if you're away for seven months, you can usually get your wife to somewhere where you're going to be. And then you can take some leave while you're there. And the navy likes this because it also keeps people on the straight and narrow. The temptation not to stay on the straight and narrow is strong: the 'little lady' thing. And of course it's awful for the wives. To be quite honest with you, I was unfaithful to my first wife. Never a serious love affair. But guys do go off the rails.

My second wife, she's absolutely terrific about the whole thing. I haven't been away for a long time, but I wouldn't dream of being unfaithful to her. I mean, there's something about our friendship that is so very different from my last one. I'm a lot older now, and she was married before as well. We're not going to have any children, no. She's great about my kids, but she doesn't want them herself. We had to take a cold hard look at finances, really, and she's not a motherly type at all.

STEVEN
RAF Officer

I have a lovely wife whom I love very much, and we get on incredibly well together, and we have a very lovely family.

She's not what one would call a 'service wife'. This doesn't worry me a bit. In fact, I find it a positive advantage because when I go home at weekends now, I relax, and the last thing we're going to talk about is anything service. That gets me away from it, and is nice. She feels badly about it, she feels she could be doing better for me as a service officers's wife, and that.

In the past ten years, I've always worked within sixty miles of my house, so she's able to stay at home, live her own life during the week, have her own interests – she likes sculpting and things like that, and has a part-time job in a shop – and a family to look after. I find that arrangement a tremendous advantage because we're always looking forward to meeting each other, and always looking forward to being together. We've had our ups and downs, Christ, in our eighteen years, but the last five or six years have been absolutely tremendous.

GEORGE
CID Officer

I've been married fifteen years. My wife doesn't go out to work. She is, if you like, the traditional housewife. That wasn't the case before we had two children – she went out to work then. But when the children came along she followed the traditional pattern in that she gave up her job and she's never gone back. . . .

I help in the house, yes. I don't think there's any conscious division of work in the house. But if I get home and, let's say, there's washing of dishes to be done, or making the beds, then I'll wash the dishes and make the beds. Hoovering I do, ironing I don't. I do clean the lavatory, yes. I think my wife's very protective about certain of the jobs. If I was to get out a duster and furniture polish I would detect, not exactly the hate vibes, but a little bit of, 'What's your game? Don't I keep it clean enough?' You have to be very careful. So to that extent I tend to leave that to her, not because I'm lazy or because I don't see that I should be doing it.

CHRIS
Bank Clerk

My wife is twenty-four, five feet three inches and very slender, which I like. She has dark shoulder-length hair which is very thick. She can't do a lot with it. To be honest, I do prefer the finer sort of hair that you can style, but then everybody wants to change, don't they?

She appears to be very easy-going, but she's quite an introvert. She's also quite stubborn and obstinate. We often argue over trivial things. The only thing I would like to change about her is her attitude to meeting new people. She's much more comfortable at home and will make any excuse not to go somewhere. We have a fairly amicable attitude to housework, though I admit I could do a little more than I do. I will dry up if she washes. I certainly haven't done the hoovering very often and I suppose I have cleaned the bathroom half-a-dozen times in two and a half years. She seems to get stuck into jobs like that, and I don't really notice when she does them. She never touches the car, which I always clean. However, she'll drive herself to a keep-fit class or, if we've been to a party, she'll offer to drive us home so that I can drink a bit more.

JOHN
Management Consultant

My wife is bottled bliss. She's alert, active, committed, critical of me, deflating, extremely amusing – makes me laugh at myself – and aggressive. She's five foot two, well-proportioned, with auburn hair, blue eyes and a radiant smile.

When we returned from honeymoon – she tells me that's over twenty years ago – the stupid little broad came out into the garden with my plimsolls and said, 'Well, now that's over put these on and I'll race you to the end of the garden.' That's what she's like. The one most important and enduring characteristic for me is that she's interesting. Men often develop a hidden deaf aid as they go on, but I can't with her. She went to one of those hairy androgynous schools in Scotland, and by God broads up there are tough.

She's good at husbandry and housekeeping and has a great breadth of vision and philosophy. She's the only woman in Britain I've ever slept with who, when I put my loose change on the dressing-table at night, can tell just from the sound of it how much is there.

She's also quite conscious of the fact – we both are – that if the chips are down she knows that I know I could grind her into the dust. . . . make her feel really small. I've never done it but I've come pretty near to it.

I sometimes think of a girl I might have married – a kind of frumpy Grace Kelly – the mere thought of it makes my glasses steam up.

Two Christmases ago by a variety of happy circumstances a whole number of remote relatives sent me a collection of clothes that all happened to be in shades of yellow, brown or gold silk. I thought I looked a million dollars, but when I flounced into the bedroom along an imaginary catwalk she looked up from her book and said, 'Good Lord, you look just like a banana.' I don't like boring broads.

PETER
Engineer

I still see her almost as she was when I first met her thirty years ago. She hasn't changed a lot in personality. I spent a lot of time in our early life trying to change her, Pygmalion fashion. I tried to make her a bit more like me as a person – physically we have always looked alike, just like brother and sister. We are both very dark. Now I'm glad I didn't succeed, because I have found her complementary character a better thing for us. The things I tried to change in her then are, oddly enough, the things I cling on to now. This is the thing I like, a Zola-like earthiness and honesty – it's reassuring. I am much more logical and cool and structured in my approach to things than she is. She establishes links with people at the level of the heart. She has not allowed life, or me, to change her set of natural

68

qualities. She seemed to reach maturity much younger than I did – considerably ahead of me. I have become disenchanted with the people I was once impressed with. I was a bit dishonest and pushed us into things I thought we should be doing, and towards people I thought we should be meeting. She was more honest and wanted a simpler life. She didn't attach the same importance to material things – the house, the car, holidays. She was always more concerned with the children, her parents and home.

I have reassured myself with other women, particularly as I grew older. But now we've fallen in love again. It's worth weathering through to something very grand. If you asked my wife she wouldn't say we'd ever been out of love.

LORD EASTBOURNE

My wife was very beautiful at eighteen and still has a remarkable figure for a woman of over fifty. She shows, on occasions, a fiery temperament. I prefer to sulk and be silent which, of course, is the worst response for someone who likes to shout and then forget it. However, the years have made us milder and less fractious. At times our relationship has been strained due to my affairs and, in particular, when I was seriously involved with the wife of a neighbour.

She's an excellent mother and has brought up our children which could be dubbed 'square' in this age, but this means we have avoided the many pitfalls around. She has no idea of money, and tends to go on spending sprees when bored. She refuses to open her bank statements for fear of what they might disclose.

Since giving up horses and riding, and with the children departed, she has not really found suitable work to satisfy and stimulate her: a little writing, instructing in the Pony Club, some charitable work, and running a house and garden with very limited help. She hates planning ahead or being tied down in a permanent job. Basically shy and retiring, she makes new friends slowly.

ALF
Trade Union Official

A strange thing about my wife is that in the courting days she just adored her future mother-in-law. After we married, all this quickly changed. She had her own way of doing things, meal-times, housework, very different from the pretty good routine I had been used to at home as a single man. She used to say, 'I'm sick of hearing about your mother', though strangely she never said, 'Go home to your mother.' The point of these remarks is that I think the early days of marriage must be difficult for a young bride.

I consider my wife to be a good housewife, albeit not a particularly good manager. She lacks routine, for example. Monday is not always washing day – washing day is when there are sufficient clothes to warrant washing. Not so with the ironing – all the clothes are kept to one side till there is a film on TV, sometimes during a morning or afternoon, never at night. Household shopping is always done on a Thursday, a definite routine for a change. She's a difficult lass to help with household chores, I have really tried over the years, but I usually get, 'Leave that, I'll do it when I'm ready.'

Her evenings are always kept free. When I get home it's never, 'What sort of day have you had?' And – wait for it – I've not even got my coat off. She starts straight off, 'I'm absolutely shattered, I have never had a minute all day', to be followed by a long spiel of all the jobs and events of the day. In twenty-five years of married life this has never changed. I always listen intently, of course – I have to. She has never been a working wife during the whole of our married life. She's a good wife, really, just like I'm a good husband, I hope.

I must say she's a good cook. There's nothing she likes better than being on her own and preparing a four- or five-course dinner for friends. She also loves going out to a restaurant at least once a week as a reward for her efforts.

Tupperware parties seem to have a particular attraction – God knows why, we hardly ever use the stuff, it's falling out of the cupboards. There must have been a better use for that money.

70

What I really do appreciate about her is she's a good dresser, always immaculate when we go out. In clothes, she will never make do with second-best. If I say, 'Well, that's a bit much, isn't it?' she will always reply, 'I'll wait until you can afford it.' By the following week she has usually won me over.

In our married life we have had three or four serious rows, nothing in my view that could not have been sorted out if she had been willing. She's younger than me, and looks it. She likes other male company (I've often wondered about this, and me going away from home so much myself). I think we have a mutual trust for each other – well, she never looks guilty.

I have never been undernourished, and I have never not had a clean shirt to put on. She's been a good mother to our daughter, and is currently thriving on being a grandmother. Has every man of my age been so lucky?

CHARLES
Chairman of Department Store

My wife has been a total support in our business career. I call it 'ours' because I could never have begun to do it without her constant support and advice. As I'm about to retire, it's truer now than ever before. It's possible for me to talk about anything to her, which I feel has been unfair over the years. I've tended to unload a lot of problems on to her. She very rarely unloads her problems on to me, because she says she doesn't want to worry me.

She gave up a career in Exchange Control with the Bank of England to care for the family, and I think she's found it all absorbing though very demanding. Being a mother suited her nature, and she takes great pride in doing a thing properly. She's very dedicated.

She's very small, under five feet, and seems much younger to me than her sixty years. Her very friendly personality and laughter have endeared her to so many people in the store that she's a positive asset to me. We are very much a partnership. She has a strong personality and strong views, and I find her

71

very stimulating – even when she takes a totally opposite stance to me. She's very anti-feminist. And I feel terribly imperfect in comparison to her.

EDWARD
Bank Manager

I have just been divorced after twenty-two years of marriage. There wasn't a sudden breakdown. It took place over about twelve years with very little friction or animosity. The problem was that I was far more ambitious than my wife and I devoted most of my energy and time to trying to be a success. I think I decided early in life that you can't be both a family person and a career person. You have to make the choice. I am doing very well and should reach a fairly senior position before I have to retire.

There are two regrets I have. One is that I have missed seeing my children growing up. Looking back, I would like to have seen more of them. And the other regret is hurting my children and my family in general. My parents have so far refused to meet the woman whom I am going to marry in three weeks' time. There's never been a divorce in my family before. My ex-wife's parents are much more accepting because they have had a relation who has been divorced.

We just outgrew each other. My problem is I am just never going to be satisfied by being average. I would say my ambition is pretty boundless. My ex-wife is a pretty placid woman – an intellectual I would say, not at all practical. Over a period of years I began to wonder what I was going home for.

Rather remarkably, the divorce hasn't affected my career at all. It certainly would have done a few years ago, but I played it all in a rather political way, and informed my director before I left home. They can't really object these days because of the sheer volume of divorces.

I could say my divorce has been a bit foolhardy. It certainly cost me a great deal of money, though I am not complaining, because I think the legal settlement was fair to my wife. I had to pay her an enormous amount of cash after we had sold our house, and I am more heavily in debt than I have ever been.

After I had met this other woman I tried to let my wife know over a period of several months. I was dropping some fairly loud hints, but she just wasn't picking them up. So eventually I had to tell her. It was ghastly, though she was remarkably philosophical about it. There were no really bad scenes; in fact it was quite amicable. The final discussion before I left went on for about an hour and a half. The worst bit for me was picking up my personal belongings and leaving home with my tail between my legs. I think it's highly unlikely that she will marry again. There are many people in life who need to be close to a man or a woman, but she is not like that. A few months later she did tell me that she was feeling much happier than she had felt before.

My new wife is thirty-eight, several years younger than me. She's well-built with enormous energy and works in marketing. She's a little mercurial and volatile, but I think I will get used to that. She's very ambitious for both of us, very well organized, and intelligent but not an intellectual. She will help me in my career, but I feel more content and happier, even though I don't have so much money as I did. We won't have any children as she has two and I have got three.

There's one drawback. We've moved out to the country, to a small village, and it means I have a long and difficult journey to work every day.

I think my new wife would be almost unbearable if she were not on the pill. Of course, it's improved women's lifestyle tremendously.

MIKE
Company Executive

I think that my wife is beautiful and if other people don't then that's their business. She's not tall enough to see over my shoulder, so if I can get close enough she can't attend to anyone but me. Her strengths are not things which make headlines in

The Times or the *Sun*. All I can say is thank God. I would find it hard to be married to a Margaret Thatcher or a Catherine Deneuve, because I would feel downtrodden and bullied by the one and continually jealous of the other.

She doesn't like being talked at, particularly by intellectuals saying things they don't really believe but think are clever. It was not easy being an intellectual and married to my wife. I gave in after a running battle of over twenty years and feel much happier for it. She watches out for any relapse and deals with it smartly.

From experience she has learnt to spot pomposity when it is but a gleam in the eye and to jump on it quickly and directly. It is rather more fun to watch her do this to somebody else than to have it done to me. I am grateful after the event or at least after the pain has died down. It takes guts and lots of love to confront an intellectual husband, and many wives would opt for a quiet and boring life.

Four children are a family that would daunt most mothers, particularly as for many years I opted out of administering much of the discipline. My wife has a vocation to be a mother and has affectionate, close and open relationships with all four. Sometimes it gets noisy and I feel worried and embarrassed but no one except me seems to remember after it is over. It's rather like a minor Italian car accident.

Sometimes my wife forgets that we have guests or that we are not at home and shouts to make herself heard, but I'm learning to tell her that she is doing so. She has a beautiful singing voice but has had too little opportunity to use it. She has become aware that she is often taken for granted, and though she used to be pretty anti-feminist she now notices the slackers and puts a drying-up cloth or vacuum cleaner in their hands.

Thank God that we are both Roman Catholics. It is the most important part of our lives and an area over which we have no disagreements. It's also something which has become very much more important to both of us in the last few years. It's the only area where I do not find her certainty unnerving and where I feel capable of discussing points with her without tension or even panic.

I am lucky to have a wife who is very loyal, who keeps secrets absolutely, and who has a beautiful laugh when I can get her to understand my sort of jokes!

Most people are not professional observers, easily able to stand back and categorize those they know well. Perhaps because husbands were so well acquainted with their wives their perception of them was imprecise and often hesitant. All the same, all of these descriptions struck me as being remarkably cool and detached; a few even bordered on the sardonic. Most husbands seemed to view their wives from afar with good-natured benevolence, dwelling on their role as wives and mothers, companions and supporters, household organizers and child minders, rather than on their qualities as individuals. Many were complimentary, but in an impersonal fashion. Some were more aware than others that their own behaviour affected their wives, but rarely did anyone talk with insight about the character of those with whom they lived intimately, day in, day out. Only one or two mentioned what their wives were personally interested in. Not one attempted to see life from his wife's point of view, nor talked about her anxieties, ambitions, talents or problems at work or in the home. None described her as a separate individual with an independent life. The exuberance of the management consultant whose wife was 'bottled bliss' and John's rather humble self-appraisal in contrast with his description of his wife, stood out from the other cautious assessments.

Chapter Five

MEN AS FATHERS

The commonest cause of anxiety for many fathers, it seems, is the lack of definition of that role, both in their own minds and in society at large. Many men told me that they felt they had no proper guidelines to go by and few clues to help them get it right. If they opted for the pattern they knew and followed in their father's footsteps, their wives and children showed quite a different reaction from any their father would have had to cope with. First, their wives were on the whole better educated and more independent than their mothers had been, and demanded a new sort of relationship based on discussion and participation. Their children, also often better educated than themselves, questioned their authority, and from an early age openly defied their fathers on a number of issues. The temptations, opportunities and problems facing their children today were often more complex than any they themselves had known. Many men who said they had longed for children found the impact on their marriage quite disruptive, and the strain in the early years tremendous.

In comparison, the role of their own fathers and grandfathers had seemed clear-cut. They had been the undisputed head of the family, the breadwinner, the decision-maker and the disciplinarian. As one man pointed out with a smile, it was not so long ago that a man had the legal right to chastise his wife or children if he thought it necessary.

In some modern families the father does not even provide the family name. Some professional working mothers, against the whole notion of patriarchy and patronymy, prefer to keep their maiden name and may even call their children by that name.

The general feeling I got from a number of men was that they were a great deal more confused about their role as father than their wives appeared to be about their role as mother. Were they supposed to do the things their wife did not do – like playing football and cricket; or share the things their wife did, but seemed to do better than they did; or was there something else they should be doing that no one had told them about?

Many men admitted to a sneaking self-doubt, fearing that they were not as good fathers as they ought to be; they felt guilty about doing so little with their children. Most agreed that their wives did the lion's share of bringing up the children, and there were complaints about this from time to time. Others felt envy that their wives had a built-in instinct for such things and that this was denied them. Air force officer Steven, aged forty-three with two children, said:

My wife never seemed to have any bother with knowing what she had to do. I think she's been a wonderful mother, she adores the children. I'm never sure where I fit in.

Most men said that, because it seemed the easiest thing to do, they followed the guidelines they had learnt from their own parents. Some had a clearer set of rules than others, and many just muddled through.

John, a management consultant aged forty-five with three sons, said:

Let's face it, parenthood is something we all do by ear. Before I got married and for some time after it, I was going round trying to cobble together some sort of basic kind of folklore

77

about what age you should have children, what gap there should be between them in age, what sexes I wanted, what relationship there should be between them, what lessons I ought to teach them. In fact, you really have to start thinking about it as a job.

Lots of men had never changed a nappy, though fewer were self-conscious today about wheeling their children around in the streets. *Their* fathers wouldn't have been seen dead with a pram, but the modern buggy and baby sling were less of a threat to their image. And it was often their mothers, they said, who would not allow their fathers to wheel the pram, on the grounds that they weren't having their husband doing a woman's job.

Unemployed men in working-class areas are used to meeting each other when they go out with their small children. It is a way of getting out of the house and avoiding the tension of being constantly under the wife's feet. One or two I spoke to had found a new pleasure in the company of growing children, and would have been sorry to miss the new closeness they were experiencing from their children's dependence on them.

Thirty-four-year-old Terry's wife was working; he was unemployed.

My little boy was crying in the night and it suddenly hit me. I just saw it in a different light – *I'm* the person he wants. I felt privileged and needed. Suddenly I could cope so much better.

But Leslie, a forty-nine-year-old advertising executive with children of four and two by his second wife, was at work most of the time so he spoke wistfully:

I think there is a problem about my relationship with the children and I can't see what to do about it. My wife only works part-time at the moment and she's at home with the children most of the day. She's a marvellous mother and looks after them both beautifully. I try and do my bit – I change nappies, make the baby's bottles, sometimes give them their meals at weekends and play with them. The trouble is that if my wife's around they both want her. If she goes out and I hold the fort, it's not long before we're all miserable. I want to have a happy time with them, but it's just at this age that they want her more than me. I expect I may come into my own when they're a bit older.

This clear sense of unhappiness with what feels like rejection by small children is the problem often forced on men by the nature of their work. The job a man does not only determines the sort of relationship he can have with his children, but much else in his life as well.

Many men I spoke to felt regret at being almost strangers to their children. These were men who left home before their children were up, and who returned just in time to see them going to bed. Young, ambitious men who chose to work long hours, to bring work home from the office, or men whose jobs demanded that they worked in the evenings, forfeited the chance to spend much time with their children. The wife of musician Geoffrey felt he had let her and the children down when they were growing up. He is a violinist with a major orchestra and now forty-eight.

I've got four daughters. They haven't told me that I haven't been a good father, but my wife has. She had to work very hard at it, particularly when they were young.

When you're trying to be a success in the music business you have to start out in a fairly humble way. It meant my being out practically every evening, and that's not very good for family life. I don't think it made it very easy, and I've never claimed that it did. One was just not doing the kind of nine-to-five job where one could come home and play with the kids. I've had more conflicts with my wife over this than I've had with the kids. They are perfectly capable of saying what they think, and do frequently, but they've never actually said that.

My wife liked bringing up children – she's an incredibly competent lady – but she's a musician as well. We met at the Royal College of Music. She was very accomplished, but she

79

didn't touch a musical instrument for all the years – about eighteen I suppose – that she was bringing up the children. My wife is continually telling me that I should have had sons. It doesn't concern me at all. Perhaps she thinks that as a father I'd have spent more time with them if they'd been boys. . . . But I feel that most of my present pupils who have young children do share their time out a great deal more than we did.

Another man who felt that his job had interfered with his ability to spend enough time with his children was Trevor, a forty-five-year-old power station worker, who has always been on the shift system. With a daughter and a son, both teenagers, he senses that he has missed something important:

Being on shifts was a drawback in many ways. It was always a bit of a dampener for the kids when they were younger, if I was asleep upstairs. I enjoyed having the children, but again it's one of those things, like everybody tells you your school-days are the happiest time, and until you leave school you don't start realizing that. It's the same with bringing up kids. The children seem to have grown up so quick. I do feel I missed something. I get on well with them. I hope if they were in trouble they would turn to me. I think the boy would more than the girl.

Some men preferred their children when they were young. They loved playing with them as babies, reading to them as toddlers, and larking around in children's games. Dick, a milkman of twenty-six, told me:

I can do all sorts of things with the children that would just seem daft otherwise. I play games that they invent, roar like a lion, and fall about on the floor. In the park, people would think I'd gone mad if I wasn't with them.

Other men with almost grown-up children were irritated by what they saw as the younger generation's obsession with their children. Don, a slightly cynical north country GP aged fifty-six, had come to the conclusion that parents worry too much.

I've had young parents ask me for advice – should I let my child do this, should I let them do that? They've read far too many books, they know far too much, and it hasn't done them or the children any good at all. They've almost lost the ability to take pleasure in the children. On the whole it doesn't matter what they do. Their children aren't really going to turn out much different from anybody else's unless they're another Mozart. Children need security, and a certain amount of routine, but they don't need to be entertained all the time. Two of my children are very well-adjusted and normal, while one's had a lot of problems, but that's about average I should say. It's my own belief that D.H. Lawrence was right as far as children are concerned: 'a little healthy neglect' does no harm. Parents should get on with their own lives and stop worrying about the children.

Older men, though, often felt a sense of regret that they had not been as good fathers as they should have been. The children were growing up exactly at the time that they were ambitiously pursuing a career in their twenties and thirties. When they had time to sit back and relax, the children were leaving home, some starting families of their own. But Charles, the department store chairman, found that grandchildren could be a compensation.

I've got four grandchildren. I enjoy them tremendously, and spend lots of time with them. Quite honestly when my own children were young I was working so hard that I never gave them as much time as I'd have liked. And I'd love to give more time to my grandchildren, perhaps to make up for that a bit.

Men who had very little time to spend with their children during the week, felt under pressure at the weekend. Wives felt time should be spent with the family, and doing things in the house. Children often wanted their fathers to do something quite demanding at the weekend, to make up for the lost time during the week. The men themselves felt they just needed to wind down and potter about pursuing an interest of their own. If this was sport, which almost inevitably took them out of the house and away from the family, it could become a bone of contention.

A car salesman of forty called Mark said:

I spend as much time with the children – I've got a boy and a girl – as possible at the weekend. If I do go to a local rugby match, which I enjoy, my wife feels I'm being selfish and doesn't mind saying so. I am a bit of a fanatic about it in the winter. Of course I can take my son and we both enjoy that. I feel at the weekends I have a lot to do to please everybody, whereas during the week I'm my own man.

Many men today have occupations in which promotion means moving round the country. Some I spoke to drove over a hundred miles each day, to and from work, because they had decided that their family should stay settled in one place. Those who worked near a major city and who were successful enough to be able to afford to live in the country often preferred to do so, for the sake of both the children and their own weekends.

A number of young men from all classes, most of whom lived in the south of England, were giving their offspring totally different experiences from their own childhoods. All those who shared the duties and pleasures of children, as equally as they could, with their wives were married to women who were working. Daniel and Marie, both in their mid thirties, and both writers, took it in turns to work one day and take total responsibility for their three-year-old daughter the next. One amusing consequence of this, Daniel explained, was that for a time the child called them both 'Mummy'.

My father was a businessman, and could never have been as involved with us as I am with Lucy. I love it, I think it's right, and it's good for us both. We were in a position to work from home, and we didn't want and couldn't afford to pay someone else to look after her. She's so precious that I feel, like my wife does, we don't want a stranger bringing her up.

David, a forty-three-year-old public school master with four children ranging from five to thirteen, and with a wife training to be a teacher, thought he enjoyed his children more than other fathers could because he was at home more. He has long holidays with them and lives near his work, so that even if late leaving school, he is home before the average father.

I keep making a mental note to myself to spend more positive time with the children, helping them and listening to them.

I particularly like picking up my children from parties. It's often the only time I have with each of them on their own. I learn a lot about them in a gentle half-hour conversation in the car, about their friends and worries, all without too much probing. I used to get up in the night to see to them, but not as often as my wife. My youngest son has Suzuki violin lessons and part of the commitment is that one or other parent has to be there too. It's a half-hour lesson, and quarter of an hour in the car there and back. I really enjoy the time we have together. I just hope that as they grow up they'll become independent people and be able to take me or leave me as a father. I think when you have a large, happy family you never have time to feel doubt about the meaning of life. This is where I am and where I have my meaning. I think when people complain about their children or think they could have had a better time without them, they're comparing an unreal dream with reality, which inevitably has lots of problems.

The men I spoke to who came from happy families themselves seemed to be the ones who were keen to have children and delighted in time spent with the family. They didn't resent doing things for their children and were willing to take them out for walks or to play at the weekend so that their wives could have some free time.

When I asked if fathers had rules for their children's behaviour or upbringing, it was working-class fathers who more often stressed the importance for their children of getting the most out of their education. Many said quite openly that lack of schooling had been a real drawback to them. Fred, a taxi-driver of fifty-five, said:

I've had a chip on my shoulder all my life actually. I haven't always been a taxi-driver – I was a person who had plenty of power, and I didn't know what to do with it. Plenty of finance, and got no idea of the value of it. But I've got a beautiful wife and three beautiful children. My youngest is at Durham University at the moment. My eldest girl got through her A-level in Russian. I made sure all the children went abroad to learn a language. I didn't push but I wanted them to take every advantage of an education that I had wanted but didn't have. My boy came back from France after seven months speaking like a native.

Dan, a TUC organizer aged forty-six, has two children. He has thought a great deal about their upbringing and has worried not only about their education but about the attitudes they learn at school.

I'm tremendously sceptical of the educational system, particularly in the infant schools. When my daughter started school I was reading about the Third Reich, and what interested and influenced me was that it said that Hitler, once he got power, had looked at the schools, and anyone who was hostile to the Fascist movement he bombed out of school, so he finished up with loyal Fascists. He was working towards an educational system totally controlled by Fascist sympathizers. And that started me wondering about the nature of our own schools and what is the nature of any society's attitude to its schools and to its educational system. As a member of the Communist Party, I started questioning the schools and looking at their influences on my own daughter. I've always been basically an atheist, because my father was an atheist and my mother was religious. He had no time for the church. My daughter was coming home and she was peddling all this Baby Jesus this and Baby Jesus that, and it was the time of Prince Charles getting inaugurated in Caernarvon Castle. And it was all our Prince Charles, and then there was the Queen. I used to develop bizarre experiments with the children. When the Queen was on television I'd sort of abuse her, and my daughter used to go mad and attack me. 'You mustn't say that, it's our Queen!' she'd say. So I could see the influence of the educational system, and at that infant stage, the impressionable age of five, they were being groomed and conditioned to accept authority, the class system, the religious system, the monarchy and the whole works. So I set about trying to counter it by ridicule.

Malcolm, a sixty-one-year-old barrister, was less worried about his children having a good education as both his sons went to Eton. He was wise enough to see that certain imbalances in society might be in their favour, but he did think there was one important lesson for them to learn.

I think one of the joys of marriage is children. I have such fun out of mine, and the first thing I taught each of my sons is that life's unfair – you mustn't ever expect it to be anything else. You've got to expect that lots of unfair things will happen, though sometimes you'll benefit. The other thing I taught them is that it's simply not worth breaking the law. Even if you get away with it the first and second time, eventually you won't, and it will ruin your life.

Management consultant John sums up the attitude of many of the well-educated middle-class fathers I spoke to:

I don't give my sons much advice. Occasionally they ask for it and I'll outline what I think the alternatives are, so they have to make their own minds up.

Within one generation attitudes towards people living together have changed radically, although marriage is still seen as the ultimate goal. No doubt an increased awareness of the divorce rate and personal experience of painful break-ups within the family have helped to bring this about. It is remarkable how many of the older generation, who would have condemned it twenty years ago, now think that for their children to live together before marriage is not only acceptable but a good idea. Ron, who enjoyed bringing his children up, said:

I wouldn't mind if my daughter wanted to live with someone before she was married. I'd sooner have her do that than get married and make a mistake and have all the trauma and upset of a divorce. I'd be quite happy for her to do that. I wouldn't like her to be indiscriminate, jumping from one to another. I wouldn't like her on the pill at fifteen, and I don't know what age would be all right. It's very difficult when it's your own.

Some men thought things had changed because young people, if both were working, were better off today. They could afford to rent a flat and postpone marriage. Nowadays working-class children seemed less likely to stay at home until they were married. Even in the most traditional communities there is a new tolerance in this respect. Tom, a Lancashire coalminer of forty-four with two grown-up children, said:

In this day and age I wouldn't mind if my children lived with people before they were married. It wouldn't bother me at all. I mean, I only found out by accident, but I knew that my daughter was on the pill before she got married. She weren't on the pill for nothing.

Even the septuagenarian funeral director, Alec, who might well have been expected to find such changes in morality hard to cope with, said:

I didn't disapprove of my youngest son living with someone before he was married. I didn't have any moral objections to it. I'm old-fashioned enough to believe that children don't have a natural place outside marriage because I feel sorry for them, a lot of them, and we do know quite a few. I don't think I've ever tried to interfere with my sons. They've never let me down – I don't think they ever would. And when I wanted support, it was there.

Dennis, a security officer of fifty-nine with one daughter who is the apple of his eye, has in the last ten years changed his ideas about young people living together.

I had such a close relationship with my daughter that when she was sixteen and she had her first boyfriend, I resented him. I told my daughter about wicked people. They don't teach them about them at school. She didn't believe me at first. She does now. I wouldn't mind if she slept with somebody. We've talked about that. Deep down I'd be very upset if she were pregnant, but I wouldn't show that to her. I don't think she's on the pill, but I don't know. I've got suspicions, but I've left that to my wife. I wouldn't like her to live with someone before she was married, but if she really thought it was right, she'd have my blessing. Perhaps ten years ago I would've said no. If my daughter had a black boyfriend I'd be disappointed, but I wouldn't stop her. I wouldn't mind a black policeman.

Many men felt naturally more protective towards daughters than sons, and were anxious about the amount of freedom that their daughters demanded today. Alf, a trade union official from East Anglia, has a daughter of twenty-three and comes from a traditional family where he has the final word. But like many fathers with daughters I spoke to, he remembers the worry of dealing with her in her teens.

The problem with my daughter was no different to what any other parent had. I suppose all daughters are rebels when it comes to a certain stage in life. It was her early teens. In my day coming in at half past ten at night was 'out late' but one o'clock in the morning seems to be the standard now for teenagers. I started to live with that. But I think I was probably more protective because I needed to be, because of the changes in society generally over the years. She wanted a lot of freedoms that I didn't have, and she got them. In my family, incidentally, it was always what Dad said. Don't know why it should be, because my wife's quite capable of putting her foot down, believe me. But what I say goes.

A retired bank manager, Stuart, who now spends a great deal of time with his grandchildren, has a son and a daughter in their thirties. He found, like many men of his age, that a rejection of his beliefs would have been upsetting, even though he felt he had already had to adapt his ideas quite considerably.

If my children had become revolutionaries or Bennites, or whatever, I'd have been very upset indeed, because it would have been so much against my background, belief and up-bringing, and I think it would have been treachery to me in those days. I think it still would, in a sense. I would find it very hard to take, that kind of thing. Although things are not as hard as they appear to be. For example, my daughter is married to a Jew. I'm very fond of my son-in-law, but if someone had said to me years before that my daughter was going to marry a Jew, I'd have been most upset. I don't know why, it's background again.

Terry, an agricultural labourer of twenty-five from Suffolk, can see things from a woman's point of view now he has a baby daughter:

A daughter will be a lot more worry than a son, because I know what blokes are like, you see, so I'll be a lot more wary when she goes out.

A large number of the fathers to whom I spoke admitted that they would find it difficult not to be critical when their daughters started to bring home boyfriends, particularly if they were somehow not up to scratch. Fred, a dustman of forty from south London, has two sons and one daughter aged fourteen.

I've warned my daughter of the type of people not to go with. Put it this way, I'd advise her to pick a boy of her own standards. If she came round here with a punk with an ear-ring. I'd sling him out. Well, you know, I'd be very upset. I don't like the idea that my children are going to get like that. I suppose there again it's going back to the way I was brought up.

Basil, a sixty-three-year-old security officer working for a car manufacturer in the Midlands, had doubts about the whole concept of fatherhood:

Women are nice to have around because they flatter the ego, but definitely not to be trusted even as small girls. Boys are all right when they're well behaved, but children altogether are a source of problems rather than pleasure. . . . I have a feeling that if I went my way again, I'm not sure that I'd want children.

I'm very much in favour of boys rather than girls. I have a granddaughter but my eldest grandson is my favourite. He's everything I want to see in a person. He's eight, he tries to please people. He must be so bright because he never says anything to upset anybody, he always says the right thing. I think that's lovely. Now my granddaughter, she'll come up and put her arms round your neck, but I don't think it's genuine. You have to be careful with little girls. They can get away with murder doing that.

Only Basil and one other informant – both over sixty – objected to their children living with someone before marriage. Basil expected them to have had no experience of sex at all. He was one of the men who believed in unchanging standards and held the unusual view, among the many men I spoke to, that children should adhere strictly to parental beliefs.

I would have been very annoyed if my children had not been pure when they got married – for both the boys and the girls.

I would have given the boys a bloody good hiding and given the girls a good telling off. I wouldn't disown them because anybody can slip up, but I would've been very annoyed. I just don't like that sort of thing. I might be funny, Victorian or whatnot, but that's it. I could have gone with other women in Italy or Africa during the war, but I didn't want to. If I'd have done it, my missus would have done the same thing over here. Whether she did or not, I don't know, but she trusted me and I trusted her.

A number of men mentioned that the advantage of having daughters was that as they grew up they brought home their 'nubile and delicious friends', as one stock-broker put it. Basil made a similar comment:

I never wanted a daughter, I always wanted boys, though now – it might be the ego thing – I'd be very proud walking down the road with a nice daughter. I think that's been brought to my attention since my son's had his girlfriend. I like to be with her. A nice girl is pleasant company.

But it was interesting how many men were suspicious of their own world when it came to their daughters finding husbands. Michael a BBC producer said he would hate his daughter to come to work for 'Auntie':

It's not a very healthy place for women. Most of the men they meet are married, and girls get messed around, and dumped. I'd really try and prevent a daughter of mine coming here.

Giles, an insurance broker, felt the same about the City:

The City is not a good place to send your daughter. I say this because I've seen girls come into the office at eighteen, as secretaries or even fund managers, and still be sitting there at thirty. It doesn't seem to work.

There seemed to be a consistently strong feeling amongst newly married young men in their twenties that, because of the expense and financial worries of a new flat or house, children should be postponed, perhaps indefinitely. Bank clerk Chris, aged twenty-five with a working wife, had planned his life in some detail.

With my parents' generation, the trend seemed to be that you got married, had your children and managed somehow. These days I think the financial side of it is more of a worry. Certainly all of our friends have set out with the idea that they will have children four or five years after they get married. The wife works at the beginning, they build a base and eventually they'll think about children, but it always seems a little bit reluctantly. At this stage, I wouldn't mind having no children at all. A lot of people have said to me that your life won't be complete until you've had children, but it's very hard to tell from the other side of the fence.

Ronald, a thirty-two-year-old VAT inspector, comes from a family where he says he had little real affection as a child, and is tired of other people getting at him because he and his wife don't want children.

I don't want children, no. I have an affinity with children and I like them, but I've got enough nephews and nieces to keep me going for ever, so I'm not actually worried about it. My wife doesn't want them – and her sister doesn't want them either – they're much alike in that respect. It could be something to do with the alarming divorce rate in their family. In a couple of those families the kids have definitely suffered as a result. I don't really know why my wife doesn't want children, and there doesn't seem to be any need to discuss it very deeply – further conversation doesn't seem necessary. I get tired of having to justify our decision:
  'How old are you?'
  'Thirty-two.'
  'You married?'
  'Yes.'
  'How old's your wife?'
  'Twenty-six.'
  'How many kids you got?'
  'None.'
  'None? Why not?'

And it's from people you'd least expect it from – even fairly close friends.

But if you take stock – I mean, collectively we've now got a comfortable income. If we had children, we'd be back where we were five or six years ago, which is when we had no spare money to do anything – not even to keep the house looking nice. In the end I'm sure I'd actually resent a child. People say you adjust quickly but I couldn't see that. I don't think we could even meet our standing orders.

David, a public school master who talked earlier about the pleasure of spending his time with his four growing children, summed up the problem for fathers:

The problem for men is that they've never thought about fatherhood as an inner vocation. They don't seem to make the final decision that it's a way of life. Life is full of trade-offs, and having children does mean there are some things we simply can't do. We can't afford to go abroad for holidays at the moment for instance, but that's not important. What is very important, and I can see this as a father and a teacher, is for children to have a good relationship with their father. I have divorced fathers coming to me at school worried about the progress of their children, and because they're worried I think they develop an even better relationship with their children than they had when they were at home. I've spoken to the children here and it's really exciting for some of these girls to be taken out alone by their father, and be given all his attention.

I think what we need is a campaign to awaken and increase the idea of fatherhood, so that men can enjoy the commitment and see the whole thing as a positive extension of their life.

Up to a point, Dan, the TUC organizer, did just that.

Initially when my wife was pregnant, I resented it. I just did not like children at that stage. I did not want them. But once the child was born, there were no problems for me. I got a tremendous amount of satisfaction from them. In honesty to myself, I think having children developed me as a person. I exploited the fact of having children because it assisted me to overcome many of the inhibitions that I felt in different directions – such as shyness. I could use them in different ways for a whole number of things. I mean, even a simple thing, like swimming. I couldn't swim as an adult and if I was taking my children swimming, they were the reason that I could go in and have a good time. So I learned to swim as an adult, through them, really. I helped them overcome their fear of the water and then indirectly I could overcome mine.

Me and my wife, we fell into the stereotype roles in bringing up the children. She stayed at home and I went out to work. I always felt that we attempted to be fair and reasoned with them. I would not adopt an overtly disciplinarian position. My attitude to children within the family unit is that once the child feels that it can control or dominate the parents, it'll develop a natural sort of abuse of the parents – you know, they're only here to furnish the comforts. . . . There's got to be a mutual understanding and respect, and not one of authoritarian dominance. I don't seek that, although when I feel I'm being abused or something, I can be quite sharp. But I don't like doing that and it does upset me.

Mick, aged forty, who works in the film industry went the whole hog and brought up his child himself.

I married a young girl who basically didn't want to have a child that early on in the relationship. I was about twenty-six and she was about twenty-one. Right from the beginning I was desperately keen to have a child because, I think, when I was a kid at university a girlfriend got pregnant and had an abortion and I was very upset about that. It's not something I've ever talked about before. I did agree to it at the time because we were very, very young. But when my wife got pregnant I was desperately keen to have the child, so I said, 'I'll marry you, anything. We've got to have this child.' She didn't want to. She didn't care.

I'd always felt this affinity to children but hadn't been aware of it until this other girl had an abortion early on. Then it really hit me, the significance of it, so I wanted my wife to keep the child and managed to persuade her by offering her a home and a family.

I felt unbelievable when my daughter was born. It was just wonderful, just terrific. I don't want to be sentimental or romantic about it but it was a wonderful thing to experience. Also I'd never comprehended the pain involved in something that is normal. I mean, it was excruciatingly painful for my wife, and she had a perfectly normal birth. The baby was given to me first and I just burst into tears, as I suppose all fathers do. I assumed that once we had the baby the marriage would stay strong, and I did the normal male things, like work, and expected my wife to look after the house, and the baby, and cook meals. My wife's studies were interrupted. She had one degree and had been planning to do a doctorate. She was going back to university, and it all just crumbled. I don't really know why. That's much more difficult to talk about.

If we hadn't had a child, I think our marriage would have survived. I think I was terribly wrong, really. I mean, I blame myself because I neglected my wife on account of the baby. I remember saying terribly cruel things to the little tiny baby. In other words, I was having a dig at my wife through the baby. I really don't know why I was doing that. I think it was a fundamental psychological punishment for the fact that my own parents' marriage went wrong. There is something very deep about it because I didn't want my marriage to go wrong. I didn't want to punish this woman who'd given me this wonderful child. But I was doing it. It was awful.

My wife needed to be loved really. She needed to feel that her life at twenty-one had not been completely disrupted, that the man she loved loved her more, not less. Since she'd actually gone through this reluctant pregnancy, she needed support, she needed caring for, she needed all the things that I didn't offer her. I've never talked about this before. This is quite surprising because we are meant to be talking about the baby. Of course, I was behaving abominably and not offering her any of the things she needed and she, as people do, behaved similarly abominably. She did things like arranging deliberately not to be there when I had to go and work. She'd say she had to go to lectures or something so that I was literally stuck there with the baby that I would never ever leave. My wife would deliberately not be there and punish me in the same way that I'd punished her. . . .

My wife was a bit ambitious, too, and of course she was very young. But she would not talk about it, she would not agree that we had to work out something. So we were punishing each other like this for a year or so, and finally the whole thing broke up.

My wife couldn't actually bear to talk about things that really are crucial. So we didn't ever talk about it. She had a difficult family, I had a difficult family. We had decided to get married and not tell anybody, and then to present them with a *fait accompli*. Neither set of parents came to the wedding. . . . Her father was always on about the fact that his mother abandoned him when he was a baby. I've thought about it before, but I've never talked about it. He was always saying, 'I've always been abandoned, my whole life', and he would use that in the context of *his* family. My wife had a very difficult relationship with him. She hated him, I think. He was a sort of slobby kind of character. He was fat and always talked about farting – do you know the kind of man? But our marriage helped her because he loved me, this fat farting father. It was not a sexual thing, he just adored me, and we got on exceptionally well. So I bridged a gap there, in the context of her father whom she hated and was afraid of more or less. The relationship between her father and her is very significant in what happened subsequently.

Anyway, we finally split up and it got to the stage where you know it's disastrous and over, and then it really becomes a physical question of who moves out, when and how. The baby was two. I was absolutely unprepared for even the remotest possibility that I would have to look after it on my own. It had never crossed my mind and not because I didn't want to. It was because I just didn't think that it would ever occur. It had never occurred to me that I would not be able to go into work at nine o'clock and come home when I'd finished work.

Around this time we'd applied to move into one of these

rather lovely flats around Kensington and Chelsea which they used to call high-income rental flats. I was earning a substantial salary, and my wife was earning bits and pieces, so potentially we were a good earning couple. Eventually this flat was offered to us, and that was when we made the break. We moved into the flat. I was working in the morning and I came home to move out, expecting that we'd have some civilized discussion about who was going to look after our daughter and how. I was assuming subconsciously that my wife would look after her, and that I would be the normal visiting supporting parent. I know for a fact that I hadn't assumed that I was going to be the parent who had her for most of the time, this baby in nappies. You can imagine what it was like. I arrived home at lunchtime and the car was packed up with all my things. Since I was going to move anyway, it wasn't that dramatic. My wife said, 'Right, this flat is mine now. I've spoken to the landlord. I've transferred the tenancy. Mine. Out. Finished.' Then she gave me the baby, and I went.

I don't think I'll ever understand how she could abandon her baby, except that it was the ultimate punishment. She wanted me to feel what it was like to have this responsibility for a baby while someone else is going out to work. I'm telling you that now, ten years later, but I didn't know that at the time. I thought she was just being a nasty vindictive bitch, and punishing me. Anyway, there I was left with the baby. I just felt panic. I wouldn't think this now, but I was wondering how the Hell I was going to work the next day. I didn't think, well, bugger that, I'll have to ring up and say I can't come in. I thought, how am I going to work? We had made tentative arrangements with the nursery at the college where my wife was studying, so I got on to them and asked them if the baby could come tomorrow. And they said she could, so she was taken to this toddlers' nursery from nine o'clock in the morning until about two or three. So I used to work those hours. I used to go and work – do everything in those hours – and then pick her up. This went on for two or three weeks, and then my wife appeared. She had lost weight and was obviously terribly stricken by it all, but was not admitting it, and I still didn't offer anything.

I regret that now. I was so in need of love and affection myself – this may sound terribly pathetic really – that I was just taking. And when she came round having behaved abominably, I just felt, God, you've landed me in the shit. I've had to fuck up my job and everything. You've really punished me. And I still didn't offer her what she wanted. We carried on in that vein. It was me saying, how dare you do this? It's all right for you, you've got no responsibility. I've had the baby, how do you think I've managed? It was not, I love you, for God's sake come back and I'll give you all the love you want.

Then for a while we had a terrible time of me going round to my wife's with our daughter when I needed her to babysit, and my wife not being there. The whole thing was played out in a ritual fashion.

My daughter was terrific through all this. She usually just laughed and didn't know what was going on. She used to panic when we shouted at each other, but that was all. She would go into a corner and have a little panic. I honestly don't think she missed her mother when she was with me. I can't remember her actually complaining about her mother not being there. I can remember her being delighted when her mother came round to see her, and thrilled to go out with her. But it seemed to work, and she was fairly secure. Because she was always picked up by me, there was no rift between a mother and a child who'd had much more attention from a mother. She'd had an equal amount of attention from me, if not more. She'd had as much physical contact with me – except the breast, of course – as she'd had with her mother. But I don't honestly think she missed her in any way that I was able to interpret. But that may not be true, of course. She certainly does not mention it now.

Then gradually things got worse and the babysitting arrangements fell through. I always had a bit of a fear that my wife might nip in and take the baby off. In fact, she did turn up one day, on one of these visiting arrangements, and said, 'We can't live together, the only way I can look after the baby is to take her with me abroad. I'm going to take her.'

I panicked and said, 'No, you're not', and I got a court order. I would have been devastated if she'd gone to live out in Italy.

From that moment on, the whole thing became a legal matter between her solicitors and my solicitors, with organized visiting on Sunday afternoons which, after about three months, she completely dropped. My daughter and I have not heard from her since. When my solicitors wanted to serve divorce papers, they could not trace her. So we're not legally divorced yet.

But the final irony is that about a year ago we were sitting in a restaurant, my daughter and I, one Saturday lunchtime, and there was this woman serving. I just got a feeling of familiarity; I didn't recognize her. My daughter said,'That woman keeps looking at me.' And it was my wife! She'd aged badly during those ten years. I looked down and saw that she was wearing a ring like this one I'm wearing.

I was a coward, if you like, but I couldn't have coped with my daughter's reaction to her. So we left. My daughter does not know that that was her mother. In retrospect, I can see that I did it out of cowardice. I was afraid to talk to my wife. I didn't want to get involved. I suppose I was afraid of all the nastiness of the legal wrangle that had been exchanged with solicitors' letters – all the lies, and all the things that *she* had said she wanted. You know, she actually tried to get maintenance off me. You can imagine how I felt about that when I was trying to struggle to keep going. I couldn't just confront the issue and say, 'How are you after all these years?' and, 'Here is our daughter. Isn't she beautiful?' I opted out. I paid the bill in a civilized way and disappeared.

My daughter is now coming up for twelve. I don't know if I'll ever be able to tell her about that particular incident. I would like to think I could, because we talk honestly about everything. But it may hurt her, you see. That's why I wouldn't. She might be hurt to think that I didn't introduce her to her mother. I might tell her when she's older, when she might understand. I would not want to keep them apart. If her mother were to write to me and say that she'd like to see her daughter again, I would do everything I possibly could to organize that, in a civilized way.

When I saw my wife in the restaurant, I didn't feel a physical attachment to her at all. In fact, as I said, for a while I didn't recognize her. I think that she'd gone through a lot of stress and, being the kind of person she is, would not admit it. She would never be able to sit down and say that she was suffering agonies from having abandoned contact with her daughter, or even with this man that she had loved. She would have to defend herself with pride and self-esteem. As, indeed, I did for a long time.

I wouldn't have talked like this ten years ago. I would have said that it wasn't my fault, that I was badly treated – fancy landing me with a baby, and that sort of thing. I would not even have thought for a moment that I might have been responsible in any way for taking this beautiful young girl into my bed and loving her and giving her a baby. I would have assumed that she was the lucky one.

I think my views have been changed by having a daughter. When you have a child, and particularly if you look after them on your own, you have to have an honest relationship with them, otherwise you can't function, really. Your adult values come into your social life as well. I mean, my life consists of working and looking after my daughter, being with her. Occasionally I socialize, but very, very little. If I do go out, it's with her. So all the values that I would expect from adult contact, and children being treated as children, don't really occur. I have a relationship with her as I would to another adult, which is based on honesty and frankness and kindness and decent behaviour and all the kinds of things that I would expect from another adult.

I think I'm afraid of my daughter being too dependent on me. I do feel this terrible fear that something might happen to me and that there is literally nobody else.

I think being a single parent has made me a much better person. I would have been abominable as I was ten years ago. I'm less ambitious, less of a careerist, less successful, less rich. But none of that matters.

There's only one factor which is like a stain in the whole business of being a single parent – the rest is just pure delight – and it's that feeling of total responsibility day and night. You're never free of it. Even with au pairs and grandmothers, it's not the same. There have been occasions when I have had someone staying with me, and I've been absolutely astonished at how well I've slept. The reason I've slept so well is that I know that, if something happened in the middle of the night, just for that one night the responsibility is shared. It's psychological, and it's impossible to talk about because most people, single parents, have problems with money. They have problems with surviving, they don't have well-paid jobs, and they're obsessed with those kinds of things: survival. But this total responsibility is the only thing that there is no release from, the only strain, and it's normally a mother's, although husbands share it.

My daughter is actually aware of my sexuality, and we have a frank, honest relationship about things like when a woman is going to share my bed. She actually stops me in restaurants and says, 'Daddy, you're flirting.' She's known three women in my bed, one of whom is the mother of my son. My daughter just took it for granted that she would be around from time to time, and that when she came she'd sleep in the same bed as me. Another was a delightful woman who had four children, with whom I had an affair for two years. And I love and respect her possibly more than anyone else. She had problems. She had a difficult relationship with her father, and relates to men as if they are all her father. And of course I'm not her father, so that didn't work out. My daughter loved her, and would come in for cuddles together with her. There has never been any difficulty in her understanding of what was going on. She's been jealous of the last relationship I've had, but it has not affected her coming into bed in the morning.

Of course there have been times when I've felt like staying at work late, drinking with the boys, but ultimately it doesn't matter – none of that matters to me. I mean I have felt inconvenience. I have thought that it would be nice not to have to go home and to stay longer in places. But it matters far more to feel that you are doing something worthwhile. I don't think I regret this lack of social freedom at all, particularly now my daughter has got to the stage where she can come anyway. There's nothing that I want to see in the way of concerts, films or theatre that she can't come to. Occasionally I get invited to dinner parties, and if I really want to go I can organize

100

babysitters. It's an annoyance, but it's not a serious matter at all. It's never stopped me doing any work that needed to be done, ever. I just have to be organized. We've had a number of different au pairs, but I've never had anyone living in. I've always avoided that.

As sons, brothers and husbands, most informants seemed cautious about adapting to the changing attitudes of the 1980s, but as parents they were much more forthcoming. Intially uncertain of what was required of them, nervous, but determined, they made great efforts to participate in their children's lives. Like many people when faced with doubts, they involved themselves even more in the activity about which they felt uncertain, striving to get it right, hoping perhaps that familiarity would make it easier.

Extremely conscious that they were cut off from their offspring by their long hours away from home, aware that their weekends were already crowded with things they would like to be doing, or felt they ought to be doing, for their wives, they still spent hours with their children, leaving little time for themselves. Devoted, anxious to help, aware of the problems, willing, enthusiastic, positive, they seemed to have taken to heart all the lessons they had learnt from their own parents and expressed so vehemently in Chapter 2. Perhaps their honesty and courageousness came across most strongly in their acceptance of sex before marriage for their own children. Not surprisingly, most would have preferred this to be with the future son- or daughter-in-law, but they did understand the need for the next generation to experiment, to learn, to find out before they, in their turn, plunged into marriage. Perhaps they were conscious from their own lives that marriage is not necessarily the consequence of love, nor is it the sole focus of a loving relationship. For some, romantic love turns out to be the very antithesis of marriage.

Chapter Six

MEN AS LOVERS AND CUCKOLDS

Over 60 per cent of the married men interviewed had had one or more affairs since marrying. When the first affair was over subsequent affairs seemed far less a problem of conscience than of the need for secrecy. Men may not be very open about their emotions, but they are highly susceptible to love, romance, sex and excitement.

To begin with many spoke of heartache, loneliness and depression, as though their 'affair' was over. But this was usually an account of their first extra-marital excursion, the one which had often caused them the most pain and upheaval. Many had had a series of affairs or several long-standing relationships over the years, about which they felt varying degrees of guilt. Only those with professedly 'open' marriages, or those who felt that once a man lost interest in women he might as well be dead, said they felt no guilt whatever.

Affairs are not confined to men of any one class, nor to any particular age-group, though there are differences in both class and age. If a man of seventy is having an affair he is more likely to be middle or upper middle class. It is easier for rich men, socially and professionally mobile, to organize affairs than it is for men who live and work in small homogeneous communities. The rich have more freedom and many more plausible excuses to be away from home.

There were some young men, mostly in their twenties and thirties, who found that the absence of what they called suitable girls made having affairs a thing of the past. Simon, an unmarried producer of TV commercials aged thirty-five, said he shied away from modern predatory women:

They all seem to want babies. It's the latest thing. All they want to do is to look at our teeth, feel our fetlocks and see what sort of father we'll make for their children. It's a question of pouring the father out with the bathwater. We men have become very expendable.

Lord Eastbourne has always loved the company of beautiful women. Large, humorous and charming, he's always had life as he wanted it, and talks of his affairs:

At Eton, girlfriends were quite unheard of. It was all talk and no action. Occasionally a boy was sacked for having what was probably a very mild flirtation with one of the maids, but as most of the maids were sixty-five, you were lucky in finding a younger one. There was a limited number of beautiful boys in the school whom everyone worshipped from a distance. The system definitely made me shyer with girls than if I'd gone to a mixed school.

It was not until later that I decided that London life was for me. I shared a flat with friends, but I never slept there. I was always at a party; I used to dance six nights a week. And in the fifties you got invitations – dinner and dancing – literally two a night. Suddenly I thought that women were marvellous. I hadn't really had any sex life up till then. The first sex life I had was when I was twenty-five, or something like that. Quite amazing, really. I went to a party at Maidenhead, with a lovely girl who had the most sexy voice you'd ever heard. We mucked about in a boat and then we drove up to London and we got under a blanket in the front of the car in Oxford Street. We've never forgotten it. She got in the train to Cornwall the next day and got engaged to someone whom she knew really well, in case she was going to have a baby, and broke it off when she found she wasn't. Can you imagine anything more uncomfortable, or stupid? It was rather sweet, I suppose.

Then later I fell in love with a singer and we used to spend every weekend together. Then her agent said she had to choose between her career or marriage, so that was that. I was a bit shaken.

I suppose, like so many people, I got married on a rebound. I think my wife did, too. It's no bad formula, in a way. You probably take a cooler look at it than you would do otherwise.

My first affair, I suppose, was about five years after we were married. I felt very guilty, yes, because there were four of us and we were all close friends. That didn't remain a secret, and it caused problems. Actually, I think I would have married her. But she wouldn't. We talked about it a lot, and I'm sure she was right. I regret to say that I wouldn't have missed that affair – it was wonderful.

It's difficult to remember the nuances now, but it was certainly more consuming than anything had been before or has been since. It could never happen again – one grows colder and harder. One goes on falling in love, but it's rather more clinical love, isn't it? This was so total, it was awful in a way. Before we were fully discovered, I suppose it went on for about two years. There was a local informant – charming – so we had an awful Round Table discussion, she and her husband and my wife and me, and we agreed not to see each other for a year, which was very difficult when we lived only a few miles apart. They forced us to agree. We didn't see each other for a year, and on the 365th day I had the best day in bed I'd ever had in my life. That year didn't make the slightest difference. And then we were discovered again, inevitably. They had to move away.

I do think marriage has put constraints on me, yes. I don't know about other people, but I just feel that with my particular nature it does. I wouldn't normally say this, but I'm talking very frankly with you. I went to a dinner party the other night and there were ten people there – husbands and wives – and, including my own wife, of course, I'd been to bed with all the wives in the room. They all knew individually, but none of them knew collectively. It amused me immensely and I wished they all knew, in a way. They were extremely attractive, very nice girls, and I'm very fond of them all, but there's no way you can say that having affairs is a man's prerogative. They were all married at the time and are married now.

I don't think I could ever be alone. I think I would have to be either married to or living with someone. I rather enjoy relationships with women and talking to women. I have had far too many, late in life. Quite often disastrously unfair and difficult but very nice. I have had to have a secret life, yes. I don't think that that's necessarily part of the fun. I've been asked that before and I've asked myself, too. If my wife discovers, she says, 'Yes, it s part of the fun, that s why you do it.' But I think it is true to say that quite often the chase is much the most exciting part of the whole thing. The success element becomes dull and then you want to move on to other fields. It's not the secrecy, it's the excitement of something different

It's usually very evident if someone finds someone else attractive by the way they look at each other You get some message that goes through Sometimes it s instant and sometimes it develops. Living in the country, the opportunities are fairly limited, which is probably a very good thing, and there s more chance of a marriage surviving. But I'm afraid I also think that casual sex with people who are attractive is quite harmless, and without any sort of scars on either side

I do mind getting older I would prefer not to. It s much worse for women than for men I've never been to bed with anyone older than myself, no. It s not a rule, but someone older probably couldn't be attractive to me I think that it starts with the eyes, then everything else falls into place.

I don't think I've ever regretted the number of affairs I've had. There is every reason to regret them, as I think they are unfair, and I do feel guilty, really I suppose I could say that I've only ever had two, maybe three affairs that anyone could call terribly serious. I've tended to have – if you call them affairs – relationships with my various secretaries. Totally mutual and enjoyable, and never totally binding – not ones that would ever be of a perfect nature. I suppose I used to choose them because I thought they looked attractive. Not now.

My wife has been made miserable by my affairs, on occasion. I don't know if she's had affairs, and I really don't mind. I wouldn't be horrified. When she discovered on one occasion, she said, 'Well, I've had affairs with two men, and it was all very good.' But I've never asked her about it since or whether she was telling the truth or whether it was a spur-of-the-moment thing. I really don't mind. I don't see why one should. I mean, I've got nothing to mind about. It's an untalked-about area between us, really. I think if she didn't know, she wouldn't mind now. But I've noticed that when I'm in London she tends to organize my life to an extent.

Sex has always been quite important in my life because it's good. It's fun and I like being emotionally involved. I tell you, from a child onwards I've always done things that I shouldn't have done – to see what happens, not for a dare. But being involved with someone – there's nothing like it. And new experiences – when you've got a relationship with a husband or a wife, which is a permanency, which is marvellous, but it's different. You don't have the new excitement coming along, and maybe part of it is the element of the chase, maybe part of it is the element of fear of being discovered. But the whole thing tied up together is very exciting.

This need for a close emotional involvement was often mentioned as a reason for their affairs by men who frequently changed partners. But the contrary need for excitement prevented them from forming long-term relationships. Many working-class men, whose jobs were local or who lived in small communities where everybody knew everybody else, found themselves involved in highly complicated subterfuges to hide an affair, not only from their wife, but from their neighbours and workmates. Having a car helped, as did a hobby such as fishing or birdwatching, which gave a legitimate excuse to leave home for a whole day, or even a weekend, without too much fuss. Bill, aged thirty-nine, married with two children, an electrician in a small Lancashire town, explains the problems:

The worst thing I've ever done is have an affair. It's going on now. I'm living two lives. There's too much pretending – it's a strain. But I'm frightened to leave them both.

I'd told my wife I was going fishing and my girlfriend that my wife was away for the weekend – neither of these things was true. I set off from work to pick up my girlfriend – we were going up to the Lakes for the night – and halfway there I realized I'd forgotten all my fishing tackle. As it was late and dark, my girlfriend suggested we drive back and pick it up, but I couldn't risk it with the wife around. I prayed she'd never find the damn things in the garage

A lot of people would say it is wrong, including my wife. I don't know if my wife knows. Possibly she doesn't want to know, I don't know. I'm just an average man – no better and no worse than anybody else.

Many affairs started just a few years after marriage, though the men who waited longer before having their first affair seemed to be the ones most likely to leave home as a result, and for whom the experience was more traumatic. Some men talked about the beginning of an affair as though it had been beyond their control Some said the woman had 'done the running', by dropping hints or sending him a message, and that he would never have considered it, or had the nerve to approach her, if she had not made it clear that she was keen. To begin with, the excitement, sexual attraction, newness and danger prevented the men from thinking clearly about the possible consequences. At that point, most men said, the consequences were furthest from their mind.

At the beginning the attraction was most often looks alone, though many men said they needed a more intellectual relationship than their wife could provide. I took this often to mean that they wanted someone to talk to – perhaps just someone new, with time for them.

Most men said their affairs were with women they had met at work. Sometimes they worked in the same office or factory, sometimes they were introduced at a chance meeting with a friend. Eric, aged thirty-seven, works as an engineering consultant.

I was doing some consultancy work in London for an old colleague of mine. There was a girl working in his office we had lunch with. She's a secretary, but a high flier; she wants to go to New York. I was attracted to her. I was working there on and off for a few weeks, and had plenty of excuses to talk to her. The opportunity was there. She has her own flat, and eventually I went back there with her. It's odd, but she's a bit like my wife to look at, but much more outward-going, more sociable. I've been married for several years and never been unfaithful, so I was both shocked and surprised, though I didn't feel very guilty at first. We met each other once a week, once a fortnight, and I stayed with her in the flat. I'm often away on business, so it was easy. It all felt very natural. I found her incredibly exciting. It made me feel very good that she loved me. I was desperate to show her off, and arranged to meet two friends one evening. We felt like a couple; they liked her, and teased me about her. . . . It may sound very selfish, but I wanted my wife to meet her too. I tried to think of a way that they could meet. I found it so hard not to talk about her that if my wife had met her it might make it easier.

Funnily enough, I didn't feel bad about it when it was going on, but unfortunately my wife found out. She had suspected something, and half hinted that I wasn't making love to her very often, so if she didn't know me better, she'd have thought there was somebody else. A friend of hers had seen us together somewhere in London, and then she asked me outright. I left home for a few days. I didn't know what to do. I didn't want to lose the girl, but I couldn't leave my children. I just phoned her up and told her it was over. She was really broken up. I've never seen her since. That was two years ago. I don't think my wife has ever forgotten it.

When it came to it, very few men wanted to leave home, and always because of the children. Giles is an insurance broker aged forty-four, and married for over twenty years. He has four children.

There haven't been many black spots in my life. I suppose one is when I fell in love with someone. It was very painful, actually, revealingly painful. I wasn't really tempted to leave home – I knew I couldn't, or wouldn't – I mean, I have four children. It was a very tricky time. I lost a lot of weight, which was tremendous – it was the best way of getting thin. My wife knew, yes, I told her. She was tremendous, and that's one of the reasons, I didn't do anything. She's a remarkable lady. She wasn't cross, no. I just had to tell her.

I said, 'Look, I've been having an affair with so-and-so.'

She simply said, 'Has it finished now?'

I said, 'Yes', and she's never mentioned it again.

I suffer from jealousy. I'm desperately jealous of her. I don't know why, and it's terribly unfair. But that was painful, a black spot.

I'm frightfully glad I didn't do anything about leaving because I know the person concerned terribly well now. She's a mess, an absolute total mess. She's been through another husband, and she's searching for an identity like anything. It was so painful, but what I think really pissed me off was the fact that she got another boyfriend. After I'd said, 'Look, this is getting out of hand', she went off straightaway and got another boyfriend. That hurt me more than the break-up.

I've been promiscuous. I think it's frightfully important to do it secretly. It's very hurtful and inexcusable to go and talk about it – I mean to one's family. I'm sure my wife must realize. She's had affairs, and I do mind, yes. I'm totally bad in the accepted sense of male supremacy – fine for me but not for her. I'd certainly rather she didn't.

There's a particular type of woman I think I'm attracted to. There's a mixture. There's the really tarty, thin blondes – the commoner the better. I see them in the streets. I don't pick them up, no, not any more. I suppose the girlfriends I have, or have had, have all been roughly the same sort – they've been quite clever, attractive, to me very attractive. I like spoiling women a lot. I like taking them to very nice places, or hiring a Rolls-Royce and saying, 'Let's do the bridges.' That sort of stupidity – 'Let's take a launch', that sort of stuff.

I don't like women who don't like me. You can tell the people who don't warm to the particular tack that you're trying. I don't like that, but I suppose it's one's ego being put down, to a certain extent. I was very frightened that you were a feminist. I'm still not certain you aren't.

Men were often surprised by the vehemence of their wife's reactions, and sad that she was not able to forgive and forget. Nick, a thirty-nine-year-old police sergeant from Manchester, had one important affair that he thinks has damaged his marriage irreparably:

I felt guilty at the time of the affair, but it didn't stop me having it. There was pleasure and excitement when I was with the particular woman, and I enjoyed her company. I found her very stimulating intellectually, more so than my wife. But at the same time, I never felt completely at ease about it I did think about leaving home for the other woman, yes. I don't know whether that would have been permanently or not I was afraid to risk it – it was a completely unknown quantity I wasn't very concerned about much else. For instance, I wasn't particularly concerned about what people at work would think. I wasn't particularly concerned about what my parents might think. I think if I'd completely left my wife she would have got over that eventually, more than she's got over the sort of incomplete thing. So I think I have a sort of cross to bear in my own mind forever, because of that. And now I can't decide whether what I did at the time was the right thing or not. The only real sort of consolation I've got is that I know I'm with the children. I think I did right though, to break up the affair.

It was a fairly traditional and conventional plot. It happened over a period of about six months. She worked with me. Things came out in the open, there was an argument between me and my wife over something, and in the process she made a suggestion that rather supposes that she was aware of part of the story. I suppose she knew from my behaviour – your behaviour must change in some way. There was a row and I did admit it. I left home at about two in the morning, and went to see this particular woman to say it was all over. Then, of course, there was a big row at that end. I went back home again, and things were pretty crazy for a few months, and to be honest, I don't think things have ever totally recovered.

Most men who had affairs seemed convinced of two things. The first is that their wife is not having, has not had, and it wouldn't cross her mind to have, an affair, and the second is that their wives have no idea and will never find out. As Wilf, a caretaker of thirty-six, put it:

Before the blow-up you think you have it all worked out. Plans of action and campaigns, some sort of incredible flow-chart. Then, when it happens . . . BOOM. The flowchart falls off the wall, and you think, where can I go from here?

The men who had affairs and yet were appalled at the idea of their wife doing so knew it was an unfair double standard, but couldn't change the way they felt. Women *are* seen by many men to be part of their property, their domain, and God help another man who tries to muscle in. I was frequently told by the more traditional men that they would kill anyone who laid as much as a finger on their wife. Bill, a fifty-five-year-old removal man, was typical.

To be honest, I did get involved with another woman while my wife was ill, though I never thought of leaving home. The affair did affect me: it put me off my wife, if you like, under-standably. I took the bull by the horns and applied for another position in another town. The affair was dead and buried by then. I did, unfortunately, tell my wife too much about the affair at the time when it was virtually dead. That was when I confessed, if you like, my love for somebody else. My wife had suspected something was going on before I told her. I would be horrified if my wife had an affair. I can't ever

111

imagine her having an affair with anyone else. If she has, I know nothing about it.

Though Ben, a bookmaker of sixty-four, thought it would have eased his conscience if he had known that his wife had had affairs too.

I got married in the 1940s, and it was quite a good marriage for a considerable time. We were divorced in the mid-seventies. I never thought I'd get divorced, never. When it happened I couldn't grasp it, it was as though it was happening to somebody else Even though I was absolutely the guilty party, there's no doubt about that I fell in love with some-body else. I'm married to her now It was all very detrimental to my first wife's health But I've paid for it, I've paid very heavily. We had a nice house, very large I like nice cars too – I've just got rid of one. Of course the divorce cost me a lot and we now live in a much smaller house. I don't recommend it to anybody, especially when there s such bitterness with it – that was the worst thing of all. Even though I was the guilty party, I couldn't believe that my wife could get so bitter She started drinking very heavily

I wouldn't have minded if my wife had said that she d had an affair. It wouldn't have worried me. It might have made it easier for me to think that I'm not the only bad one.

A number of men were surprised that having an affair had led to the break-up of their marriage, and they seemed very hurt by that. Victor, a thirty-one-year-old teacher in a comprehensive school, said it had opened his eyes to the sort of changes he would have to be prepared to make if ever he remarried:

I married when I was comparatively young, twenty-three I'm still wondering what went wrong. I think I was extraordi-narily selfish, because I didn't change my lifestyle one iota. So we tended to have very separate lives. She was a teacher too, in the same school, and a sporty lady She played a lot of tennis in the summer and I played a lot of rugby in the winter Then I had an affair, with another girl who was teaching at our school. I couldn't cope with it. I had to tell her, you see, I don't know why – though I would again. I had always told her everything. I didn't want to keep a secret. She was very hurt, understandably, and we just didn't patch it up together because there wasn't enough between us at the time – we'd grown apart anyway, in terms of our lifestyles and what we did. I still feel guilty about it because I let somebody down. And it turned out not to be just one person, but my parents-in-law as well ... they're tremendously smashing ... I still feel wretched.

Strange things like the marriage vows seem like a laugh at the time, but now that worries me even though I'm not religious. If she'd had an affair, I'd like to believe that I'd have been philosophical about it, but I think men are much more sexually jealous than women. Much more. So I think I'd go and smack the bloke one.

If my girlfriend walked out, it *would* matter, but I'd be quick to find other people. I've got a quick recovery rate.

If I marry again, I know I'll have to make changes. They might be quite difficult. Although I wasn't malicious, I was definitely selfish. I didn't actually make any sacrifices as such, and I do think you have to make sacrifices. You have to give to that person and be prepared to do certain things. I think I should have made much more time for her, and insisted that we do a lot more things together – she wasn't very good in that area, either. And at parties, and so on, perhaps I should have kept her company more. But I'd be off to see people and leave her. But domestically, in the house, I got ten out of ten. I always cleaned the lavatory, and I taught her to cook.

Victor was typical of many men who spoke as if the women in their lives fulfilled a necessary function, but were clearly interchangeable. Apart from 'My wife was wretched', and 'It made her very unhappy', men offered very little evidence that they understood how their wives felt about their affairs – wives were expected to forgive and forget – nor how their lovers spent their time when they weren't there. It was often a case of, 'Well, she knew that I was married and I've never talked of leaving home', or 'If it ever started to threaten my marriage, I'd end it immediately'. Even at the point at which they were most deeply involved with someone else, some men locked the affair very definitely away in a separate compartment from the rest of their life. This was the way in which they could prevent it from becoming too disturbing or damaging.

The most frequent reason for ending an affair seemed to be that their wife had found out. Then there was the showdown with the mistress, who might get the message and leave him alone, or could cause enormous and embarrassing trouble. One man came strictly to the defence of his wife and sent for the police when his mistress waited outside the family home to attack her.

Some men tried to end their affairs honestly by telling the other woman face to face, but others found this impossible. Weak resolve made them afraid that she would talk him into seeing her again, and more often than not men said they 'hated hurting people', so a clean break with no possibility of discussion seemed best. They did this by telephoning, or by getting a friend to telephone to break the news. Then as far as possible they tried never to see her again. Some said this avoided the painfully recriminating discussions that inevitably took place, and possibly this was a weakness because they knew there would be some criticism to face. Van driver William thought it was the manly thing to know how and when to call it a day:

I suppose the things I'm most ashamed of in my life are my illicit romances. I suppose there's a possibility that I'll have more. I would certainly never up and leave my wife, like some chaps do. I would never let myself get that emotionally involved. I think I have enough will power to see that if that was happening, I'd knock it on the head. That's how a man's supposed to be when all's said and done, isn't it? I mean, you're supposed to be able to see how things are going to end up and then just stop it. I would hate to see my wife or children hurt. And I could never walk out on my young daughter. I'd sooner see my wife go than lose my daughter.

Only a minority of men interviewed had left home, wife and children to join their lover, and some spoke of the remorse and guilt they felt for some time afterwards.

Lord Eastbourne, the peer mentioned at the beginning of the chapter, said that he accepted that his wife had had affairs and implied that he did not mind. But most men took being made a cuckold as a serious betrayal. Sam has a small private income and works part-time at running a wine bar. Married for the second time, he recently discovered his wife was having an affair with her boss.

I suppose I'm not very ambitious – the average Englishman, really. I haven't worked full-time for about ten years. My mother owned a couple of hotels in Hove and I sold them when she died. It raised enough for me more or less to live off. I met my wife on the rebound from a showbiz romance. She used to get her photograph in the papers on this guy's arm at all the premières. She's very affectionate – more than I am. I love her, but I find it difficult to show it. I can't fling my arms round her – it seems so corny somehow. I seriously think she'd have liked me to go down on my knees when I proposed to her. I can't bear the idea of splitting with her or my daughter.

I suppose my wife needed some life really, and I wasn't going to object to her working. The extra cash was helpful, and I liked looking after her daughter. I did the school run, I like shopping for food, and I do a fair bit of the cooking, even hoovering. My wife has this job as personal assistant to a guy in a video company. The trouble is, he's done incredibly well. I don't think it will last – but he's off to America half the time on Concorde. He took her on the last visit. She gave me some nonsense about meeting the people he had to deal with, and I thought she deserved a break. He's an ugly little fellow – no personality, really. I didn't rate him as competition. They went off to the West Coast. She came back describing some hotel in California where the lifts shot through the ceiling and went outside the tower block, and I said, 'Yes, darling. How fascinating.'

A few nights later I was looking for a match to light the gas, and I looked in the pocket of her parka and found these incredible letters. Really old-fashioned love letters about her breasts and her scent, her honesty, how he couldn't live without her. Really corny stuff. It's amazing how easy it is to con a woman if you put your mind to it.

It absolutely threw me. One moment I was a happy man, the next I really felt suicidal – really sick and ill. I'm not sure quite why, but I decided not to say anything. I tried to hold on. I think, actually, she half knew I knew. There's that terrible secret code between two people when things are going wrong – a sort of hidden dialogue: phrases, abuse, justifications, which are rehearsed in the mind, and you sometimes don't remember whether you've said them or not. I had imaginary arguments with her in my half-awake dreams. I hated her and I loved her. One night I would think I would leave her, and even speculate about who else I might go out with. The idea of a first date with someone new filled me with horror. I couldn't speak to any of my friends. Only my daughter could comfort me. Her embraces were sweetness itself.

But I couldn't contain it. A little thing triggered it off. My wife said something derogatory about her boss and it suddenly came out. I said, 'What did you say about me to your previous boyfriend when you first started sleeping with me?' There was this total collapse. She just crumpled. I think she saw her whole life collapsing. Her boss was her passport to glamour. And her job, of course. It was something she could talk about at parties. People would be quite interested, too. Or was it losing me that she worried about? Inevitably, her boss is married. Married men are much more passionate as lovers, aren't they?

It was the most terrible long night. We shouted and screamed. We took it in turns to cry and half comfort each other and half forgive each other. We said terrible things. I really can't remember most of them. I do remember she said

116

he was the most fantastic lover. I threw her typewriter against the door, and I think it must have woken our daughter. She came into the bedroom; bedclothes were everywhere. I was half dressed and half packed, half meaning to leave. The thing was, my daughter came to me.

I don't know what's going to happen. She says she can't give him up yet. She says she will, but not yet. I just can't envisage starting another life. This is my second marriage. I live from day to day now, from hour to hour. Thank God for the wine bar. I get distracted for several hours a day. It must get better. Nothing can be worse than this. I told her yesterday that soon I won't care any more. I can't go on caring as much as I do now.

This is a point of view that many women will recognize.

Sam admitted he had occasional girlfriends himself, but he was stunned by his wife's behaviour. Brian, a van driver of fifty-two, saw red, and took the law into his own hands and murdered his wife for having an affair.

I'll have done eight years in January. It's a long time, it's a big chunk of your life. I'm here because I killed my wife. I'd been married to her for two years. I'd been married before, as well. I was twenty-nine when I first married. I was in the army when I met my first wife. She wasn't a wife at all, she just wasn't a wife. She wouldn't let me touch her: I blame her mother. I was stationed in Berlin for three years, and then stationed in Cyprus. I think army training has helped me survive prison. At the age when I came into prison, my ways were set. Probably if I'd been in my teens, it might have affected me, being in prison. But I'm still the same fella as when I came in. I'm just an ordinary man. I just like things to go easily along. All I want from life is a nice home, a family and a steady job. That's all I wanted from life. I was no big dreamer.

I met my second wife through my sister. She lived about five, six doors away. I met her through a party that my sister had. We got married pretty quickly. She'd been married before and she had two children. My [second] wife was two-timing me. I didn't know this. I found out because she boasted about it and I just blew my top, and that was it. I did it with a

117

knife. I stuck my knife in her. I treasured her. And I trusted her. I was out at work with my truck, and she got the kids off to school. The man she was going with was a neighbour. And, like the judge said, he says, 'You put your wife on a pedestal.' I did. And he says, 'You shouldn't put your wife on a pedestal.' Well, I don't agree with him. If you can't put your wife on a pedestal, who can you put on a pedestal? I don't know why I didn't kill her lover instead of my wife. It happened, just like that. Well, I'm a person what's got morals and principles. The Assistant Governor said the same: 'You set principles for people, don't you?' he says.

I says, 'Yes, I do.'

And he says, 'Do you think that's wrong?' I says, 'No, because I set standards for myself.'

I don't think that makes me hard to live with. I think I'm very easy to live with, to tell you the truth. I love people. I enjoy talking. I've not got a temper. I have if it's pushed hard enough. I can control it but there's a point, if someone pushes hard enough, it will go. No, I'm a pretty placid person, really. I'll look at all angles in things. But, as I say, the one thing that brought me in here, was just a thing that just – VOOM. When she said that, it just all went, and that was it. I don't remember how I felt afterwards. I gave myself up. When I was in the police station I was very upset and emotional, and I was upset and emotional for about a year, realizing what I'd done. I went off in weight. I couldn't eat properly. My sister had to have a good talk to me on her visits.

The murderer was interviewed again later, after his release from prison.

I'm a sincere person, I always have been. I think this is why things happened with my wife. I loved my wife very much. I'm a sincere person and when I love somebody, I love somebody. My wife had been playing about and I didn't even know. But I don't feel bitter about it now. It's all past, it's all gone by and I'm living my life now, and it's all forgotten – even being in prison.

A lot of people don't know about me. I'm courting a girl, I am, and she's a lot younger than me. She's eighteen. I've known her for about four months. She works at the same firm I work for. I only told my girlfriend about my past about two weeks ago. I thought it was only fair that she should know. I couldn't go any further without telling her because she means a lot to me. I said, 'I've got something to tell you, Gina, and I just hope you're not disappointed but I've got to tell you. I can't go any longer without telling you, 'cause you're meaning so much to me.' I can't remember exactly how I put it but I told her that I'd been in prison and that I'd killed my wife and how it came about, and it wasn't an intentional thing, it was just a heat-of-the-moment thing. I told her all about it, and she could decide. And she decided. She was pleased I told her and she didn't want to hear no more about it. And I'm very pleased about that.

I look forward to being with Gina. I don't get a lot of leisure time, but we go out when we can. I haven't met her parents, no. I'm a bit doomish about this, actually, because of the big difference in the ages. Her father might actually be younger than me, I'm not sure. This is a problem, I think. It's an unusual situation in a way. I'm very pleased, though – I think a lot of her, and she thinks a lot of me. She does, because she wouldn't go with me otherwise. She could have younger men, and she knows all about me. She likes my mother and she likes my sister, and my sister likes her very much, she does.

Marriage is a long way off, but I don't know if the differences in our ages will be a problem. It's a thing you can't say. I've always said that I didn't want to get married again. I don't want to get hurt again. But things might change. It's a bit early.

From what I've heard about my [second] wife since – I've been told a lot more about her by other people – it sounds as though she was just a prostitute. You know, nobody deserves to be killed, and I don't feel that she deserved to be killed, no. But she was a rotten thing. But if you can't trust your wife – the one that's closest to you – it's a big drop, a heck of a drop. It's like a ton of bricks dropping on you. I'd have never forgiven it because I'd given her all. And if somebody lets me down, that's it.

I have to drive past the house quite often, where it happened. Funnily enough, I don't think about it any more. I'm more interested in the garden. I loved the garden. I'd like to look and see how my peonies are doing.

Extra-marital affairs seem a normal, though on the whole secret, part of the majority of men's lives – though men who were having, or who had had, affairs themselves frowned on other men whose wives or children were being visibly hurt. The strictest rule of the game is secrecy, though a man might well let it be known to male friends that he was having an affair, and would be happy to be seen in certain public places with his mistress. There was not a lot of thought for mistresses, or what they did in their 'time off', birthdays, weekends and Christmas when family ties made it impossible to meet. Many men ended affairs abruptly if their mistress became too demanding or started to talk of marriage. All the informants seemed well aware of society's disapproval of what they were doing and the right of their partners to object; few flouted convention lightly, most suffered guilt in one form or another. Most men objected very strongly to the idea of being cuckolded, and were pretty sure it couldn't happen to them. The majority found affairs irresistibly exciting, stimulating, and good for their ego. Only the thought of hurting or losing their children held them in check.

Chapter Seven

DIVORCED MEN

Affairs may blow over or they may not, and one side may pretend not to notice or may condone a partner's behaviour, but if the tensions and conflicts in a marriage become too great then recourse may be had to the courts for the formal ending of the marriage. More English men and women stay married than get divorced, and a very high proportion of those who divorce marry again, as already shown. They may not have made it work the first time round, but they have no basic objection to the institution. Far from diminishing the general desire and respect for marriage and family life, provision for divorce is now regarded as an integral part of any sensible system of family law, but a divorce is not always obtained with ease. When the decision has been made, and divorce is the next step, when the lawyers move in and the courts are involved, what happens next can be a very different experience depending on whether you are a man or a woman or, perhaps even more relevant, a father or a mother.

As so much has been written about divorce, this chapter deliberately stresses the effect of the present legal system on divorcing men and their children. This is what the men themselves most wanted to talk about, though the effect of the trauma on every aspect of their lives was apparent: the sense of shame at the public display of failure, the feeling of bewilderment, of 'I didn't

121

know what to do or who to turn to'. The misery and the genuine surprise applied to all, even to those divorced more than once. We are ill-prepared in our society to grapple with emotional crises, confrontations and distressful upheavals. Even though divorce has become so common, the shock of 'it can't happen to me' was apparent for each individual.

Of the divorced men interviewed, half had been divorced by their wives on grounds which they often found hard to comprehend. Some men found their marriages never went right from the beginning, and divorced soon afterwards. Others found that, after the children had grown up, they and their wives looked at each other and found they were strangers. Yet others confessed they had never put any effort into their marriages and so a relatively minor affair had been the last straw from their wives' point of view; and men like Robin, an insurance salesman of forty-eight, told a common story of the gradual deterioration of their relationship over a number of years, ending with constant acrimonious rows:

I left home after about seven years. It wasn't traumatic, leaving. Like all men, I had the car, and I threw my seven years of marriage into a suitcase and slung it in the boot – a couple of baggy suits and a couple of pairs of shoes – and looked back at what all my efforts had entailed. . . . By this time I had a boy of about nine and a girl. I told them as best I could. I was pleased to leave because of the rows. They started in private but then eventually became public, and we rowed in front of the children. Eventually we didn't know anything other than rows. It didn't matter who was there. I suddenly found that I was speaking to her in front of other people as I would in private, and she was doing the same. The rows were getting more exasperated and more violent, and I could see these two poor little buggers sitting there looking at each other with their eyes rolling. I came home one Friday evening – I can remember it as yesterday – and I'd just

122

finished off the house. To get myself away from the marriage I'd buried myself in this do-it-yourself. I've got a garage and a room above. And I made this damn great house double-fronted. It was beautiful by the time I'd finished because I'd put into it all my feelings about marriage. I'd just had the place recarpeted, on the never-never like everything else, and I looked at her and I said, 'I can't possibly visualize spending the rest of my life with you. I don't like you as a person, and I don't love you.'

She said, 'And I'll be even more frank. I hate the sight of you.'

There was no feeling left between us at all.

Some men who had divorced their wives told of the constant attacks, the nightly telephone calls and threats of suicide, the problems of dealing with women who had simply collapsed, or who had ended up in a mental home, and the problems of the guilt engendered by their treatment of them. These were stories of men who might look to the outside world like monsters, but had themselves lived unhappily for years.

Recently husbands and fathers have organized themselves into vociferous lobby groups to try to change the divorce law so that it protects the interests of men. The Campaign for Justice in Divorce, a group of ex-husbands, successfully pioneered the Matrimonial and Family Proceedings Bill which deals with what they thought were over-hefty alimony payments to defaulting wives and their families. Families Need Fathers is an organization which helps men understand the law and campaigns for custody and access to children to be more evenly distributed between parents. Many of the divorced men who were interviewed were so appalled at the cost of their disputed divorce that they had become minor experts in the law themselves, and were willing to go into enormous detail about what they saw as anomalies and the unfairness of divorce law in its treatment of men.

In most divorces, custody is granted to the mother with 'reasonable access' for the father; arrangements about 'staying access' may also be included. Of the divorced men interviewed the majority were upset that this system too often deprived them of their children.

George is a GP age 38 who married in 1977. He has two children. He runs a busy NHS practice single-handed and has a number of private patients. He says he has always worked extremely hard, and was aware that this was a strain on family life.

One of my problems is that I'm a manic-depressive, and I've been under the care of a psychiatrist. I had a bad accident a couple of years ago and was off work for several months. Things began to go wrong then. Although I wasn't having an affair I was seen around town with various women and we were leading a reasonably separate life at home. My wife got a lawyer to send me a really vicious letter, quite out of the blue, accusing me of saying the word 'fuck' in front of the children and demanding a divorce. I had no idea that things were that bad. We went for a time to a couple of marriage guidance counsellors, basically sex counsellors, but they were so frank about the way that we'd behaved towards each other – they brought it all out into the open right away – that my wife walked out of the second session.

I couldn't consider divorce because of the children. I couldn't see myself walking out either, however bad things had got. We had a hefty mortgage and a large house with a lot of building work being done. But my wife was absolutely adamant. I was told by my solicitors to plead guilty to adultery – it would get the whole thing over in three or four months. We had both gone to the wrong sort of lawyers. Now that I know so much more about it, I wish I'd gone straight away to a divorce specialist. I had accepted the fact that we were going to be divorced even though I was against it. At this point my wife's side started delaying tactics, and there was total confusion on the submission of petitions. She wanted more money than I'd got right from the beginning. She ousted me from the family house a year later, got an order to forbid me to go there, and threatened to have me sent to jail if I did. Her greed became excessive. Like other women in this position, I think she hoped that if she'd been in sole possession of the house for long enough before it came to court, then she'd have squatters' rights and I'd have nothing. Throughout the proceedings she has continually wanted to see me in prison.

After two appalling years we got the decree absolute. I had had a series of nervous breakdowns and had had to take a fair amount of time off work. Thank goodness my practice hasn't suffered too much, as my staff and patients have been extremely sympathetic. I didn't keep it a secret from them – anyway they could see I was ill: on top of it all I had high blood pressure.

I had to sell the house. Half of the proceeds went to discharge the mortgage, and my wife was awarded about three quarters of the amount left. From my share, I had to pay both sets of lawyers and the taxman and discharge a massive overdraft. I was ruined, but I thought the judge, who was a woman, was very good. She gave my children the best settlement they were entitled to and said my wife should go out to work again.

I think the hardest thing for me was that she was given custody of the children and I had access once a week. My feelings against my wife were bitter. To tell you the truth I wanted her dead – it would have solved a lot of problems. She made it harder and harder for me to see the children, and gave me no say in their schooling or what happened to them when they were ill. I've had to take my wife to court again and we've seen a conciliation officer to discuss the matter of the children. She has sole custody, but I was determined to maintain my relationship with them. I wanted staying access, because it was the only way the children and I could go on growing together. When we did have time together I was always looking nervously at my watch, hoping I'd get them back to their mother in time. We were always just killing a day out.

My wife is now moving house and recently asked me to have the children for a whole weekend. It was marvellous, though I can see some frightening behaviour in the children, like my daughter at four saying there are things she wouldn't tell Mummy.

I've learnt a lot about divorce and how much lawyers make out of it. Now I've read all the books, I realize that I ended up fighting the law rather than my wife. She was just sheltering behind the misery they had created.

The same story with some cruel twists and variations was told by others. These were men who, whatever the nature of their marriages, loved their children, but were forced to sell the family home to finance their wives' settlements, legal bills and alimony, when their wife had been the one to demand divorce in the first place.

The stupidity of the court system as it presently operates was evident everywhere. Reginald is fifty-two and was married for twenty-five years before his wife petitioned for divorce. He ran an import-export business which has recently collapsed. His two sons of twenty-four and eighteen were always under his wife's control and left home with her. He has no idea where they are living now, but was recently taken to court by his ex-wife to pay his son's university fees. He has already spent a fortune on their education – partly abroad – and cannot believe that the family who have left him penniless and broken, and who, he said, 'have disappeared like fugitives', should be aided by the courts in their continuing demands for financial support.

For Danny, now a thirty-five-year-old television and hi-fi retailer, going through a divorce was the first major crisis of his life, and the attendant feelings of searing jealousy and emptiness were new and startling.

I'm thirty-two, we'd been married six years and had one small daughter, Caroline, when the bombshell fell. I'd walked out of a very well paid job and set up my own business with my partner. A week after the new company was going I found out he and my wife were having an affair.

When they told me, I was sitting here playing the guitar on

a damp Sunday afternoon. He was in the office next door. She'd gone out, I thought to see a friend, but she'd gone to the corner to call him on the second line, said she couldn't take the pressure any more. I was happily sitting here and he came in. She had come back by then and was visibly distraught. My feelings had been that I didn't want to see him around all the time, we worked together all week and I wanted to get away from him at the weekend. But my wife had once said, 'But he's my friend as well.' It's funny how what you hear at the time is different from what you hear afterwards. I felt competitive with him in business and didn't want him to know all about my life. He came in, he was very sane, not drunk, and he pronounced his love for my wife. It was a total shock. I'd no idea. She said, 'That's life, things happen like that.'

I got rid of him very quickly, I paid him off. But the stupidity of the two of them letting me do it, that was unbelievable. It was total shock. I had no idea. I'd never messed about. I really freaked out, it was the let-down, not only of a wife but the betrayal of a best friend as well. Two best friends, and when you're married you have very few good friends. The feeling was total emptiness. Totally wiped out. I had a head here and I had feet at the bottom, but there was nothing in between.

My immediate reaction was 'It's not fair, it's just not fair, I've never done anything wrong'. I believed until then that you got out of life what you put into it. You work hard, you're a good husband . . . not perfect, who is? I was never out at nights. Kept her very comfortably. She said it was my fault, said I didn't understand her, hadn't seen the problems. Maybe I wasn't receptive enough to her feelings. She'd said she wanted to go out to work, and I never really wanted her to. Then she said she'd been shamming in bed for the last three or four years. You think you know someone, and you go to bed with them every night and you live with them, but I don't think you ever really know them.

Well, one half of me thought we've got to make it up, for the kid's sake. But then anybody who can do that once, can do it twice. Someone said to me that if she's ever late by five minutes you'll start thinking, and it's true. She went to a lot of support groups later and they said it was not her fault, so she tried to put it onto me. I thought that was stupid because if you were writing the headlincs they would be,'Woman goes off with man's best friend.' That was how I'd write it. There's very few other ways you can see it.

I actually went round to kill him, which for a sane person is a terrible thing to say. Luckily he wasn't there. The only reason I didn't do anything to her was because I knew Caroline would always need to have a mother. Whatever her mother was like.

I felt a sense of failure. All of a sudden my work, my family, everything just collapsed.

He got her a flat and she moved out. He walked out on a wife and two kids. Her mother never knew the real facts, it would have hurt her. It hurt my parents a lot. They had no experience of it. I think their stability helped me get through all the very painful times. Their feet are very firmly on the ground, very Jewish.

I began to wake in the mornings having drunk a lot at night and reach for a drink again. I used to shake and at nights I'd be scouring the streets just to try and find the two of them. She kept my daughter one night and it nearly drove me insane. They're still together and from what I see of her she's not the woman I married. She's changed, I mean she's a screwed-up lady.

I had no experience of divorce at all. None at all. It was never mentioned by anyone I knew. I was the only one of all my friends who was getting divorced. I don't think it's shaming but your social circle changes. Friends who were so friendly you just stop seeing. One of the ways I got through it was to talk to people. It helped me get it out of my system. This talking was a new thing for me and I found it difficult at first. I'd tried any means to get her back, tried anything that was in my power, almost to the point of embarrassment. Then she started to get very aggressive about our daughter. So I started proceedings straight away. It was a wise move, he was a tough lawyer. I could have taken Caroline then. I came very close to taking her. My wife was not stable enough to deal with her: in retrospect I'm sorry I didn't do that at the time. I could have made her have a breakdown, and then I wouldn't have had any problems keeping the child, which I had later. Even to this day my biggest worry is that she'll pack her bags, take Caroline and go. Even though we have joint custody. I didn't give her alimony. I bought her out. We negotiated and I gave her £15,000. That's the law; it stinks. She walks out when I'm starting a new business and I have to give her money. I had to give the two of them money. They set themselves up in business with my money.

Reaching the agreement was very very painful and took a long time. We went to the Conciliation Court and talked to two social worker types. They're totally impartial. You sit round in a room and talk and it all comes out. They didn't think we'd have to go to court, and I'm all for an easy life. So we reached an agreement, made a deal, but she changed her mind. She kept on doing that. The only reason I suffered any of it is for the sake of the little one. We did end up in court and it took two years, all because I had to struggle for joint custody.

My one consolation is Caroline. I take her to school and pick her up. If she was with me twenty-four hours a day it would be marvellous. Divorce was an education for me. An education in the way you can change your lifestyle. It's the chance to live a different life. But the pain is such that in a way death would be better. Death is final but the death of a marriage lingers on, all the painful things, the house, the child, your friends, the way they look at you. Some people are even afraid you're going to rush off with their wife.

The experience has not made me more cynical but more knowledgeable about marriage and about myself. Not more knowledgeable about women. I knew I was fairly strong before but I didn't know how weak I could be. You really have to be very very strong to get over such an experience and not get hardened. If you do get hardened it tends to rub off on the next relationship which I don't want to happen.

I cried a great deal. And I worried even more when there were no tears left. I was very down, any little thing could break me. The pain of jealousy,of one's hurt ego, I still can't think about that. Another man, MY PARTNER, with my wife. It's a feeling of numbness, the emptiness is almost indescribable, it's something you can't get rid of, it just goes round and round inside you. You hope you'll wake up feeling different and you don't. You have your garden and it's all neat and tidy, you don't want somebody coming and stomping across it. And you're stuck with the feeling of jealousy because he's there.

But the biggest joke of all was my record collection. I'd amassed it over years, it meant more to me than money, but the last thing she said she wanted was two hundred records. There were thousands altogether, but that was not the point. A collection is a collection. She wanted to choose which ones she wanted to take, and I think that creased me more than anything else.

Over half the children of divorced parents, and that comes to nearly one hundred thousand children each year, soon lose contact with one or other parent; because of the way the law operates it is most likely to be their father. The legal system, and the lawyers who operate it, often create such acrimony between divorcing couples that it makes all hope of future co-operation almost unthinkable. Recent changes in the law may sweep away some of the old anomalies. Whereas in the past maintenance payments could be re-assessed and resurrected whenever there was a downturn in the ex-wife's fortunes or an upturn in the man's, a threat hanging over the heads of many men like the sword of Damocles, the law and the courts are beginning to emphasize the importance of certainty and finality in matrimonial settlements.

Today fathers are showing a growing interest in the possibility of reconciliation through 'out of court' conciliation services. Support, counselling and help are offered away from the stigma of the law and the courts. For, as many men feel with regret, they might have avoided the pain, the costs, and even the divorce itself if they had known whom to ask for advice at an early and appropriate time.

Chapter Eight

MAN VERSUS WOMAN

A great many men confess to being mystified by women. And many seem to be in despair about the demands that women make on them and the problems they pose. The words I heard men use to describe women included admirable, wonderful, extraordinary, competent, strong, good fun, illogical, irritating, gossips, incessant talkers and bitchy, but above all the descriptions often expressed uncertainty, lack of understanding and a certain awe which sometimes sounded more like fear.

In the minds of men women are associated with emotion: they are seen as liking to talk about their need for such abstractions as passion and love, sympathy and affection; they will argue about despair and loneliness, misery and happiness. Men feel ill-equipped to grapple with such conversations because they feel that they have been discouraged from discussing such matters, or displaying outward signs of such feelings, from an early age and they do not intend to begin now. As a result, men tend to slither round such talk or to avoid it altogther. If they do try, they use words which express emotion in such a completely different sense from the way in which women see it that the ensuing dialogue can sound like a conversation between two foreigners

Jeremy, the young Jewish estate agent who described his home life so succinctly in Chapter 2, explained how it began for him:

I was terribly embarrassed about girls from ever since I can remember. Literally if I was walking down the street and a girl came over, I would blush and hold my head down. Girls were so remote from me I knew nothing about them. I knew nothing about the way they thought. It wasn't part of my daily life and I resented it. . . .

I asked a girl to dance at our local girls' school. She was probably more embarrassed than I was. She sort of giggled a bit and then rushed off, and that was it. I was just left standing there, desperately hoping that nobody had heard. It was my second experience of dealing with parties and social affairs with women, and it was just as shattering as the first. I thought, That's it! That's it! I'm not going to do that again! It must have left its mark. I didn't begin to dislike women for doing these things to me; I always interpreted it in terms of myself: *you're* a failure, *you're* the one who can't cope, *you're* the one who's going to have to come to terms with it somehow. I didn't know enough about women – I didn't know the way they thought or the way they felt.

The problem does not necessarily become easier as men get older, as Geoffrey, a forty-eight-year-old violinist, was honest enough to admit.

I don't understand women and I'm not actually very good at having women as friends. I know people who are terribly good at it but I find women very difficult and always have done. At one time I think I was terrified of them, because there weren't any of them around. I was one of three boys and went to a segregated type of public school. One never actually got to know what made girls tick. I don't think I've found out since, though I have made quite an effort.

Rodney, an officer in the army, is forty-two. Sandhurst-trained, and intent on getting to the top, he has married a foreigner, which on reflection he fears may well have damaged his chances of promotion to a very senior post. He grew up in a rough working-class district of a large city but has now assumed the camouflage of the British army officer, complete with cavalry twill trousers, shining brogues and pale cashmere sweater. Ill-at-ease with me and, I should say, with all life beyond the strictly male quarters of the army, he expressed his fear of women as more of a controllable phobia.

When I say frightened of women, I don't mean a running, terrified sort of thing, but more like some people can be frightened of water, or whatever. I mean, you might still swim. I do find men slightly easier than women as a rule.

Bob, a seventy-four-year-old, has been married twice. His first wife died soon after they were married, when they were both young. To him a bisexual make-up is more normal than one that is completely heterosexual.

Although I don't feel threatened by women, I think I have found, progressively through my life, women more mysterious and more difficult and more illogical than men. If I was feeling in a bad mood I would say more stupid. Maybe this is a kind of concealed resentment about the fact that, in a sense, they have given the more practical difficulty in my life. I've never found women very easy. I find relationships with women much more difficult than with men.

Larry, a taxi-driver of thirty-eight, told me he didn't understand his wife at all, adding with a smile that might be because she was Italian. He thought it was better if women weren't too clever, and certainly not cleverer than their husbands, because that could lead to trouble.

Women have lots of tricks that men don't understand. They do it to confuse you – and get your money out of you. So you've got to let them know who's boss. I give my wife a certain amount of money each week. She doesn't know what I earn – just as well – and she never asks any questions. I wouldn't answer 'em.

Then he went on, pointing at me,

Now I wouldn't care to be married to a woman like you, it'd be like having a piranha fish in the pond.

He turned round to look at the road again and I was left to draw my own conclusions.

Lionel, a company director, serving a two-year sentence for fraud, had an equal mistrust of women, though he'd had to leave his wife to keep an eye on his company, and partly relied on her to make sure he wasn't being fiddled while he was inside. He'd had a lot of time to think about women recently and saw the relationship between men and women as a con.

I think men are suspicious of women, men have to live up to something with women, because I think men sell themselves to women, and in every sales patter there's always a hint that the customer's getting a better deal than what they are. It would be unnatural if men didn't sell themselves to women.

Uneasy and tense in female company, many men felt that women ruined male fun. They were an inhibiting presence for Tim, a thirty-two-year-old coalminer, who feels he cannot relax if there is a woman in the room.

I like women's company, but I like the times when I go down the road for a pint with the boys. I find that if I go out with some friends and there's three men and one of them's got his wife with him, it spoils the evening, you know. Though you're not going to do anything wrong, you're always on your guard. It's important for men to have time on their own because they talk about different things from women. They drink different, they talk different, they swear different.

Being able to say what you like without fear of offending women seems to be a popular element of all-male company, and that often means swearing. Swearing and male camaraderie frequently go together; swearing is what they will do with their friends but not in mixed company. Many men expressed to me their

134

need to be able to swear freely and without inhibition. 'Letting go', as they called it, was one of the few permissible ways in which they could express their feelings. Another miner, Tom aged forty-four, drew a clear distinction between the way he talks in the male preserve of the coalmine and the language he uses at home.

Down the pit I'll swear a lot. Everybody does that but at home I don't. Swearing in front of a woman might not bother me down the pit but it does on the surface. I don't know why, but it's something I don't like. I don't mind a woman swearing, but it depends on how far she goes with the swearing. My wife, she doesn't like swearing, and her mother – well, she deplores it.

But a thousand feet underground in the Lancashire pit where I first met some of the miners I later interviewed, the air was hot and grit-filled and the conditions were cramped. The very harshness of the work and surroundings causes men to behave crudely and roughly, hiding their strong regard for and reliance on each other. There can be no real quarrels underground; your life cannot depend on a man with whom you have had bad words. These men are probably closer to each other at work than at any other time, and many of them have worked in the same gang for years. They live in an all-male world where for them women have no natural place.

Other men, like Walter, aged fifty-four, a train driver, think that if there are women around men will have to change the very topic of conversation so as to interest the women.

Where I come from, in the north-east, there used to be quite a number of pubs which wouldn't let women in at all. Now I can be accused of being a male chauvinist and everything else, but I did prefer the men-only bars. There's times, and not for any reason that's anti-feminine, or anything like that, when you just like to get away from women. Just to be with men, and talk about politics and football. And with all due respect to women, once you start talking about politics, they get very upset that you're leaving them out. There are some things you could talk to women about till kingdom come and they would never understand. Not all women, you know. There's exceptions. But with a man you just have to wink and nod and he understands everything you've said. In a lot of respects no matter which strata of society you come from, men will see things in the same way, from a different standpoint than women do. I don't know why.

But Frank, aged sixty-two, a golf-playing Cambridge professor, finds like others I spoke to, he is sometimes offended by all-male behaviour.

When men get to the clubhouse they seem to regress to childhood. It reminds me of prep. school, with the awful jokes, giggling, aggression and showing off. Of course they don't want women to be there – it would be too shaming. I don't quite see why, but women don't seem to feel the need to compete with each other in this particular way. I don't mean by playing golf, but the conversation and ribaldry in the clubhouse afterwards. It's awful.

Quite a number of the single men I spoke to voiced the confusions they felt about where and how to meet the right sort of girls, and how to talk to them in order to interest them. Ray, aged ninteen, who is black and has been unemployed since leaving school, spends most of his day in a largely male youth centre. He feels conscious that if he spends too much of his time out and about on the lookout for girls he will run into trouble from white groups, or from the police. When with girls he feels the need to raise the tone of the conversation to suit them.

When you talk to your mates, you talk blunt, you know, like things just naturally come out. But when you talk to girls you have to sort of, like, change. You don't talk to them as if you was talking to your mates. I don't know why, but if you talk to your girl the same as your mates, she's just going to think you're a complete idiot. I suppose when you talk to your mates you're just a bit thick and childish, and things like that. So when you talk to girls you got to step up a gear and change a bit. That's the way I see it. I think they expect it.

But if women do spoil men's fun, it seems to be agreed that they often improve men's behaviour, and according to Oliver, a City broker aged twenty-five, who was propping up the bar in a pub full of pinstripe look-alikes, are fairly indispensable.

I like having birds around. It makes men behave. It's amazing the effect that women have on men. They're bound to make men more competitive, I suppose. That's instinct. I think they do improve a chap's performance and behaviour. And they're a vital part of life for one's comfort, entertainment, anything else.

'Anything else' more often than not was sex: basically many men felt that that was really the only thing that women were good for. Clive, a hotel manager aged thirty-six, confessed to having had hundreds of different women in his life, in many different situations, and more than one at a time. He was married once but now feels that 'it would be difficult for me to have a friendship with a woman for anything other than sex'.

Sydney, a retired further education lecturer, had apparently had enormous success with women all his life. He now lives a quiet suburban life playing with his grandchildren, but in the past never took no for an answer.

Any young, lusty man is only interested in one thing; having it off with a woman if you can persuade her. I mean it's all nonsense about respecting women, and all that. It's just that if you get a chance, you avail yourself of that opportunity.

Many men said they genuinely liked the company of women because women were good and sympathetic listeners. No mystery here, for if one sex is trained to listen and be sympathetic to the other from an early age, and the other is trained to talk, of course men will find women more sympathetic listeners than men.

A few of the men to whom I spoke told me that they had what they called a feminine side, though they were not at all homosexual. One such was Julian, an author, who rather favoured the company of these more sensitive men. Such men often found their own sex tedious because of the taboo on the discussion of feelings, seen by them as a sign of weakness. Instead they were happy to be open with me. Writer and broadcaster James, sixty-eight, on his own admission started life as a male chauvinist pig, but as he has grown older he has become enormously sympathetic to the female sex. He said to me, after a long and frank account of his life:

There's no reason why I shouldn't tell a man everything I've told you, but I would never dream of doing it.

I'd like to think I'd tell the same story to any woman who asked me these questions, but I can't imagine a man asking me these questions and me telling the same story, and I don't know the reason why. I favour women's company simply because I find it easier to talk.

Chris, thirty-five, is slight of build, fair, with a small moustache. While he walked his large dog I talked to him about his job as a tennis professional. He told me his job could have given him the perfect excuse to get near as many girls as possible but, he went on,

I almost never get the opportunity to sit down and talk about myself. And this is mainly because I am a little reserved in that area. I don't wish people to know too much about me. I did get quite close to one girl over a very short time, and I found myself that night telling her a great deal about myself that I'd never told anyone before. I don't know exactly why it was. It's just that I felt very warm to her in a short period of time. Men don't open up to each other. I think men are very frightened of being exposed, whatever their weaknesses are.

Women on the whole find it easy to open their hearts to a friend. They find it therapeutic and comforting, because they trust the friend not to repeat the private feelings disclosed, not to use the information against them at a later date. Men are always teasing each other, so perhaps they feel a greater need to guard themselves against divulging secrets to their own kind in case such intimacies are revealed when they are at their most vulnerable, in front of their friends or their families, in a pub or at work. Like stags battling for supremacy before the herd, men ceaselessly spar with each other in public. Henry, aged fifty, a hotel doorman for the last twenty years, was well aware of this.

I enjoy women's company but I prefer men to work with. I objected to having a woman boss most strongly at first, instinctively because she was a woman. I suppose I like women because it's all to do with my ego – you know, the fact that half the time they want to listen to you, and I don't mind talking. Women are better listeners than men because they'll take every last bit out of you. Men are basically aggressive and when you're in male company there is this constant sort of pecking order that bores me, because I want my social life to be relaxed. If you're in a group of blokes they try to score all the time. Men are very competitive. When I relax I don't want to feel that I'm in competition. And the only time you can get that feeling is with women.

These last informants praised women for listening so well when men feel like unburdening themselves. But men like to think that this seldom happens to them, and that they are strong and silent. It is women whose tongues wag ceaselessly, who talk too much, who prattle on about children, schooling, relations, shopping, friends and neighbours, who become excited about the latest bargains to be had, who gossip endlessly over trivia. Listen to this from a Conservative back-bencher, aged sixty-two:

Have you noticed the difference between men and women on the telephone? Men use the telephone as a machine for a purpose – to give a message and then put it down. Now my wife, if she was waiting here for me and we were going out to dinner, and there was five minutes to go, she'd pick up the telephone and ring somebody. Always. At London Airport waiting to be called out to the plane, straight to the telephone. I *hate* telephones. I use them for the purpose of passing a message or receiving information – that's all.

Telephones irritate me about women. They really do. A friend of mine was listening to his wife on the phone the other day – we were having a drink in here – and after five minutes he said, 'So far that call is totally non-productive.' I thought it was rather splendid. I know I'm being unrealistic and unfair.

Fred, forty, a dustman, who prefers talking to men about sex and sport, finds that much women's talk is beneath him.

I talk to some of my wife's friends, and I join in the conversation if it's about a television programme, whether it makes much sense to me or not. Mind you, things like *Crossroads* and *Coronation Street* are for women in my opinion. Soap operas.

Ralph, a tycoon in his seventies, is married for the third time to a woman much younger than himself. He is proud of her, considering her attractive, high-powered and professionally successful, but he still alluded to 'people' and 'women' as two separate categories. Although he told me he adores the company of beautiful women, they nevertheless annoy him.

Women talk too much. I think I rather like the sound of my own voice, and although I'm prepared to like the sound of other people's voices and women's, I know some who prattle on and never stop. And it's women I happen to like but it irritates me.

The peer who has already talked about his affairs with women has impeccable manners and a convincing air of listening to every conversation with interest, but showed that this can be a skill to hide behind.

I think some women's conversation can be desperate, absolutely desperate. I just shut my ears and ask after their children. And I know that for the next twenty-five minutes I don't need to listen to anything at all. I can just think about what's going on in the world. There are wives like that who live in quite high walks of life, but they're totally besotted by their children. I belong to a dining club, mainly political. A men's club appeals to me because you get the same sort of conversation that you get after dinner when the girls have gone. In this case it's mainly political, but it needn't be.

The fact that we women are illogical is not unknown to us. The concept that everything is measurable in logical terms is an interesting one to which many men cling. Some scientists believe that everything, even beauty, is in the end capable of being measured, and disagreement with this seems to lie at the basis of many misunderstandings between men and women. Women say to men, 'But you don't understand what I *feel*', and men reply, 'But you're being illogical.' Ralph explained to me what he meant by 'women's own sort of logic':

They believe that whatever suits them, or whatever they want, is morally right as well. Men often feel guilty that whatever they want is probably wrong. Women always seem to have morality on their side. If a man leaves a woman, her girlfriends automatically designate him a shit. If a woman leaves a man, nine times out of ten she is doing the right thing. But then they do need support and allies.

I adore women. I find them so much more *original* than men. Perhaps they need to be, as they seldom have other advantages like power or position, which always makes people marginally more interesting. Of course if they are beautiful they have more power. I usually find very beautiful women a bit boring – rather like a company chairman who thinks it's enough to be just *there*. . . .

I really have no criticism of women as a race and of course they *are* a different race. But I dislike some of the species. For example, small, fluttery, 'poor little me' women I can do without. Also arch moaners, particularly if they're getting on a bit, but that's true of men as well.

What do I most admire? Apart from their originality, I admire their stoicism. I love too the pleasures they can take in things. I love their sensuousness, their silkiness, even sometimes sulkiness. I love their qualities of perception. I like to see the world through their eyes – how the world I see, through tired eyes, strikes them. They usually see things more perceptively than most men. A man has to be very intelligent to be as perceptive as many average women. Men are usually programmed on existing tracks.

Of the men I spoke to it was very much those from the middle- or upper-class group who appreciated this element of surprise in a woman's viewpoint. Others said it was very refreshing to be given a point of view that would never have occurred to them, and women were often intuitively better judges of people than men. This could be helpful in business, as Eric, an engineering consultant, told me:

If I'm interviewing people for a job here, I let them spend a little time waiting and talking to my secretary. She'll often come up with some marvellous insight afterwards, and I think she's often been right about them. I don't think it's unfair to do this – it makes her job more interesting.

When pressed, several interviewees see-sawed between admiration for women's practical abilities, as drivers, organizers and professionals, and their wish to see women as totally impractical and in constant need of a man's help. Unlike Ralph, quite a few found the 'little woman' image rather appealing. Was this because they could patronize her and render her powerless, or because they enjoyed being knights-errant?

Many men found the successful businesswoman or executive bearable to work with, but not at all appealing as a partner. At home they preferred someone who did not challenge their opinions or disturb their life too much.

Colin, a sales executive with a large international company, is now fifty-five and suspects he will not be promoted further and, according to his colleagues, is at present floundering in a job beyond his capabilities. His wife, who is thiry-nine, works in a similar, but even larger, company, on the development side. Her career is blossoming and she frequently travels abroad to set up new 'green field' projects. They have no children, though both would be happy to have a family. His wife's increasing success has made Colin unhappy, but for reasons he found hard to express:

I don't think I'm jealous of her success – I'm pleased she's doing well – but somehow it just causes too much trouble. She gets anxious, she's away quite a lot of the time, she gets very tired. When she comes home at night, often after me, she's preoccupied with thinking about work. I'm an easygoing sort of chap, but frankly I can't be bothered to listen to her talking about it. I'd rather think about something else.

But she was willing to listen to his work problems:

Well, yes, in fact she's helped me solve a couple of problems here. I just feel she takes things too seriously.

The fact that women could not only surpass men at work but could also be sturdier in other respects was well known. Several informants felt women were better able to bear both emotional and physical stresses and strains than they were. That this was so filled a member of the government, aged forty-five, with admiration for his wife.

I don't know how she manages to do all the things she has to do. I'd say she's far more resilient than I am. She has a full-time job where she's very successful, and looks after the family, cooks, entertains, and sometimes picks my underpants up off the floor. Women just are better than men at keeping lots of different things on the go. Women are marvellous.

Sydney, the retired further education lecturer from Yorkshire, was also convinced that men were frailer.

I think men, on the whole, are much weaker than women, much weaker. I feel about men like women feel about men, in one part of their characters – 'Oh men, they make me sick.' I feel just the same. I'm much happier and more relaxed in a room full of women than in a room full of men.

All those who mentioned it were unanimous in admiring women for their ability to endure physical pain, particularly during childbirth. Some had witnessed the spectacle but others had firmly avoided doing so. A cheerful bus driver had organized his shifts with care to ensure that he was working when his children were born.

I don't think I would like to have been a woman. I don't think I could have stood having babies for one thing. I didn't worry when my wife was having children 'cause I was working when my son was born. I wouldn't have liked to have been with my wife 'cause if there's anything I hate, it's blood. If I see blood, that's it – I faint.

This was a sentiment with which Tom, the forty-four-year-old Lancashire coalminer, heartily concurred.

I don't think I'd like to be a woman, no. I wouldn't have the patience. My wife can have flu, or something like that, and can plod on, she can. I can't. I moan and have to go to bed. She wouldn't do that. She's tough and she'd carry on. I don't know why that is – possibly women have to. Although I do a tough job, I think women are tougher in other aspects.

144

Sturdiness was not all: men looked for sympathy in their womenfolk, for softness and understanding, and frequently mentioned their need for generosity and comfort. Both lovingness and affection were qualities much admired and so were good looks, although this latter was passed over in a somewhat shamefaced fashion, as if it should not have been important although it was. Roving eyes noticed small details; glances were keen and appreciative. Young and old enjoyed having their egos boosted by being seen around with good-looking women. Gavin, a florid young army officer aged thirty-two, spoke with great honesty:

I can think of very few ugly girls whom I like. I really can't think of any. But then someone you think really isn't very attractive, when you get to know her better and you like her, then you think that she's attractive because you like her. I like very little make-up. One notices quite quickly whether it's a good bird or not as to how she's done her make-up.

John put looks high on his list too.

I'm a terrific admirer of women. I had a lot of fairly severe romances when I was at Oxford. I developed a philosophy then which can be clumsily summed up as, well, finding the right girl was going to be a matter of trial and error, and the more delightful errors I made the more I liked it. And I pursued that very seriously.

I've always had a fairly strong idea of aesthetic values – visible, visual beauty. This is the coward's way out but it's terribly easy to identify in yourself. So I always liked to have girlfriends who were very physically attractive. Beauty in itself is just delicious. Money can't buy it; it is a delicious commodity and you're privileged to be near it. I think it was indulgence in the beauty of women that I liked.

John was unusual in his lively use of language. Just as most husbands found it hard to describe their wives, many men found it difficult to explain exactly what kind

145

of looks they appreciated most. Their vocabularies were meagre, often falling back on 'nice hair' or 'pretty eyes', although a few became more venturesome and volunteered ' a good figure', 'shapely legs', 'slim hips' or 'generous lips'. But they knew what they liked when they saw it and were sadly aware of its rarity. Jack, a forty-three-year-old trombone player in a popular jazz band, realized the tribulations and trials being plain could bring.

Although I'm petrified about losing my hair and getting a potbelly, I think it must be harder for women. Sometimes you see the most ragged sort of guys who you might not look twice at, but they're surrounded by beautiful women. But women have got to be pretty or have an awful lot of style or something to get by. Otherwise they'll be on their own. Women are more likely to go for men's character or niceness or personality than they are to immediately say, 'He's great-looking', whereas a man will go for a woman because she's attractive and therefore a sort of attribute to him. A lot of guys need that – almost like a possession for them. It's a very disgusting thing.

Women suffer from that thing. It's what they're complaining about, having to look like models in newspapers. The pressure there is cruel and awful.

Ray, an unemployed West Indian some twenty years younger, looked for something different, though he knew what *he* liked in a girl:

I prefer to have a white girl really. It's a matter of competition – who can take the best white girl? I prefer brunettes to blondes. They say blondes are stupid, but I don't think they are. They just don't appeal to me, not like brunettes – they're nice, they've got a nicer personality. The first thing I notice about a girl is the way she talks. If she talks softly and she's a bit shy when she looks at you, then you know you can talk to her for a long time without getting bored. After that, I just look at the body to see if it's all right, and then, who knows?

146

There's nothing wrong with a plain girl. If she can cook and has got a nice personality, I would go out with her. I wouldn't mind. Some of these girls nowadays, they can't cook.

Quietness, femininity and moderation in behaviour and dress scored highly. It was great to have a good-looking girl on your arm, but not to be the cynosure of all eyes. Nobody wants to be laughed at, singled out or made embarrassed by the bird he is with, particularly in a public place. That girls could wilfully upstage men was well known to most men from their adolescent days when, as uncouth youths, they had often suffered from such antics. Memories of hurt feelings made some men complain about what harridans women were, shrewd harpies who could make life Hell, not only for men, but also for each other.

Stuart, a retired bank manager of sixty-six, dealt daily with scores of women, both customers and employees, so he should know.

Women as a group together, just women on their own, tend to be a bit bitchy, which I don't like. Men are bitchy too, but I think women can be more spiteful than men. It's the way women tell you things. I think they tend to be a bit more wily about these things. If you do the sort of job that I do, a lot of people talk to you and it's the way they talk to you, sometimes it's got an edge to it. I'm not suggesting that all women are like that, but I think when you get a group of women together there's possibly more bitchiness than there is in a group of men.

Sydney had even stronger feelings on the subject. Had he lived in an earlier age, he might have hurled around such epithets as trollop, hussy, jade or minx. To him, women are malign tarantulas, sharp-clawed felines: bitch is hardly strong enough.

When I think about some of the things I know women have done, I just stand back in amazement. Women are like

147

elephants, you know, they never forget. And they wait and they wait and they can wait for bloody years and then, WHAM. I've got a great admiration for women, but the way women behave ... I mean, they're so absolutely cold-blooded about the revenge they take. I remember talking to a police inspector and he said that all the worst murders were committed by women: the most horrible, the most vindictive and the most carefully planned.

Those who have been at the receiving end of feminine anger are, not surprisingly, bitter about it. Richard, a twice married man in his forties who works in the theatre, felt the fury of a woman spurned. He also echoes the feelings expressed by many men, that much of this seething feminine rage is caused by disappointment that men have not maintained the confidence trick of their masculinity:

I'd much rather be treated badly than treat someone else badly. You can get indignant and you can get sad, you can do all sorts of things, but this slow agony of treating someone badly. . . . I didn't marry the lady I left my first wife for – she left me very badly treated. Because women can be vicious. . . . They don't mind. They look at you and say, 'You're disgusting, you're not even a man. I'm leaving you.' And that's terrific. You sort of shake for three days. In my experience women are very, very vicious when they think you've let them down. They think you're going to be terrific, and when they discover you're a silly fool, the indignation is tremendous.

Clearly it is difficult for one sex to be objective about the other, but the comments quoted in this chapter were sincerely felt. Many men did see women as bizarre beings to be admired from afar, to be handled with kid gloves. They saw them too as gossipy and aggressive. No wonder they felt that female company inhibited their own behaviour.

I had expected to find that men were conscious,

though defensive, of their attitudes to women, and was surprised that so few of them had ever really examined their attitudes at all. Women as separate beings were not something they'd ever found it necessary to think about. They knew that women expressed their needs in a manner which irritated them or made them feel inadequate, but this was seen as the difficulty engendered by getting close to one woman in particular, and not as a significant difference between men and women.

Rather a small number of men spoke of their almost unbounded admiration for women. The majority of those who talked to me were plainly frightened of women in one way or another, and many weren't afraid to admit it. They recognized the power women had over them and expressed it in a number of different ways. Some were just abusive about the stupidities of women, and admitted that in normal all-male conversations they made insulting remarks about women. It was a way of getting back at them. Some men were angry about the sexual power that women had. One man wrote to tell me that women, in his view, didn't like sex as much as men and withheld it to exert this power. Women were sexually inhibited. Once a woman had a child she could lavish all her affection on it. This was her way of getting her own back on her husband for always responding with sex to her need for affection.

A number of men were aware of women's constant dissatisfaction with them as they were. As soon as a woman had got her hands on them she wasn't satisfied, she wanted changes made, and things she'd tolerated during courtship became battle-grounds after marriage. Some of the men I spoke to simply said they wished they could be 'left alone' more often, and found at home that their priorities differed fundamentally from those of their wives. Many admitted that the attractions of all-male leisure pursuits were pure escape. The kids were fine, but in small confined homes the noise was too great, and some resented the fact that the only time they did have with their children was spent in trying to discipline them, under pressure from their wife who had them all week.

Overall there were very few men who seemed to have worked out a truly sucessful relationship with women, and some of those who felt they did have things to their satisfaction were the ones who never allowed any woman to get too close or to become too important to them.

Chapter Nine

SEX

Today sex is talked about intimately, generally, publicly and freely; we can read about some aspect of it daily, if we so wish, in almost any magazine or newspaper. Most informants said that sex was a natural topic of male conversation. Discussions might centre on local women of interest, or on someone who had just come into a pub; it might take the form of bantering about a friend's sexual prowess or of another's failure to pull women; all said there was a strong element of competition in such talk. Despite the ribaldry, men seldom escaped a sense of inhibition when talking about what really went on in their lives. A few intimated that they seldom mentioned sex specifically themselves – it was usually their wife or girlfriend who brought it up in a conversation they would rather not have been having. Talking about sex in this way implied that something was going wrong and, as with so many aspects of joint life, men felt such a discussion was an implied criticism, did not solve any problems and frequently made matters worse.

The immediate reply of a number of men to any questions I asked about their sex life was either 'What have other men told you?' or 'What's the national average?' Trying to explain the male reticence about discussing such important things as shared life, Tony, a gay solicitor aged thirty, said women and gays created a framework of reference for themselves within which they

151

could talk about their social experiences, pleasures and problems, including sexual problems, but that this frame of reference did not exist for men:

The other night I had some friends round here. They happened to be a straight couple, a lesbian, and four gay men. All were chattering away when I suddenly realized that we – the lesbian, the wife, and the gay men – were all talking furiously, and the married man at the other end was looking on in amazement. I thought he might be feeling a bit left out – not a bit of it. The husband said, 'I was absolutely fascinated and intrigued, I hardly understood a word of it. I didn't know what you were talking about.' I suddenly thought that we had been talking about our own social experiences, our subjective experience which was totally different from his. He'd been saying that he felt rather voyeuristic, that he wanted to join in, but he knew he couldn't, because he didn't understand the frame of reference.

A heterosexual would have had no experience of what it was like to be in the minority, and perhaps this husband was also surprised by his wife 'talking furiously'. But today many women have found freedom from the old and expected sexual silence and passivity, have found new pleasures in knowing what suits them best and in experiencing the freedom to seek it; and a new confidence to say no to the accepted male sexual dominance. Some women have learnt to talk about sex with each other in a frank, open and often humorous way. Doctors, counsellors and agony aunts everywhere also urge them to talk over their problems with their partners. However, judging from what men have said in these interviews, frank talks with husbands and lovers may have proved a somewhat unsatisfactory and less than humorous experience. Candid conversations about sex produce anxiety in men, with fears of criticized performance, of no longer knowing what pleases women, and even impotence. Such talk made Sydney angry:

Men never worried about whether they satisfied their girl-friends or their wives sexually. Now they think, 'Christ, was that good?' you know, and I think it's all wrong. I think it's a disgrace. I think we should go back to the old way.

However Clive, a twenty-six-year-old policeman, had no such inhibitions and was only too delighted to describe his activities with joyful exuberance:

I remember the first time I had sex: I met her in the swimming pool. She was about five foot two, blonde and twenty-four; I was sixteen. I didn't think she was as old as she was. She was fantastic. We did it in bed first, after that all over the place. It was wonderful, but I was absolutely petrified. I rushed home afterwards and scrubbed myself, had a bath. I didn't know about catching things – I just felt, not dirty, but I don't know, I can't explain it, I thought people would notice. I think I was shaving once a week then, I was a real man! I went out with her for about two months, and got up to amazing stuff. She was into pain, being burnt with matches on her chest. I carved my initials in blisters on her chest. I've not done that sort of thing since. I don't remember enjoying it. I don't remember the dialogue, but she was perfectly willing. I mean, I was a baby really, I did not know anything else. I don't remember being shocked. I tell you what I was shocked about, when she asked me to lick her ass. That to me at sixteen was absolutely unbelievable, that she wanted to do it to me; they were both equally abhorrent to me. I just could not do it. I could now! I shaved her, I burnt her. She taught me that I was there to please her rather than the other way round. She showed me what a clitoris was. I think probably a lot of my success is due to what she told me and taught me. I was having a great time anyway, and she taught me how to control myself, how to come.

I think my first sexual act probably took as long as ten seconds. She just taught me to relax – I was very tense. I practised, we did it a lot. I actually came five times one night. I can't do that today. I can go much longer now, you see. I do go much longer, have a drink or something and then go back to it.

153

I make love to my wife once a fortnight. She complains bitterly. There are often nights when she wants to make love and I don't. I think it's work, because when we are on holiday, particularly this last Christmas holiday, I was at home all the time, because I was studying for exams, and we were doing it twice a day usually – every day. I wanted to do it, I was not being forced, I just felt like it. Day to day during the week I've got no inclination to do it; if I go to bed, I go to sleep.

With my girlfriends it's entirely different. It's not that I do something different. No, I do the same thing, it's just different people. In fact, I made a New Year's resolution that I would try and cut it down, because I was going with so many girls. There are two here at work. They don't know about each other. There must be four or five at the same time and I'm always looking for another one. I think sex at home – married sex – is less exciting and less interesting.

I think about sex every time I see a woman, almost immediately. I think about going to bed with them. I like to think that I can give them pleasure as well. I think most women like to be led and dominated – I don't mean overbearingly – but they like to be shown the way. They want to be treated firmly but with some thought – some understanding and tenderness at the same time.

I think I'm a good lover but I have had complaints from my wife. She says that I'm too quick, but I think that's the familiarity thing. I can't be bothered with too much foreplay – just get on with it. It's sometimes a bit inconvenient if you want to get on with it. Sometimes, with my wife, a quickie will be fine and it will just happen like that. I'm afraid we have got very boring now, we make love in only two or three positions. I find standing up very uncomfortable.

I think I've had between one and two hundred sexual partners. That's a lot, I know, but when I was living here as a single man I was at it every night virtually. If I could do it again, I would. It's dangerous – I mean, I've contracted some unsocial diseases, which is one of the main reasons that I decided that I really must cut down, because I had the same problem with it re-occurring. They call it NSU; it's not really painful, it's just damned inconvenient. It just re-occurs,

154

because now I'm weakened and susceptible to the slightest thing. So a change in sexual partner could start it off. Then, of course, I could give it to somebody else. My wife knows – I had it when I met her. I've never had anything more serious. Christ! I'd like to think that I would choose my sexual partner carefully enough to avoid that. Again that's one of the main reasons that I decided that I really should cut down. The trouble is, I like it so much! It makes me feel nice, it's a beautiful physical sensation. It's being inside, and coming – it's the whole thing really. I have been with some very chesty women and some very flat-chested women, and I don't find the flat-chested ones unsexy; in fact, my wife is very small. I think personalities are sexy – people with big tits could be unsexy.

I was once in a threesome, it's unbelievable. A man and a woman. They were two friends of mine. I stopped and had a chat, and I got into his car; he was in the driver's seat, she was sitting in the middle and I was in the passenger seat. There was a bit of conversation and what have you, and I suddenly became aware she was giving him a blow job. Amazing. One thing led to another – I was a bit embarrassed at first – but then I felt this hand on my fly, and she undid my trousers, and I screwed her while she was giving him a blow job. I could barely control myself, it was so exhilarating. I got out and left them to it – I don't know what happened to them after that.

The biggest fantasy I have is to go to bed with more than one woman. I have never done that. It's something that I desperately want to do. Well, perhaps not desperately, but I'd really like to go to bed with two women who were quite willing to do whatever they wanted to do.

I've never really had a homosexual experience. But once, after I got married, I was with another guy, and we happened to stop off at a local toilet for a pee, and there was two guys in there, playing with each other, and it gave me a kick, I felt quite excited by it. I was horrified to feel this. I do have a slight fantasy about going with another man. I don't know what I'd do – just fondle, I think. It frightens me, because it's not right, it's such a taboo for me.

I don't understand these guys who dress up and that sort of

thing. It's pretending, it's not – sort of – real.

I have been to massage parlours and that's quite pleasant. They go through this charade, they ask you if you want talcum powder or oil, and they massage you all over, and just getting close to the squidgy bits, and then you turn over and you've got this enormous great erection, and then they proceed to massage you all around it, as if it was not there. They just totally ignore this enormous penis sticking up. Then they ask if you want any extra or things like that. Masturbation is quite pleasant, very pleasant indeed, and you can lie there and be done, and it's very nice.

I masturbate quite a lot – I think that's normal. I was quite slow starting, I mean, most boys are at it from the day they get a pubic hair. I'll get a girl to do it for me if I can. There are girls here in the station that will do it for me. I just ask them. There's somewhere that we visit and I say that's where I'm going and she knows what that means. It's quite exhilarating really. I suppose it's the thought of being caught.

If I'm criticized it's for not being passive enough. If I don't want to do it, then nobody else is allowed to approach me with a view to it. I can enjoy a stranger taking the lead. I once went to see this girl who had had her car stolen and we were sitting in her flat, and were just talking, and she said something like – she was a big girl, very attractive – 'What would you like to do?' And I said, 'What do you mean?' and in the end she said again, 'What would you like to do?' So I said, 'I'd like to make love to you', and she said, 'No, you can't do that, but you can have a wank', so she took my trousers down and did it for me.

I've thought about prostitutes and come very close, but we're not supposed to associate with them. I can't talk for other men, only for myself. It's just a different person, that's all.

There's lots of girls that I have made love to and have no idea what their names are. I just love ladies. I love making love in the open air, I don't mind hairy legs or hairy armpits. Periods are no problem either. It's not dirty, I think, as long as you have a decent wash afterwards.

The only reason I think I have so many women is because I

just like it. I like sex, I like sex with different people; what other reasons could there be? Inadequacy, I suppose – I don't know. I fall in love very easily and I think that's part of the problem. I fall out of love equally quick. I remember going with one particular woman – I didn't actually sleep with her – who I thought within days of meeting that I would probably marry. And within a fortnight, I didn't want to speak to her. Just got fed up with her. I say fed up, that's probably the wrong word, it makes her sound bad – I tired of her for one reason or another.

I would like to be less dependent on sex – I suppose it *is* a drug, isn't it? I don't have to have it, but I like to do it. I'm quite successful with women – without a doubt – I'm not being big-headed. I'm just honest with them. The only trouble is it's all very temporary – my affairs don't mean anything other than sex. Although I'm unfaithful to my wife, I don't feel guilty about it; I feel guilty when I get caught or nearly caught.

I don't need to talk about it to other people. I don't want to. I've never told anybody else who I have been to bed with. I've got a dreadful reputation anyway, because I'm a flirt and I'm very outgoing, and people think the worst of me. If I was as bad as people think I am, then I'd be in my grave: I would have fucked myself to death a long time ago. I'm not as bad as they think I am, I don't do it as much. I sometimes wonder if I would like to be a little less sexually aggressive. But as I get older I find it easier to chat women up than I ever have done.

I think my idea of Heaven would certainly involve golf, but sex as well. Golf is not a sport, it's a disease, without a doubt. It's the course, it's hitting that little white ball. I love cricket, and I love squash. I used to play well, but now I'm limited by the size and shape of me. I've deteriorated physically over the last couple of years. I stopped smoking three years ago, and put on two stone, and not been able to get it off – I'm fat now really.

There have been problems on a couple of occasions, when girls have tried to contact me again. In the end I had to be quite firm and just tell them to piss off. Since Christmas there really has been only one lady, apart from my wife. There are a couple of ladies here at work who massage me at lunchtime sometimes. But I don't have sex with them. I did before Christmas. But I made a New Year's resolution, and managed to stick to it, which I find very difficult.

There was this stunning woman, and we went back to the section house, and she insisted that I wear my full uniform while we made love – she was absolutely stunning to look at, she really was. So we did it, boots, helmet, the lot. All she wanted to do was to screw a policeman in uniform. She did and that was that; she was gorgeous.

Not everyone's first experience of sex was such a happy occasion as Clive's. It certainly wasn't for dustman Fred, aged forty.

I was about fifteen or sixteen when I first had a regular girlfriend. I was seventeen when we first had sex. It was a bit of a wash-out. I didn't know what I was doing and came before we started. That's the way life is. Women can always lay back and enjoy it, and let the men do all the work, and they're still doing it now, of course. The girl didn't enjoy it the first time. I've seen her since, just for a chat. I've often wondered if I should put the proposition to her again [twenty years later] – I've been tempted.

Some were too nervous to try even though they were jealous of those who had, as Matthew, a local government officer aged forty-five, admits:

I remember the first boy in our class to sleep with someone was seventeen when it happened. Rather late compared to today, I think. We were all envious and impressed and wished we had done it. It was a minor public school, Catholic, and my girlfriend was Catholic too. There was certainly no serious petting with her. I couldn't touch her at all.

Getting started was quite a problem. Sydney, aged seventy-two, comes from a middle-class family.

My mother died when I was young and my upbringing was a bit piecemeal. I was handed around the relations, and there was absolutely no talk of sex in those days. But I first made love, or fucked, rather, when I was fourteen and the unfortunate girl concerned was my cousin. She was fifteen. She was a nice girl. I've always been very interested in sex. It was an experiment – I enjoyed it, though I don't think it did much for her. I worried for days afterwards that she might be pregnant. The idea of telling anyone was out of the question. I didn't know anything about abortion, of course. I considered running away and joining the navy; but thankfully she wasn't. I never had to do a lot of persuading of girls. I know a lot of boys did, and they considered it a great triumph if they managed a grope, if they got the girl to wank them off. But then, it was quite true to say that nice girls didn't do it. By nice I mean middle-class, of course. As far as we knew all the working-class girls were at it like rabbits, but we didn't bother with working-class girls.

And from another generation Jimmie, aged thirty-eight, a heroin addict from Liverpool's dockland, might agree:

I had my first sexual experience when I was about eleven. There used to be a girl down our street, and her mother was on the game. The girl used to drag three or four blokes in the house. We was about eleven, she was thirteen. She was educating us. I suppose I was thirteen, fourteen, by the time I was mature enough. I couldn't really honestly tell who the first girl I slept with was. From twelve, thirteen, fourteen, where there was a crowd, you used to go out with different girls. Some were a bit younger, some were older. It would all be like going round a block of flats, up against the wall, bang, bang, bang, goodnight. I had a few years where you just drifted, but when I got with girls, I seemed to stay with them. By the time I was fifteen I was with a girl for four years.

Others had not had such accommodating neighbours, but several had found co-operative older women to initiate them into the complexities of sex. It was often someone they knew well – a friend of the family or, as in the case of George, a north country CID officer, someone soon to become a relative.

The first time I had sex it was very strange. Certainly the breasts were very nice but the experience of the vagina was very peculiar. I remember the occasion insofar as it was with my brother's fiancée. I think I was taken aside and 'had' rather than the other way round. It was an older lady. I didn't know what I was doing, I can really only remember entering her and coming and then feeling very embarrassed. I'd heard that one must satisfy the partner, having no knowledge of what one must do, you know. I was aware of pregnancy. I was aware of Durex but never purchased them or had any particular knowledge of them. I certainly then worried about pregnancy at some stage but I suppose I hid behind the fact that she was engaged to my brother, so that if anything did go wrong it could be thought of as his. My brother never knew about it. We would often fondle and I thought she sought my company because my brother would be forever working, or again, drinking out with the boys. I was a single man and when I had weekends off I'd come and stay at their place. I suppose we had intercourse about four or five times. Again, I don't think my performance was up to what I know now.

Middle- and upper-class boys who started their sexual adventures at a slightly, or sometimes considerably, later age had the advantages of owning a car, often the place in which they first made love. They also often came from largish houses where there was room for privacy, particularly late at night when the parents had gone to bed. Jonathan, chairman of a sweet manufacturing company, who grew up in the early 1950s, said:

I used to take girls home after dances. Because we all lived in the country, they often had to stay the night. It was all very proper, or so my parents thought. My mother used to leave a tray of cocoa out in the drawing-room, and we'd tiptoe in after midnight. I never took a girl to bed with me at home, but we certainly used to indulge in a sort of struggle on the sofa. Looking back it was rather awful, but wildly exciting then. I'd try and get as much of their clothing off as possible: they'd sort of protest but not for long. There was a lot of splendid

160

underwear then – rather harsh bras, and suspenders which you had to learn to negotiate. We never actually made love, but we got jolly close. One or other of us would end up coming, usually me, I'm afraid. I wasn't too clear about my technique then.

Some older middle- and upper-class men explained that they had got married because it was then the only permissible way to have sex. This was particularly true of men whose public school education and lack of contact with women had made them repressed and extremely nervous about the whole experience. These men were almost apologetic when discussing their first sexual experience, as Arthur, a retired rural dean of seventy, said: 'I was twenty-five when I first made love to a woman. That's rather late, isn't it?' Some said they had been homosexual at school to the extent of indulging in some mutual masturbation, but didn't think that this had ultimately affected their heterosexual development, although it had made them late starters because they had taken time to learn how to approach girls. However Richard, in his forties, was certain that being educated in an all-male institution left permanent scars.

My first experience was with a tart in Paris. It was extremely grotty – the most alarming experience. I went with my friend and he never had sex with a woman again. I had lunch with that friend the other day, and he told me about how he's met this girl recently – she tried to seduce him – and he couldn't do it. If that can happen years later, it made me think actually what a dangerous moment the first time you have sex is. You've probably been thinking about it for years, and there it is – this thing you've been dreaming about. I mean, we were terribly repressed. And men who were brought up like me, at a public school, remain infantile. I'm embarrassed by nudity. All this business on the beaches at Brighton, the idea of ladies without their clothes on, excites me like a peeping Tom.

I married when I was very young – twenty-two, twenty-three. My wife was nineteen. I can't imagine why I got married, except I was rather rich and rather spoilt, if I wanted something I had to have it. I wanted to sleep with her and the only way to sleep with her was to marry her. So I married her.

Jeremy, the Manchester estate agent of twenty-nine who lives on his own, also found early gaucheness hard to dispel. He is not gay, but has always found it hard to become intimate with women.

I certainly do remember my first sexual experience. I have to remember. In my life any relationships with women are so few and far between, I remember them all intensely. It was at college. It was sad more than anything else. It was very short-lived and I couldn't cope with it. It was almost as though I was saying to myself, 'Well, you're twenty-one, for God's sake, isn't it about time?' I always remember really sympathizing with that guy in *Here We Go Round the Mulberry Bush* – there was that feel of the sixties with the Spencer Davis group playing, and a sense of hopelessness. There was that great world of sex before us, and it was all a mystery. Well, it's remained a mystery for me. I can't cope with women. I find even talking about it very embarrassing.

Beginners' difficulties were not unusual, and various ways of solving them were explained to me from experience to experimentation and fantasizing, as local government officer Matthew put it:

I had terrible difficulties with sex when I was a young man. I had the wrong image in my head of what I wanted and it never worked. I always went for tiny little, fragile, blonde women. I could never make them happy, nor myself. By accident, in desperation, as everything was so bad, I ended up once with a very big, dark woman and had the experience of my life. It went on for a whole weekend.

After that I simply experimented with everything and anything. It was part of my growing up and took several years. Because I was willing to experiment, I kept meeting people all over the place in the oddest situations who understood how I felt. I was open to everything, and I suppose it showed. I remember on a train being in the same carriage as a young girl. At her station, she said, 'I have to get out. Will you come with me?' I went and stayed overnight.

I remember going to bed with a man and a woman, and we all had the feeling that everyone could do anything they wanted. It didn't matter who you were kissing or holding or touching. We didn't feel at all inhibited.

I've been with prostitutes – it was an interesting experience. I have enjoyed going to prostitutes because you can be totally irresponsible, do what you want. Prostitutes have lots of experience, they know things. Yes, I always talk; I don't sleep with people I don't talk to. One prostitute became a friend. It was all a game. I found total freedom.

A lot of my male friends never did all the experimenting with sex that I did – some married their first girlfriend. Some of their marriages have ended in divorce, perhaps partly because they think there must be something more. Something they haven't experienced.

Those kind of things don't happen any more because my experiment is over. It ended with my wife. By that time I'd done everything I wanted to do.

Peter, a fifty-two-year-old engineer from a redbrick university, said that as he grew older his fantasy life had become richer. He has been married for thirty years, a marriage which has gone through some very bad patches, but is now as happy as it has ever been. He has had a few affairs along the way, mostly when he felt he was suffering from the male menopause, and needed constant reassurance that he was still attractive to women. Now he is less sexually active and fairly content with his life.

I think fantasizing is very pleasurable. In fact, I would go so far as to say I think it's something people ought to learn, to be taught. I'd like a class on how to enjoy your fantasies more. Fantasies can add colour and excitement to your life, in a perfectly harmless way. At my age I'd say my fantasies

163

concentrate on lost opportunities. I look back on my life and think, why the Hell didn't I? What was holding me back? So I recapture real themes, and real people. I think a lot of people who fantasize build that fantasy around someone very real. We don't give our fantasy life nearly enough importance.

Fantasies varied widely, and some were explicit. Andrew, a thirty-eight-year-old hospital orderly with a slightly careworn face and red hair, sat slumped in a chair in a friend's flat.

We've been married for seventeen years, and although I've only had one affair during marriage, I often wish I was making love to somebody else. I fantasize about all sorts of people: for a time it was a student nurse; she was incredibly beautiful. Sometimes it's just an imaginary woman; sometimes, if I see somebody on television that I like, I'll think about them. Usually the woman I imagine is very free – she knows what she wants and is uninhibited. I would like a woman to take the lead.

Other people fantasized about sex symbols or film stars but most fantasies were much more mundane. Geoff, a designer of fifty, kept his well within the bounds of possibility.

If I fantasize, it's always with my wife in mind. I just place us in more exciting surroundings. We live in an old, draughty house, which isn't very warm, so we usually make love in bed. I think of making love to her in the sun out of doors, perhaps on a swing or on the edge of the sea with the water lapping round her. I'm rather romantic at heart and I dress us up in romantic clothes in beautiful surroundings. I do talk to her about this as we make love – I think she likes it. If I'm going too fast and in danger of coming too quickly, I think about what has to be done in the garden. I happen to know that a friend of mine always thinks about playing cricket – it helps to calm him down a bit. Sometimes I think about somebody else watching us make love. Nobody specific. It makes it rather exciting.

Jim, a shopkeeper aged forty-six from a small town in the south of England, to whom I talked in a bar at lunchtime, said he was surprised to be talking so openly about sex, that he loved his wife and had been faithful to her since they were married over twenty years ago.

My wife doesn't like me to bother her too much with that these days. The children are grown up. I don't honestly think she enjoyed sex overmuch. From what you read today I may have been to blame. But she had a very strict upbringing. One thing, you know, she would never take her nightdress off. I think it's a pity. Well, fantasies, I would think most men fantasize a bit, I think they enjoy sex more than women. . . . Well, if you're asking, I did have a fantasy for a time that I'd be watching her masturbate, and she wouldn't see me. But I would doubt she would even know what the word means. I could have had other women, women who come into the shop, but I haven't.

Just as women may enjoy the quality of power in men, some men find it equally seductive in women. Several middle-aged men from quite different classes fantasized about making love to Mrs Thatcher. She was described as a good-looking woman by more than one man. A well-known City figure said the combination of the woman and her power was quite tantalizing. Fifty-nine-year-old security officer Dennis was turned on by her combined strength and femininity.

She doesn't have that lesbian quality that I dislike, that's the strange thing. She's not a cuddly woman. I used to think she was, but I think you'd have to ask permission. Even her husband must say, 'Shall we have sex tonight, dear?' and put in an application.

Clive, a hotel manager of thirty-six, had a rapacious sexual appetite. He said he had made love to hundreds of women, although he also said he thought he was incapable of love. I interviewed him on his day off when he had just returned from the tennis court. He was small, fair, self-confident, and highly strung, with a nervous grin; his fingers toyed first with his pen, then with the gold medallion round his neck. He too fantasized about sex with more than one woman, but had also lived out the actuality that other men only dream about, that of sleeping with a black woman. A number of men wished they had had the opportunity because they thought black women were sexier, less inhibited and 'real goers', as one young architect put it. Clive told me:

Sex is very important in my life. I'd find it very difficult to live without it. I am highly sexed. As far as sex itself goes, looks in a woman don't matter at all. Only to a very small degree. I have made love to women I don't like, certainly. It's for the sexual side. Making love with someone is very enjoyable the first time – a new person. I don't necessarily need to be with someone five or six times to really enjoy it. In fact, I probably enjoy it more the first time than the following times. It's just more exciting, it's in the mind – that's basically what it's all about. I enjoy sex in different situations. I often take risks, sure I do. I've made love in my office on more than one occasion. It's just that I think at the time: if I don't take the opportunity it may not come again. There's certainly a degree of additional excitement in taking risks – I can see this in the hotel here.

I think away from home women loosen up a lot more, and their attitude to sex changes. I think a far smaller proportion of women are promiscuous as against men. It's the fear of being known, of being found out. It's not so great for a man. I would rarely try to approach a woman that I didn't think would be, or possibly would be, inclined to be thinking along the same lines as I am. The fact that they're married doesn't matter. On a number of occasions I've made love to women who've been staying here with their husbands. There has to be a certain magnetism there. I wouldn't dream of approaching someone with a husband here if I thought she was going to say no.

My sexual fantasies are usually about more than one woman and myself. I mean, one woman herself is a very beautiful thing, a very great thing, but two women is the greatest stimulation. They have to like each other, of course. There are several fantasies I have in which the three people would be completely uninhibited, and they would be able to perform anything with each other. I think another big fantasy of mine is just to watch two women. I've been with two women before, but I've never been with two women that have actually had a lesbian scene with each other.

I didn't make love to my first black woman for a long time. At first I was put off. A totally different taste, a totally different smell. A very much stronger taste, very strong musk. Not distasteful, just different. And that, at first, is a little difficult to conquer – or at least *I* found it difficult to conquer. I consider myself to be a very clean person, and I don't like certain body odours and body smells, and so forth.

That a man's enthusiasm tailed off after the first encounter was not unusual, although admitted rather sheepishly. Some said that the excitement of the chase was all; winning was not of much interest. Others enjoyed variety, particularly those with someone steady in the background – a wife, a regular if independent girlfriend, or a lover.

A successful and attractive interior designer, Nick, aged forty, lives with a woman two years older who has her own business and often travels abroad. He enjoys his highly active social life, had dozens of current invitations on his mantelpiece, and often goes to three parties a night. He frequently gives parties himself, and moves in a number of different social circles.

I think there are an awful lot more attractive women around than men. I adore women and I adore sex. I usually only want to sleep with them once out of curiosity. I rarely sleep with anyone more than twice. I do feel rather ashamed about the way I treat them, even more now I'm getting older. I just don't contact them again. I know there are girls waiting for phone calls, they do send messages, and worse still, presents, and try and contact me, but I manage to escape. It isn't something I admire in myself.

But if some men had a guilt complex about the number of women they had made love to and never contacted again, there was one man who had no such feelings. Philip, aged fifty, a smartly dressed tycoon, was tall and powerfully built, had neatly cut greying hair and wore an expensive aftershave. He has been married once and is thinking of marrying again. He talked from behind an enormous, highly polished desk whose top was totally empty.

I like the company of attractive women. If I go to bed with them, I presume that's what they want *too*. I've certainly never forced anyone. I've always kept myself fit, and I think I enjoy sex more now than ever before. I think I'm attractive to women, partly because I'm honest with them. I don't make any promises. There are one or two women I see regularly, one girl in particular. We have a very good time. I can still make love all night, and make her come as often as she wants. I don't like making love in the dark. I like to look at a woman's face, and know she's being well fucked.

Sex is very important to me – not in the sense of trying to prove myself; I actually enjoy sex very much. I like it. And I have no conscience, either, which is something else I discovered; I don't feel guilty in the way that other men feel guilty. But after an office party, or when the chaps have been out on the town, you can see the ones that are players and the ones who aren't. You can tell the chaps who are really enjoying it and looking for women, or whatever, but you tend not to discuss it too much. I suppose very close friends do, but I don't know if that's typical. I don't really have a *best* friend, no – I have a lot of friends, though. I certainly wouldn't talk about a girl in detail to anyone else, no.

I think all this talk about women not wanting to be dominated is absolute rubbish. Women like powerful men. I should know. I don't think the average woman would admire a man for being too deferential or even gentle. Women like you to give it to them hard and regular. I suppose you're a feminist and would disagree with all this, but believe me, there are an awful lot of women who are not feminists.

But if this man was a type, and one I met in different guises up and down the country, he was not typical of all the men I spoke to. Cyril, a bookseller aged sixty-six and on his own after two marriages, had spent a lot of time thinking about the differences between men and women. Distinguished and stooping, with a shy smile, he hated the idea of speaking into a tape recorder, but he persevered.

Sex is a mystery, and always will be a mystery. I don't agree at all with all that talk about men wanting to dominate women. I couldn't disagree more. As far as I'm concerned [the word] dominant is idiotic. It makes me fearfully embarrassed to say it, but I want to disappear into the female, because the female is immensely bigger and amorphous, and it's marvellous to lose oneself. Men are modified by women. I desperately need to be modified by women, and union is terribly important.

But sex is an extraordinary thing to do, isn't it? Most of our life today is so completely artificial that when we come across this thing that is life in action, it's amazing, shocking. Men try to neutralize the terror of sex by using all those obscene swearwords, trying to make fun of it. I have always wanted to break away and live in a cave on the side of a hill – to be wild would be marvellous. A man is more constrained and more limited than a woman, and lives a more unnatural life. For this restrained and inhibited man, sex and obscenity are linked. Sex is a wild and unconstrained thing.

When I asked men what worried them about sex, their anxieties seemed to be remarkably similar. Initially and understandably they were a little embarrassed to talk. Some said it made them feel coy; some said I had asked them a cheeky question; some said they had had little opportunity to talk about sex in a straightforward manner, and if I did not mind, nor did they. Many men who professed to be happily married said that their particular anxiety was being uncertain if their wives were content with their sex lives, but not knowing how to broach the subject. A surprising number of those who had been married a number of years had never found an opportunity to talk about such matters. Apart from what happened in bed, they were anxious because they couldn't always judge whether their wives wanted sex or not.

Harry, a fifty-four-year-old silversmith, who remarried five years ago, felt it had been easier before he was married.

I think one of the problems about sex is knowing accurately when your girlfriend really wants it. It's almost a matter of tact *and* tactics. Funnily enough, this is easier when you're *not* living together. If you go out for a meal you only go to bed together when you're both keen on the idea. It's easier to avoid any misunderstanding. Some married couples I know have little secret signals; if she has a second vodka and tonic, you know you're on. My best man friend tells me when he's in bed with his wife he strokes the underside of her foot with his instep – a signal that can be rejected without him being hurt.

It's absolutely marvellous when we make love together well. If she's happy, it's as if her flesh melts. I love making her come. I see this as my main job around the house. Of course, I sometimes have to control it and sometimes *not* think of her – to *stop* me coming. It's very nice when she makes love to me. It's not because I'm particularly passive; but it means she really wants it. And she can go at the speed she likes, and I know I'm not hurting her. If she sits on top of me and thrusts down on me, I know she must be motoring along at about the speed and strength she really wants.

Anxieties about not knowing when to make love were compounded by anxieties about how to make love. A number of men, some newly married and some married

170

for years, didn't really know what most pleased their wives. They felt they would like to be more experimental, but if the odd hint was not taken up, did not like to spell it out too clearly for fear of ridicule or rejection. The more men I spoke to, the more obvious it became that, although they may seem to be confident and dominant lovers, their feelings are easily hurt and their egos are perhaps even more vulnerable than those of most women.

A clearer guide about what pleased women most would have been appreciated. Mick, a forty-year-old who works in the film industry, divorced and not presently living with anyone, said:

I like it if women know what they want – I certainly don't mind them telling me. If I'm with someone new, I always ask them, as gently as I can, what they would like me to do. It's Hell if you don't know if you're doing it right. I only really enjoy myself in bed with a woman if she's enjoying herself too. Sometimes I'll suggest things that she may not have tried, that can be exciting for us both. But there shouldn't be any fear or anxiety. It can spoil it completely.

Colin, an advertising copywriter, now forty-six, twice married and sexually very active, thought the new openness – particularly amongst women – was marvellous.

From a man's point of view, it's terrific. I love uninhibited women and there are more about than ever before. Thank goodness for all those articles in *Cosmopolitan* telling them all they should know.

I've always enjoyed sex, but when I was younger always with working-class girls. Sometimes with prostitutes, but middle-class girls made me nervous. In a funny sort of way, I'd say I'd changed classes sexually over the last twenty years – gone up-market. Years ago men may have been ignorant about female sexuality, and about women physically, but honestly, it's my experience that women were just as ignorant about themselves. Well-brought-up young women had never explored their own sexuality – they weren't exactly frigid, but they were certainly inhibited. I have a strong suspicion that girls of my daughter's age – she's twenty – have no questions left to ask. They know it all.

Men do have a general interest in, and anxiety about, the size of their penises. Public school boys, who saw each other naked more often than did boys who went to state schools, spoke of comparing the size of their cocks and explained that being well-endowed could create envy, whereas the reverse made for misery. Phil, a pop singer aged twenty, had this problem.

I've always worried about my penis being small. I was teased about it a lot at school. I'm not very tall, but I know it hasn't really got anything to do with that. When I make love to a girl, I feel I should stimulate her in as many other ways as possible. I've always worried about my penis just not satisfying her. I know all the magazines say that when they're erect there's not much difference, but I don't think that's true.

David, thirty-six, who works in television, unmarried, large and fair, with thinning hair, and a loud and nervous laugh, told me that he had done pretty well in the 'cock-measuring stakes' at school. He seemed pleased and self-confident, and yet a little embarrassed. He mopped his brow in an exaggerated fashion, and said, 'Phew – what an explicit conversation.' No, he had not had any complaints from women; he thought they liked that sort of thing. He also said he had not noticed much difference in women's tastes sexually.

Men expressed a number of different anxieties to do with sex. Some men said that marriage immediately made sex less exciting: they felt it was less secret, more humdrum, and they were not able to look forward to it in the same way as before. They objected to the way that sex settled into a routine that was hard to break. Other men were anxious about sustaining an erection for the considerable time it took to arouse their wives. It meant learning to keep their excitement under control, and this often meant they had lost interest by the time she was ready.

Ian, a dentist of thirty-three from the Midlands, who loved his wife and enjoyed sex, spoke in tones of baffled disillusionment:

I think that having a wife who's slow to arouse is a problem. It never used to be because we went out ballroom dancing, and it was exciting – we'd want to make love as soon as we got home. I know women take longer by some trick of nature, but there are times when I'll try everything to make her ready but it doesn't work. It isn't a lot of pleasure for me. It puts me off starting sometimes.

Tension at work could affect a man's ability to perform. Derek, a thirty-one-year-old lecturer in a polytechnic and a parliamentary candidate in the last election, who failed to win a seat, said:

We hardly made love at all for months leading up to the election. I was exhausted. I felt under a tremendous strain, and just lost all interest in sex – all my energy was used up. My wife was pretty understanding to begin with, but I think if it had gone on for much longer she'd have had cause for complaint.

Hugh, a young country solicitor was not unusual in worrying about the deterioration in his sex life after he and his wife had started a family. His wife had seemed to lose interest in him since the children had come along.

My wife often says she's tired, and I don't doubt that she is. We both work pretty hard. It's hard to make love anywhere but in bed these days too – we used to be more experimental. We've got a live-in mother's help, and I can't quite see her stepping over us as we make love on the stairs. I do feel a bit jealous of the children, yes. They seem to get most of her attention, and she probably finds all the cuddles and physical contact she has with them quite satisfying. She says she enjoys that side of the children very much. It's all a bit bleak. . . . To be honest, as that's what you seem to be asking, I have been having a bit of an affair. I work away from home sometimes, and the opportunity arose.

I think men are more promiscuous than women generally. I mean that sex is more important to them. The crucial factor to the woman, it seems to me, is the feeling and the closeness and the relationship other than sex. The mental togetherness.

Men of all ages and classes were quite emphatic in their belief that men had a stronger sex drive than women, and therefore felt marriage placed constraints on their natural sexual instinct, which was not to be monogamous.

Some men suffered a great deal from knowing that their wives had had previous lovers; it wasn't that a wife taunted them, but just that the knowledge itself made a husband feel insecure. Was she comparing them as lovers, was she thinking of the past, had she really wanted to be with him? This situation seemed to play on a natural insecurity that some men, often those with unhappy childhoods, had about being lovable and desirable. Don, a north country GP, aged fifty-six, who believed with some reason that his mother had always disliked him, said he was still unable to trust his wife when she said she loved him. It had made both their lives miserable until he had sought professional help.

I love my wife and I married her knowing there had been other men: one in particular that she'd been very fond of, and I think she'd had an abortion. This was all a long time ago. But I always worried that she married me on the rebound, and that *he* was the man she really loved. For a time it was so bad that every time I made love to her I imagined I was him, and that she was thinking of him. It makes me look ridiculous, I know, but that was how little I thought of myself. He was a popular local figure, and I hated him intensely. Eventually he moved away from here – this was all some years ago. I still wish more than anything else that she'd never met him.

Paul, a teacher in his thirties, seemed anxious to talk but had to steel himself to do so. He sat with his legs crossed and both hands thrust between them. He occasionally released one hand to run it through his hair, bite his nails, and shove it back between his knees again.

There's one thing that really irritates me about my wife. We've been married just a short time with a rather intermittent sex life; now, we make love about once a fortnight, if that. She's a teacher, and she's just been promoted, and she's working very hard. We haven't ever talked about it – I can't imagine having that sort of conversation. She normally wears a nightdress in bed, but if she wants to make love – or perhaps feels she ought to, I don't know – she comes to bed with nothing on. So for nights and nights it's nothing, then I'm supposed to perform. It puts me off, and sometimes it makes me feel quite violent. I think, Why the Hell should I, why should she control when it happens? I'm afraid I have indulged in quite scathing remarks about it.

Graham, a thirty-eight-year-old economist, gets upset because his wife has a stronger sexual drive than himself, and insists on discussing it. For most of the time we were talking, he looked past me out of the window, his seeming nonchalance masking considerable inner strain:

I can't honestly think you find any of this interesting, but the highest problem my wife and I have had to cope with is sex. I suppose we've deliberately skated round various problems. In a sense, it's never worked for either of us. I think the deep-lying reason is probably my wife's dreadful fear about not being thought feminine – although, in fact, she's a very attractive girl. She feels her breasts are too small, men can't possibly like her – that sort of thing. It's a feeling of inferiority that she can't possibly attract, and that has made it more difficult for her to be

175

fully easy on the sexual side. At the same time, she does have a very strong sexual drive, there's no question about it. It's somewhat stronger than mine, and I must admit it's produced a simple conflict. She places more importance on it in her life than I would in mine. I have perhaps felt threatened by that. When we have sex there aren't too many problems as such, but it's more the climate in which sex can be had and enjoyed, that's when the problems arise. It does not take place quite as spontaneously as we both feel it should do. There's an awkwardness about going to bed. It's a problem; it's not a side issue. My wife has suggested, quite insistently, that we do something about it; I can't honestly think it would help. It's just that sort of relationship. I don't see why relationships have to be on an even keel all the time. So it doesn't bother me that it oscillates. I think it's pointless to demand something that can't be given. I don't think that on such basic things you're really going to fundamentally change your character. Which may be another way of saying I have not tried very hard to change myself in that particular respect. Which is true. I don't think it would be a very rewarding thing to do. I somehow think that would not be me. I'm not basically interested in discussing it because I feel it might force me to turn my attention away from things that I would quite honestly rather be doing.

Jeremy, a successful young photographer of twenty-nine, smartly dressed in Italian designer clothes, who enjoys London's night life and visiting the most fashionable restaurants, was honest and amused enough to talk about the things women had criticized him for.

I enjoy oral sex more than anything, but it's sometimes caused a bit of trouble with girlfriends. They don't want to experiment as much as I do. I enjoy going down on a woman, I enjoy her sucking my cock – it's more exciting for me than the missionary position that most women end up in. One girl, who was a bit of a feminist, said oral sex was all right, but she thought I liked it so much that she was suspicious of my motives. She said I was detached, and she never felt really

176

close to me, and that so much oral sex was a way of keeping my distance. She may have got rather near the knuckle when she put it that I was more like an actor giving a performance, that I made love by numbers like a bloody sex manual; other women had said something along those lines too. I don't always feel totally absorbed in making love. I 'watch' myself doing it, and it's also possible for me to think of other things at the same time.

A consultant psychiatrist told me that there is an increase in the number of men seeking help for impotence. There were, he thought, several reasons for this: women had in some cases become the sexual aggressors, asked men to make love to them, and wanted more love-making than some men could cope with. The pill has affected social mores in a number of ways but to many men it has meant an end to the pleasure of flirtation as all too often the girl could now say yes, something not all men welcomed. Impotence could also arise from boredom – they loved their wives but no longer thought of them as sexually arousing. There were also periods of high anxiety in a man's life when making love became impossible for a time. Dominic, a forty-four-year-old manager of an office equipment company, was ambitious and hard-working and had devoted most of his energies to his work. His wife divorced him and, with four small children, sought a large amount of alimony.

I resented my wife leaving me and taking the children. I had to face the prospect of being much poorer. I had a girlfriend but she expected to have a nice time and be taken out a lot. I felt she was critical of the mess my life was in, and things began to disintegrate pretty quickly. I got very low and just couldn't make love for a time – I couldn't get an erection at all. It had never happened before and I felt very sorry for myself. My girlfriend wasn't very sympathetic – she wasn't very patient and that made it worse. We broke up – I haven't seen her since.

177

A lot of the men I spoke to, including a cabinet minister and a dustman, talked about having a 'strong sexual drive' and thought that sex was 'very important in a normal man's life' (they used almost exactly the same words). Kevin, the unmarried dustman in his mid thirties, keen to find the right girl to settle down with, went on to say:

Sex is one of the main things, isn't it? I mean, it's what you go to work for and earn some money so you can go out and meet girls. Everything really is more or less based round that. I think men do separate sex and love. I mean, you can go out with a girl for months and not feel any love for her, but find her attractive enough to have sex with her. If I go out with somebody, I don't expect sex straight away. I'll expect it eventually, I suppose. I wouldn't think less of a girl if she wanted sex the first night we went out. If blokes can do it and not think bad of them, I don't see why women shouldn't be able to. I know women do get a bad name for that, and to me, I don't think it's fair.

Some men said their strong sexual drive made them much more sympathetic to women whom they found sexually attractive. Urbane Miles, a merchant banker, was slow to discuss his obsessions but when he did his eyes lit up:

Sex? Yes, it's been enormously important to me, it's been the key playground of my life. I love beautiful women, and the idea that they might do this extraordinary thing with me still seems amazing to me, even in my late fifties. I love seeing their faces as I make love to them. I do like to please them as much as I can. I suppose this is ultimately selfish. On seduction, I never really use my hands until late in the game. Eyes, of course, and words, and perhaps the lightest of touches at the elbows if we're going into a restaurant, but one always knows nowadays. In the fifties, of course, one wasn't always sure. It made it more intriguing.

I suppose my oldest friend is my cock really. I hope you

don't mind me talking like this? Sometimes it's on automatic pilot, as it were. It almost has a character of its own. The most important thing is that it hasn't got eyes. Nowadays it's a bit of an old clubman, quiescent much of the time. When I was young, I used to get erections the whole time.

Now I have two or three girlfriends, partly I suppose because I won't mind too much if one defects. It's terribly expensive, of course. But going into a restaurant or a casino with someone very pretty still gives me great pleasure. I just wonder why they do it. Sometimes I think they don't really like us, but are they driven out of boredom or competition with their girlfriends? Or is it the endless search for someone who might possibly *really* listen to them and care for them properly?

John said he'd enjoyed sex 'one hundred and one per cent. And when I die I want them to put just three words on my gravestone – "IT WAS GREAT." ' He had been happily married to the same woman for twenty-two years and said he felt men so often sadly missed the point about physical pleasure.

For me, sex just can't get better – it's been very important in my life. Men need to learn about their feelings – 'First know thyself', said Socrates, and he was right. We can learn to preserve that almost hedonistic freshness and excitement that a young man feels every time he makes love. But I find I get sensuous pleasure from all kinds of things. Physical exercise is very sexy. There's sensuous pleasure in watching things grow in the garden. We should keep the excitement in our lives going, stitch in our own silver lining, have a treat lined up on the horizon.

According to some men the strength of their sex drive was quite different from any feelings that a woman might have. Richard, who works in the theatre, is rather shy. He had been educated at a public school and is twice married and divorced. He said he had never been lucky enough to marry the women to whom he had been strongly attracted, so had ended up marrying women he 'didn't feel much about at all'. He underlined my growing impression that some men could view sex with enormous detachment, and did not even want to associate it with any deep emotion. Far from being a life of erotic pleasure, it was often rather miserably unpleasing.

It's like masturbation – either the awfulness of it stops people doing it, or they go on because there's no emotional involvement. I mean, men will go on having bad sex, men will go on mutually masturbating – not with each other, but men will go to tarts. Men will have bad sex with people they're not attracted to – well, they're attracted to them, but they wouldn't want to have good sex with them, they wouldn't want to have emotional sex with them. I think, with the majority of women, one would prefer to have bad sex rather than good sex, because you don't respect them enough. I think women are much better at this. What women do is that they discover, maybe when they're younger, that they have bad sex and they don't like it. They feel disgusted, they feel, 'I've let myself down.' Men feel that too, but they don't learn. And you always know that you're going to feel bad. I think that some women are just as capable of wanting naff sex, but are much better at knowing that it's not going to be any good, and knowing that they're going to feel grotty afterwards.

I think men really do want people in a way that women don't. They can be enormously attracted to somebody – it might be a film star or a tennis player, could be anybody – and it's serious. It's painful to a man – he fantasizes long and hard about the person. Women are much more practical; they don't do that. I mean, I'm *serious* about Chrissie Evert. I want Chrissie Evert desperately. A woman doesn't get like that. It's not just because I'm middle-aged – I've always been like this; it's getting no better and no worse. On a beach, say, there would be at least twelve ladies who, without speaking to, I'd go off with if they asked me.

There was much talk about strong male sex urges, about deep desires for women and about rich fantasy lives, all of which centred round straightforward heterosexuality with the male dominating. Few talked about unusual, bizarre or perverted cravings, none said they were transvestites, only a handful mentioned pornography and only three admitted to being bisexual. (Apart, that is, from those who have been mentioned earlier as having had early experiences of homosexuality but who later became heterosexual.)

A member of a rugby club said he went to their monthly pornographic film shows but that what he enjoyed most of all were the funny and obscene remarks shouted out from the audience. I asked if that happened because they were embarrassed, and he said:

Well, yes, I suppose it was embarrassment. I can't just imagine us sitting there in silence and watching that stuff, though there was nothing kinky or nasty, just straight sex and beautiful women.

Another who mentioned pornography was Bob, a retired gynaecologist, who talked openly about being bisexual:

I married because I think I couldn't live alone. I am totally bisexual to the extent, I should think, of being 40 per cent hetero and 60 per cent homo. I like male sexuality 60 per cent better than female sexuality, but this varies seasonally. The curious thing is that in the summer I become more homosexual, and in the winter much more heterosexual. This is for purely physical reasons. Young adolescent males reveal much more in summer than they do in winter; it's a matter of physical excitement. Girls are much more mysterious in the winter.

Even at the age of over seventy, I am completely knocked out by seeing attractive boys walking around: it's a sort of metabolic change, a kind of gasp, a total physical feeling that invades one's whole body. It's extraordinary; I don't know if I'm unusual about that.

One of the things about being a victim of purely physical

attraction is that I can feel attracted without knowing anything about their mental ability at all. In fact, on the whole, I feel attracted to people of what used to be called the 'lower class' to whom I probably can't talk at all, though occasionally perhaps one finds that they are at the same time very interesting people. I am rarely attracted to people in their fifties and sixties. This is annoying. Life would be enormously easier if the two things could come together and if I found myself madly in love on all levels – on an intellectual level and a physical level. But that happened only when I was young, and since I've got stuck at always liking adolescents up to twenty-fivish kind of people, progressively the whole thing's become much more difficult. On one level it's rather nice to see absolutely marvellous people and have fantasies about them, but on the other level it's fairly agonizing. I don't feel guilty about these fantasies; I only feel that they're rather a waste of time.

One of the most powerful memories I have is of my prep school where the head boy let it be known that he was going to exhibit his cock at a certain time. It had to be arranged very carefully so that none of the masters knew. And for some reason or other I was excluded, and that *really* affected me. I mean, it has had the most extraordinary effect on my whole life. It is absolutely absurd that it should be so. Later, at a rather extraordinary school there were certain times when we swam naked in the pool. I remember my observations of other boys as intensely exciting, disastrous to concentration on bookwork, a stage in a lasting obsession with cocks. In particular I remember one boy, now famous, who was completely hairless and very pink, fascinating because lavishly endowed.

I think that an enormous number of men – many more than would admit it – are bisexual. A long, long time ago I jumped to the conclusion that bisexuality is normal, really. If somebody says to me 'I'm perfectly normal', I would think, then you're bisexual. Maybe you don't admit part of it, but it seems to me a very much more common thing than is admitted.

I remember when I was a medical student there was one

182

student who was very thin and unattractive, who used to go along the back row in lectures undoing people's flies and wanking them off. Yes, I did enjoy it. The trouble with being young is that you always think something better is going to happen, but I now think that one of the few advantages of being older is the ability to accept the imperfections which qualify the moment of ecstasy.

I find pornography totally acceptable and interesting. A very large proportion of pornographic films are lesbian, and it's just accepted as a perfectly normal kind of sexuality. I find them exciting, provided the girls are attractive. However in New York I went to a lot of pornographic films and there were certain things that shocked me. I think sexual behaviour becomes shocking when it exploits, where people are obviously paid, particularly if they are children, to perform.

I've always thought that the act of buggery was unattractive and it features in pornographic films now far more than it used to.

My own fantasies have always included images of beautiful boys, either walking through a wood or standing outside a shop. They're wearing shorts and they want me to feel them.

My very first hetero affair was with a black lady when I was twenty-one – very late, really, in modern terms. I didn't know it at the time but she was very well known for liking young men, boys. So she whisked me off to various places, but I suffered of course from the usual young man's complaint of premature ejaculation. In the end, she said, 'All you young Englishmen, you're obviously homosexual, and I know exactly what you want.' And she then proceeded to do what in fact was a very correct assessment of what I did want, which was to be sucked off. That was very successful but I was deeply ashamed, and am still ashamed of the fact that I never actually made it with her. And that is quite a shaming thing. It wasn't till I was about twenty-six that I actually got control of it.

If you are bisexual, you are under two kinds of pressure as opposed to just one kind of pressure. I do quite consciously feel it would be very much simpler if one wasn't attracted on both levels the whole time. The fact is, that in any given hour of one's life one can be assailed by male and female sexuality and equally disturbed by it. I do envy someone who can go around undisturbed by this totally physical thing. I wish I could be like that but the ways in which I get disturbed are *daft*. I often almost dread a really sunny day because in the background of my mind a sunny day represents all kinds of things going on all over the world – people on beaches, on top of haystacks – all these things going on. It's terribly disturbing. If I can be left here in the country for a weekend I'm very happy, until suddenly comes the thought that at that swimming place there's marvellous things going on and that I must go and have a swim. The ulterior motive, the sexual motive, is very strong. So I drop everything. It's as powerful as that.

One's sexuality must be glandular up to a point, but then, of course, it's a combination of the things that happened to you when you were young. Compared to other people I've had quite a lot of sex. Compared to other friends of mine, I've had nothing. There are men I've met whose whole lives are just devoted to sex, and they can have three boys a day – in places like the Philippines. So compared to that, I haven't had a lot.

I have paid for sex, sometimes just with presents. But I think it's more honest just to treat it as straightforward business, and pay for it. It's no different in the heterosexual world; presents of various kinds mask whole areas of disguised buying. A housewife can be just as much a prostitute as any other, in a way he's paying for sex by marriage, and by giving her presents.

It's a *fantastic* thought that civilization has become so free about sex. It's an extraordinary development during the lifetime of someone like me. Now it seems to me that one is allowed to have a totally free sexual life, whereas when I was young this was not so. So one tends to feel everything is so much easier. But I also realize that a totally free sexual life brings its own problems.

I feel a lot of envy for people who stay with the same sexual partner all their lives. I think it would be *marvellous* to be able to do that. They must be rather special people. On one level I feel they have missed out on certain levels of experience, but I should think probably they are happier people.

If I walk into a room at a party and I see some man across the room who attracts me, my immediate reaction is not to want to get together with that person. I think that there must be so many people after that person I don't stand a chance, that I'm not going to put myself into the tortuous situation, and possibly the slightly humiliating situation, of joining hundreds of people who are scrambling away after him.

On the whole, it's a terrific relief to have the kind of relationship with someone that is not a sexual relationship. Sex gets in the way of proper understanding quite often.

I often wonder if people on the whole are happy with their own characteristics. Part of the maleness which I hate about myself is body hair. As compared with orientals, Europeans are covered with body hair. I hate that. I hate it about myself. I've always found that I disliked everything about myself. I disliked my type. I disliked my hair, my nose, my colour, everything. People have told me that I'm handsome, yes, but I've never believed them because what I've always found physically attractive is the opposite of myself.

Looking back on being young, I think I spent too much time thinking about my own physical appearance. I think that I have not properly used my ability. I have not focused my enormous energies in proper ways. I've always been interested in doing too many things. I've wasted an awful lot of time.

Only one or two informants mentioned scenes where the male played a passive role. One was Richard who had spent time with prostitutes. He had observed that an enormous number of their male clients are rebelling against that male role.

They want to dress up as women, they want to be beaten, some of them want to put on nappies, or whatever it is. They want to be relieved of the male role; they're completely passive. It's extraordinary. Most want to be thrashed and tied up – a sort of nanny thing. And that's rebelling. Even the ones that aren't perverted, they want not to be men, not take the lead. And they are very passive, these frightful men. In the massage parlours they come in, they lie there like fishes and long to be tended to. They clearly feel they can't do this with their wives. Now if you opened a brothel for women, in which they could come along and rebel against the female role, where they could dress up as Marines, bark orders and drill each other – in fact, behave like men – there'd be no takers at all. I myself don't rebel, I like to be manly, actually, in a relationship, and I feel quite happy doing that. But I think an awful lot of men don't.

If, as he suggested, men do feel the need to be more sexually passive, then it wasn't something they wished to talk about. The pressure on men to be masculine, strong, in charge, is so deeply ingrained that they seemed to loathe to destroy the image. I can only say that I sensed men's unease with the stereotyped male role on many occasions, although it was rarely expressed in words.

In some circles celibacy has its own social vogue, in others it is a chosen and disciplined way of life, but certainly one which does not just ignore sexuality.

A monk from a Roman Catholic order, aged thirty-nine, said that not having a wife and children of his own was a great sacrifice.

I come from a very large family and I sometimes think, how have I got myself into this way of life where I'm not going to have any of these children? . . . It's more of a sacrifice, now that I realize what I'm doing, than when I was twenty. I've had crises, thought about leaving lots of times. As far as sex is concerned I feel this is something that is closed off to me, part of the problem of talking about it is that I've missed it and I'll never know. One obviously retains a kind of longing about it, and a kind of curiosity about it too. When I was young I was quite fascinated by the idea of trying to build a relationship with one woman, on a long-term basis. I went to Oxford. I had the opportunity.

I think one of the problems of being celibate is that it's very

186

easy to become selfish. What has dawned on me from listening to some married men talk is how important sexuality has been in breaking open their selfishness. But I don't feel I'm celibate in any way because I didn't want to get married. I'm inclined to think that NOT wanting to get married is a disqualification. I take it as being the purpose of man's life to discover that his real self comes from being unselfish.

For most people their major opportunity to crack their selfishness comes aided by this sexual drive, which drives them on to meet someone else. For me this conversation is quite important because, in a sense, the aim of a celibate life and the aim of a non-celibate life is the same. It's to give yourself away. I think the art of celibacy is discovering this different way of giving yourself away. I suppose there's bound to be some part of my personality that remains untouched, because my life is not expressed through a relationship with a woman, and as I think the whole of my life is going to be involved with being celibate, I was going to say something rather pious, that that part of myself is kept for God. I don't mean I shift my normal affections onto God, that is not how you become celibate. One retains one's normal affections and gives them out in a different way.

Initially I was surprised by the candour with which men talked about their sex lives, even though some said it was the first time they had had such conversations. Then I was startled by the number who found the whole subject fraught with perils and problems. There were anxieties about learning the ropes as young men, worries about the lengths of their penises, fears about not satisfying their girlfriends, more distress over performances within marriage, further disquiet over the need for fantasies, for excitement, for the thrill of the chase; there was mortification with lack of success and anguish over the boredom of endless marital nights. And that was for heterosexuals. For homosexuals, sex could seem even bleaker and more fraught with problems and fears.

Men said that because the male sex drive was so strong, monogamy was an unnatural state for them. Many felt the need to 'prove themselves' to make sure that they were still attractive to the opposite sex. Sex was seen by many as pure fun which fulfilled a strong need, and the pleasure was unrelated to the need for profound relationship, or even to knowing the person concerned. The pleasure was often short-lived. It seemed common for some men to have made love to a number of women (not prostitutes) whose names they had never thought to ask. The opportunities for this kind of sex were always there. There were also girls in the office who enjoyed a 'quickie' as much as they, and always somewhere just private enough to make it possible, if risky. A policeman had girls in the station quite willing to masturbate him whenever he felt the urge, though he was often too tired after work to make love to his wife.

Views ranged from that of the seventeen-year-old apprentice: 'You're not a bloke until you've done it, it's got to be done', to those of maturer men who took great pleasure in pleasing and understanding the needs of their lover. But throughout, I had an impression of men's deepdown confusion over emotional involvement with another person. They wanted to make others happy, to please, to perform well, but though they were uncertain what women wanted, and were aware that they might not be interpreting the signals right, they still declined to discuss such matters in words, even with those whom they professed to love. Huge communication gaps yawned in this area of men's lives. Vulnerable, afraid of appearing inadequate, determined to keep their outward image untarnished, most did what they thought was expected of them, as best they could.

Chapter Ten

HOMOSEXUALITY

The heterosexual opinion of homosexuality tended to be that something had happened to gays which made them incapable of making love to a woman; perhaps some kind of early trauma had taken place, maybe they had had domineering mothers or possibly it was the result of a public school education. Most men said they had no time for homosexuals and laughed and joked about them, if they were present at work. Heterosexuals who said that they had no experience of homosexuality whatsoever were usually the most vituperative, perhaps because they did not wish to recognize that side in themselves.

Ron, senior foreman of a large factory and a highly regarded trade union official, said:

We had a couple on the shop floor, and I think one's still here now. Now and again people make jokes about them, but they're treated all right. They're accepted more than they were twenty-odd years ago. . . . I wouldn't like it if my son came home and said he was gay.

Nor would anybody else, it seemed; Fred is a dustman and, like many others, thought gays were tolerable if they left everybody else alone, but some violence of feeling underlay what he felt:

If my son said he was queer, I'd kill him. It's up to them. I've got no time for them at all. Personally what they do is their business, providing they don't interfere with me. If they talk to me, I'll show them as much respect as anybody else. But I do like to keep a distance. It's the same with lesbians – I find it hard to believe that other people have to be lesbians or queers. I don't know, not having done it, what their pleasures are. I mean, why do it with someone else when you've got everything yourself. You might as well play with yourself. It doesn't make sense.

Many men fear the more feminine side of their nature that they recognized and despised in gays. There is also the fear of being mistaken for a gay, though, as this cabinet minister clearly explained, it was more because of his friends' feelings than his own.

I've never been intolerant of homosexuality. I mean, both at school and in the forces there was a certain amount. One has, inevitably, friends who are. I've been partly influenced perhaps by my wife, who finds them very entertaining. What I dislike is the flamboyant homosexual who camps around. I mean, I'm embarrassed to be with him, partly, I suppose, because I suspect I might be treated as one myself because of it. That's a terrible fear that men have, to be mistaken for one. It's because, I think, one suspects that all one's friends are more anti than perhaps one is oneself. I really don't mind.

And then there was a game that many people seemed to play called 'spotting gays'. The same cabinet minister explained drily:

I can never spot them. This is so odd. My wife can spot one instantly. I never can unless he's flamboyant. I think it's a hunch my wife has. There probably are quite a few homosexuals in my world, but I'm so bad at identifying them. I mean, one starts suspecting everybody over the age of forty who's not married, which is probably very unfair. Usually he's got a very good housekeeper who boils his eggs to perfection and he knows no wife would ever do him so well.

A number of the older middle-class informants who spoke about homosexuality thought something inexplicable and awful had happened to such men. Some of them talked of horse-whipping, others of even more violent punishment to 'put them right'. Bob, a prison officer who had been violently anti-gay, said he had changed his mind, and could see that treatment did no good at all.

I don't think you can help being a true homosexual, a bona fide homosexual, any more than you can alter the colour of your eyes or how tall you're going to be. It just happens, it's in your make-up. There were so many in this prison because it's a psychiatric place, where a number of sex cases and alcoholics, drug addicts, people with personality disorders, psychopaths, compulsive gamblers go. I don't think it's done any good. I don't think there's one whit of evidence to prove that anyone who's been here has in any way benefited by it. It's a sop to the politicians.

Many men were in favour of legal curbs on homosexuality because they feared it would corrupt the young. This view was denied by most of the homosexuals I spoke to, who said that unsuspecting youngsters were not tempted into relationships by older men.

Homosexuality in the armed forces is still punishable by law and the seriousness with which men view their own sexuality and any attack on it was underlined by Neil, aged thirty-six, a naval officer who thought, just like some other informants, that homosexual approaches to young ratings could be far more damaging to them than the gropes that the average girl might have to put up with.

We've had a very big disciplinary problem on board. One rating was assaulting other ratings, at night. Just having a quiet tickle. The guys were waking up and by the time they got the bunk light on the guy had gone. Suspicion fell on almost all the ratings. Fortunately it didn't fall on any of the officers, it was obviously one of the lads. It caused an awful lot of bad feeling in the ship – the young sailors concerned were terribly upset. These guys were in tears. I mean, if a girl gets her bottom pinched, it's usually by some guy with a slightly inflated view of his own sexual presence; from the girl's point of view, it might be offensive but at least the guy thinks she's attractive. It certainly isn't degrading. But if you're a young sailor who's sixteen or seventeen years old, probably just forming your sexuality if you're a late developer, he thinks, God, some other guy finds me attractive, perhaps I'm gay and I don't know it. Now the reason why the services weren't included when the bill came out in about 1968 was the problem of corruption of young men. An older man could convince a young man that it was perfectly acceptable, that it was a sort of tradition. We have got a more enlightened view in the service now, so that if a guy goes along to his division officer and says, 'I'm queer, please help me', which very few do of course, he would be discharged without any disciplinary proceedings. He would just be eased out of the service with the minimum of pain for everyone.

Dennis, a giant of a security officer and ex-policeman who, like many big men, had a gentle side to his nature, said he numbered some homosexuals amongst his close friends, but hated the business of arresting them.

I've arrested hundreds of homosexuals. But to catch two men in the public toilet together, masturbating together, I don't understand it. We used to catch hundreds of them, people from good homes. It was pathetic. I phoned up one quite well-known person, and I said, 'I've got your son here. I've arrested him, I'm sorry to say.'

He said, 'What has he been doing? Stealing or what?'

I said, 'No, caught in a public toilet. Masturbating another man.'

The man fainted! It was terrible.

George, a CID officer now too senior to be involved in

arresting men in lavatories, voiced the feelings of many men I spoke to.

The idea of two women making love to each other does excite me. The idea of two men, of course, is abhorrent.

Boys' public schools were often mentioned by men of all classes as being at the root of much English homosexuality, though those who had been to such schools, like this aristocratic old Etonian, often thought it was just part of growing up.

For most men a homosexual period is part of boyhood. I don't think school made one more homosexual It never occurred to us that we were homosexual. It was just mutual masturbation – a lot of that used to go on It was a bit secret; we were definitely doing something a bit furtive. There were a limited number of beautiful boys in the school whom everyone worshipped from a distance. There was one in our house who was sacked. Anything between a senior boy and a little boy was frowned upon heavily

Richard, who works in the theatre, thought there was little connection between homosexuality at school and sexual behaviour later in life

There was homosexuality at my school, I don't know what it s like now We didn't think we were homosexuals. But people who were the most homosexual then are now the most heterosexual. We were just larking about, sort of getting some sexuality I don't think it was tremendously exciting.

A member of the House of Lords in his late seventies agreed and said that his own early homosexuality at school had not affected his ability to have a number of successful and enjoyable sexual relations with women it had merely been expedient

I was utterly homosexual until I was about twenty-three Yes, then I thought women were totally different creatures – monkeys. I gradually got to know them and like them more I

193

remember at Cambridge a contemporary brought a woman along to my rooms one evening, and we thought it was rather unnecessary, not the done thing. But at school, being homosexual meant I could get off games, and out of all the things I didn't want to do. I didn't mind it a bit, but I wasn't a real homosexual, it was just convenient. Other men I know are totally homosexual. You'd be surprised if I told you who they are.

I was very much in favour of the change in the law. Why ruin the lives of a lot of very talented and creative people? A distinguished colleague of mine said at the time, 'You're doing something I detest, legalizing these buggers.' I think Winston Churchill had a streak of homosexuality in him.

John is forty-five and married. He remembered the cruelty of some aspects of homosexuality that he had witnessed at Oxford.

There was homosexuality at Oxford – my God, there was. I didn't like it because the particular manifestation I observed had an overlay of social divisiveness in it. The public school-boy, who was very suave and debonair, started behaving towards the grammar school boy in a manner which was very demeaning for the grammar school boy. And he started to treat him as the sort of manservant-valet figure he ultimately wanted to have. This didn't really come into the open until one evening when we'd dined in hall and were all guffawing and laughing and the beer was flowing round in these silver tankards we had. All of a sudden 'Jones' (we'll call the public school boy) swung round on 'Brown' (the grammar school boy). He said, 'Brown, you may leave the table.' Brown got up quietly, meekly, with a blush coming very slowly to his cheeks, and walked quietly out of the dining hall. It wasn't prearranged; there wasn't that kind of cohesiveness. I was appalled, because I thought it stank. In a sense I liked the qualities they both had, but I hated this grinding the cigarette under the heel bit. The other guys in the group didn't say much. Most of them were public school boys anyway, and I'd been to a hybrid between the two, and I couldn't give a damn. I thought, Well, I'll have to talk to Brown about this, since nobody else will. Talk about how to lose friends and depress people! I spent a long time one evening with Brown and, to my amazement, he hadn't really been aware of what was going on. He'd undergone a kind of homosexual hypnosis in the relationship. And he floated out of the thing as though he was under some kind of spell. The next thing that happened was that he went straight up to this homosexual friend of his, and said, 'I'm never going to talk to you again as long as you're in the bloody college.' And the only tangible reaction yours truly got was that the dominant partner strolled up to me one evening in a similar situation to that in which this crucial episode had occurred, and shouted at me, 'You keep your nose out of other people s bloody affairs. This is none of your business. Everybody knows you re a pain in the arse. Fuck off!' So, that was that. I had two friends before it started, I thought, and I haven't got any now

When Harry was at Cambridge, his homosexuality was a way of moving into society He s now fifty-four and married

At school and unviversity I was inevitably homosexual It was pure sex, not yet deviation For a time when I was an undergraduate I allowed older men to take me to restaurants, the theatre the opera. My homosexuality was mainly economical then I couldn't afford the kind of life I wanted. I didn't go to bed with these older men, I just let them take me out, rather like a girl really When I made my first money as an undergraduate selling books rather successfully from door to door and later advertising, I became straight overnight and started taking girls to nightclubs. The transference from one to the other was effortless. I remember thinking my first night with a girl was rather messy, but I never went back I remember my tutor saying to me, 'Harry, you re just coming to the age when you will be particularly attractive to women, and you must fuck and fuck and fuck He was rather an unusual tutor really

Very few heterosexuals realize how many gay men live for years in a steady 'happily married' state like

Edmund, retired master from a well-known boys' public school, who until recently had lived as part of a homosexual couple, out of necessity secretly. David, his lover, a successful professional man, had just died. Edmund, aged sixty-nine, had never in his youth heard of homosexuality. Contrary to popular opinion that homosexual relationships are short-lived, he and David were together for thirty years.

Before I met David, during the war, I had a terrific love affair, but in a way it was highly romanticized because it was one of those situations where neither of us knew what to do about it. This was in the army. He was of similar rank. He was marvellous. That sort of thing wasn't accepted at all. Those things were never talked about at home. The word 'homosexual' I found in a book – I'd never heard it spoken. So my generation tended to grow up with very vague feelings about homosexuality. You couldn't define the thing. Looking back, I suppose I did subconsciously know for a long time that I was homosexual, but I suppose one didn't face it until the war was well over. I would've been about twenty-six, or something.

Men did seem to recognize that I was homosexual, and they sometimes tried to pick me up. I was uneasy about that.

Growing up for me was a traumatic experience. I used to look at maps of France and think, Oh, Paris, James Joyce, and all that sort of stuff. I was very much an outsider in my family. Everyone else seemed to me to be tough and good at games, and all that sort of thing. I was hopeless.

David actually made the running. I'm not so good at these things. David was so strong. He'd got a fixed idea of what he wanted to do and he would do it. He wanted me and it was all absolutely right. I wanted it too, and we both seemed to want to have a stable relationship. So it was just good. It went on for thirty years. It worked wonderfully, though we weren't actually living together all that time. It was a perfect set-up in many ways. He'd come here every weekend, and I'd spend all the school holidays with him. I had my separate life here and he had his there. Lots of things that disrupt a relationship are often caused by people perhaps being too much shut in together. When we started living together we were so used to each other and so easy together. Sex was never any problem. But you can never have a perfect relationship. Everything has a little compromise. Obviously David had one or two flings on the side. I did mind about those, but if I look back, I wouldn't be the same now. I'd be more understanding. I'm terribly faithful, actually. I wouldn't have had an affair while I was with David – it would have hurt him so much. We used to talk about it occasionally, and he'd say, 'It'd do you good. Why don't you have an affair?' Most of our friends were heterosexual; we did know a lot of homosexuals, but neither of us wanted particularly to be just with homosexuals. I'm sure we just felt that we were normal people, and our friends were married but they were normal too. There have been friends who would have us to stay and put us in a double bed. I thought that was very nice of them. They treated us as a married couple.

David's flings didn't happen very often, and there was only one which was rather serious. I knew about that because you can always tell. I didn't really have it out with him, and it was a tricky period. It went on for about three months. He behaved in a different way towards me, in a slightly guilty way. He kept buying me presents.

When the law regarding homosexuality was changed, it was of no consequence to us. But I can see it must have helped a lot of people who could have been blackmailed. That *was* always a slight worry I suppose I could have been blackmailed by somebody here saying, 'You're working in a school with boys, and you're a homosexual.

When David died, I thought that there would never be anyone again. That's one of the sharp lessons of life, I think, that it *can* happen again. You don't want anything else to happen, you don't want to stop grieving, you don't want to ever forget. Of course, one doesn't stop grieving in a way, but you absorb it somehow. I haven't ever wanted children, no, not at all. I hated family life; it wasn't a very happy family. And I'm not a family person. I hadn't ever felt I wanted sons; I've never felt that – passing on the name and all that sort of stuff. But I am good at looking after boys, difficult boys at

197

school who have problems. They often get sent to me. That's paternalism, I suppose.

Even though the law has changed, fears of blackmail have decreased and attitudes are less extreme, there are still problems for those who are gay. I talked to some who still lead secret lives, but they did not want to be identified or quoted. A few were grappling with the tensions of 'coming out', which still requires considerable courage. Coping with belonging to such a minority means facing daily slights and hurts, snide comments and scathing glances.

Barry, a twenty-five-year-old gay musician who had recently arrived in London from the Midlands, said:

I do feel persecuted by society because I'm gay, yes. I feel that outside my own group people just can't accept me as a person. They make jokes, and there's a lot of avoidance, at least where I come from, as though one had a nasty infection. The police persecute gays, too, when there's no reason to; for instance, there's a very famous cruising area – Holland Walk. If you go down there at one o'clock in the morning there's just all these men lined up, and it really is like going to a supermarket. You walk along, and they're just leaning against the wall, and you just walk past them thinking, Oh, I like him, or He's all right. Now the police are always going up there and arresting people for no reason at all. I mean, what harm am I doing? What harm am I doing anybody by standing in a pedestrian walkway at one o'clock in the morning? The only harm I do is to myself, if I get mugged or something, but I'm not committing an immoral act. I mean, if I start screwing someone in Hyde Park at one o'clock in the afternoon, I think then they have justification in arresting me. And it's the same with clubs – they're always being raided. I'm quite sure that we're the most maligned minority there is. I don't know why it is. You find a lot of gays that are hyper-intelligent people, and yet they're still prepared to be used and manipulated and humiliated for no reason at all.

My most down-to-earth homosexual informant was Shane, a male prostitute of twenty-five from Manchester, now living and working in London. I talked to him in a small overheated room in Soho, where the sound of the traffic outside made it almost impossible to hear our conversation. He was on the top floor of a building where at street level the entrance hall with its permanently open door was slightly more scruffy and paper-strewn than the street outside. He was dressed in jeans with a grey pullover and a Levi jacket with the collar turned up. His dark hair was cut short and bleached, and he wore a ring on the little finger of his right hand. He had attractive eyes, and a small mouth with an amused and slightly self-mocking downwards twist.

I've been in children's homes all my life. I was put in a home when I was a little baby. My parents had separated. I was fostered when I was five up to eleven, but I didn't get on with my foster dad. I used to run away. Then I asked to be put in a children's home. I couldn't cope with him; if I didn't do things right he used to hit me. So I was in a home up till I left school. My foster mother was a singer – she used to work in a club. I liked her a lot. I used to put her wig on and stand up and sing. Some of it was happy, some of it wasn't. One time I ran away from my foster parents and I went to this old lady. She had two cats and a poodle, and I got on really well with her. I went round to her house and I was in tears and I was telling her what happened and she was really nice. The Social Services got me a flat and I lived there for a couple of weeks. But I didn't like it, I didn't like living by myself, I didn't like the landlady. Then I stayed a month with my dad, but one of my brothers' wives told him I was gay, so he threw me out. He hit me. He said I was dirty because I went with men.

I knew I was gay from about the age of sixteen. I'd been interested in girls but just as friends, not for sex. I'd had girls before but it just didn't turn me on.

My first gay sexual experience was with someone I met in a club. I was sixteen. He picked me up; I quite liked him I suppose. So I went back with him. I was a bit scared. I thought it would kill me. I never really liked it, that side of it. I was passive when I was young – people take advantage of you when you're young. I didn't really enjoy it but I just took it because I liked him. I'm mostly active now, more dominant.

When I first started I was by myself. I didn't speak to anyone because every time someone tried to talk to me – the other gay boys – I used to give them dirty looks. Well, you've got to be careful or you might get ripped off. I'm not really frightened of violence, I've been threatened but that's about all. If it happens, it happens. You only live once. If a client gets a bit rough you just push them, tell them to get out. There was a coloured guy, we went back to his place and had a session. He paid me and as I was getting dressed after he'd gone out his friend came in and he locked the door. He wanted to go with me too, and I said no. So he started chasing me round the room and I tried to get the door open. When he wouldn't open it, I went into the kitchen and brought out a carving knife. Then he opened the door.

I started because it was easy money. In them days I charged £15. Now it's £25 onwards. That's for about an hour, or half an hour. Sometimes, if you like the punter, you do more. You do a lot, but if it's someone you don't really want to do it with, you just do as little as poss. You find clients want a number of different things. Some want to be screwed, some want to be sucked off, and I don't really like doing that. I don't object if they want to screw me but I'd rather do it for a regular than a one-off. Some take you back to their place and want you to put on a pair of shorts, or strip down to your underpants and just walk around while they masturbate. I think it's a bit stupid, but you get a lot like that who are not active. Some of them want to check to see if you're clean, and some of them smell, but you just grin and bear it. I went back with one client to his place in the country. He wanted me to cane him. He had three different sizes and showed me a special way of doing it without hurting him too much. I spent a couple of hours doing it, it was very tiring. I've got one client who's really nice and respectable, he's middle-aged and says his wife and

200

children know he's gay and accept it. He pays good money, £100 for a night. But in this country you can get away with very little sex if you don't feel like it. When I did six nights in Europe once I worked far harder. The English are shy so they're easier.

When the punters are out looking for somebody, they eye you up. You don't go for them straight away because they're a bit nervous. If they walk on a bit and they look back, then you follow behind. Then you start approaching them. Sometimes some of them are bold and you walk straight up to them; some of them just smile and walk off. Then you get some who just stare at you. Then you go up to them and they say, 'Oh, no.' Some of them, they'll spend ages talking to you, ask you what you do, how much it costs, where you live, who with, then they go home and have a wank. I call them window shoppers. It's really annoying.

If I'm going to a club and pick someone up then we talk about what we like straight away, because it's like picking someone up from a meat rack. Either they ask for it or you tell them what you want. I pick people up in nightclubs most of the time. But the other night, after I'd met no one during the week, this guy on a bus kept looking back at me. He got off the bus before me, so I looked over and he smiled at me. I got off at the next bus stop, and he came up. He asked me if I wanted to go back to his place but I said, 'It's best to come back to mine.' I'd rather be in my own place, it's safer. At least I know where the kitchen is. It's not so far.

When I take somebody back I won't do anything I don't like. I just put my foot down. There are perverts. I don't like clowns, or the kind who just wear the same hair-cuts and wear leather – he-men, trying to be butch.

I've done it once or twice in a back alley, but it's very nerve-racking looking behind you all the time. You're afraid that a copper might just walk round the corner any moment. You'd be done for indecency. That's the worst thing. I've been done for importuning. Got a £30 fine. The police here are really bad, they're always pulling you in. It's pathetic, you just get fined. They should legalize it. And because they're trying to clean it up, the police are getting worse, punters are scared, and some of the boys down there are ripping them off. They aren't gay at all.

In France you don't get hassled by the police. There's more money over there. In Paris the rent boys all have their beat. See, *here* we accept anybody on our beat, really. The French boys don't like the English boys working in Paris. They don't like any foreigner working their beat. They chase you off, half-a-dozen of them.

I work mostly on Piccadilly Underground. I've been a rent boy for about five years. I heard about it on television. You have these documentaries about London. It was before *Johnny Come Home* because I was here when that was on television. I thought that was a load of rubbish. A lot of it was acting, wasn't it?

I'm attracted by different sorts of people. I'm not that keen on blonds because they are not that good in bed anyway. They are attractive but they are not as good as dark-haired people, they're not as passionate. They are all trying to keep themselves perfect. I'm attracted by men the same age or a bit older – not too old. Sometimes you get them younger, but not too young. Eighteen or nineteen.

I get foreigners and English approaching me. Foreigners usually pay more, and they're more friendly. They want to know you more. They tend to want to see you again. It's better that way; you don't have to go about so much.

The English don't like to tell you what they do for a living, and you can meet some very important people – politicians, civil servants, quite well-known sort of people, even television people. There's enough work around – we're everywhere.

I had an Italian who worked in the embassy. He was very discreet. I met him in Hyde Park. He always parked his car half a mile down the road. Sometimes people take me back to their place. It's different if they've got nice houses. Men have wanted to keep me but I don't like being kept. I'm too independent. I had a sugar daddy in Manchester but he's just a friend now. When he comes to London he sometimes gives me money, and if I'm skint he'll give me money. Another one took me to Holland and Belgium for a holiday. He had a hang-up on what he wanted. He wasn't sure if he wanted a boy or a girl. He works in a straight place and if they knew he was gay he'd lose his job.

I'm not interested in bisexuals. You can't have an affair with them – it's a quick session because they've got a girl-friend. There's no competition; a girl can't compete against two gay guys – she feels inferior.

I like women as long as they don't try and make a pass. The only women I like are the most beautiful women – tartish, and get away with it. I love Marilyn Monroe, her personality, her looks. My background is almost the same as hers.

I have a check up at the clinic about every two weeks. VD isn't too bad, and I'm not really worried about AIDS, because if you get it, you get it. It can take two years before the symptoms start showing. You see, gay people tend to go with different people all the time, because there's so much oppor-tunity, plus you're looking for someone – the right one. You could call us sluts, really. Even straight guys don't really mess around as much as us.

As far as getting the money goes, sometimes they give me the money first, sometimes afterwards. If I'm seeing some-body regular they keep on paying. I won't ever go with dirty-looking people. You can't be *too* choosy, but them sort you don't go with. They look the sort that would rip you off anyway.

There's no pleasure in it, really, it's a job. It comes auto-matic to you eventually. At first it's repulsive, you don't react or activate, and then you just do it automatic, get used to it. Then when you go out with boyfriends, you've got to relax and you don't always relax as much, because you're so used to doing that. I did want to give it up but it's easy money.

Some queens are 'size queens'. We call them size queens because they're into big ones. Some of them get really turned on. It may be painful but they get used to it – they really enjoy it. Some real queens are just into that. It becomes pure plea-sure. We can take more than what a woman can.

I used to like hairy men but I'm not choosy any more. Japanese are slightly feminine when it comes to having sex with you. Americans are into a lot of sex. They're a bit loud

203

and try and impress you, a lot of them, and they call you sweet. I met this American down Piccadilly. He chased me around and I thought, Well, I won't stop him, and he came up to me and he said, 'Are you working?' I says, 'Yeah', and he says, 'That's a shame, you're rather sweet. See you some time.' Some Americans turn round afterwards and they won't pay for it.

Being gay is not as bad as it used to be. Five years ago the hassle I used to get from people, calling us queers and all that. We used to have fights but now no one seems to bother. It's been on the news and people have become more tolerant. Sometimes, for a laugh, I go to a straight club. Me and my friend wear these pink T-shirts in the summer. We saw this guy and we said, 'Oh, he's nice. . . .' and the barman knows us and he said, 'Right, drink your drink and get out, you couple of lesbians.' He came round the bar and told us to get out straight away.

I used to wear drag, but it's a bit risky. Doing business is a bit hard, you know, making all these excuses and saying it's your periods, and all that. And I don't like to give a mouth job.

I've only got two real friends. One's working as a rent boy, and he's taking drugs – he's getting registered. The other works for London Transport. They know he's gay. If I was in trouble I don't think there is anyone I could turn to. I had a boyfriend once, when I was seventeen. It was really bad, I really loved him, and it finished. I was really upset. I was in tears, and I just played this tape of love songs and cried a lot. Someone said it's not worth crying, sort yourself out, there's plenty more fish in the sea. You've got to snap out of it.

I don't think I'll ever settle down. I'm afraid I wouldn't like to have somebody living with me because people who have lived with me have always had arguments and I've lost them all. The longest relationship I've ever had lasted a month.

I don't really want to think about children. I don't want to be responsible for them being called nasty names and all that. I'd be called a nancy, and all that, if I had children in the house.

I worry about losing my looks a bit. I use face packs and all that – my cupboard's full of all sorts. I used to wear make-up but I grew out of that. You grow out of that after about nineteen. If I won a lot of money I'd buy a lot of clothes, Italian clothes. And I'd run a bar, a gay bar, but not in this country because of tax and inflation, and it's hard to get a licence.

I do feel a bit sorry for older gays. Well, they start buying, don't they? They start buying boys, they do down Picadilly. Some of them become a recluse and hide, some kill themselves. It depends. I'd hate to be an old man by myself. And I'd refuse to pay for it.

When I'm a retired rent boy I'll get a job, I suppose. I work in a club now, which seems good enough. I suppose sooner or later I should have a permanent job before it's too late.

Under most circumstances it seemed that men found talking about sex naturally and openly almost impossible. Victor, aged thirty-one, a comprehensive school teacher, put it like this.

I think men are definitely inhibited in talking about sex in many ways, and they normally make reference to their own sexual prowess or they talk about being hopeless and confused and unable to cope. But it's all done under the guise of humour, really. I suppose it's a form of showing off.

When talking of homosexuality, they spoke as if it were one simple, identifiable form of behaviour. None of these men considered that there might be as many types of homosexual behaviour as there were heterosexual. Although in society as a whole there has been a genuine liberalizing change in attitudes towards homosexuality, it still has a long way to go, judging from the comments made to me.

Chapter Eleven

WORK

If men found it difficult to talk about their emotions, when asked about their work there was no such reticence. They visibly relaxed, and began to discuss a subject they knew something about with a sense of relief and an air of confidence. In fact, it was often hard to stem the flow of technical detail, ranging from cleaning the inside of boilers to trading in cocoa and coffee at sums beyond the imagination. Very few of the men interviewed led lives which were not dominated by their work, and many seemed to derive their greatest satisfaction in life from the long hours spent fulfilling ambitions through their profession or job, though there were those whose work was so humdrum and boring that all thoughts were of time off. Work not only provides the wherewithal to satisfy material needs, it also provides a social identity (which may or may not have high social status) but which fulfils the individual's need to feel significant. The effects of redundancy, unemployment or forcible retirement can be seen everywhere.

For many of my informants, the word 'work' was used in its traditional, old-fashioned, narrow and unambiguous sense of a job done for a certain number of hours each day in return for money. It was usually carried out away from home and consisted of a task that that person would never have chosen to do freely; earning a living, being engaged in wage-labour for another, or performing a service for a fee or a salary was work. But people who ran societies, brought up children, dug gardens, cooked and dusted without monetary gain and who might be said to be expending energy and working, were not always considered workers. This strange paradox no doubt lies at the root of some women's resentment of men. Others who were lumped in the working but not workers category were criminals, who made great efforts at a number of activities but were not thought to be doing a real job.

To start with the exception, Johnnie, thirty-seven, spends long hours and well-organized days earning a good living through a life of crime. I met him in a part of London where he is not known. He's of medium height with short, blond, well-cut hair; a self-confident, stocky man who is very successful as a crook, but no longer uses the methods he describes here.

I was born in 1948, so really my childhood was just after the war when the East End was all bomb sites and debris. I suppose we was the last ones of what I call the real East End because we grew up with people who had been there through the war and just after the war. It was still old houses and little streets when I was a kid. They're all gone now. You always get these people that say: 'I'm from the East End and it was hard and it was rough.' Well, it's *not* hard and rough, because when you're brought up in that environment, you think everyone's like that. It's a good life in the East End, it's like a village. . . . I left school at fifteen. I never took exams; we was never encouraged to. They was closing down a lot of the East End schools, the small schools, and turning them into comprehensives. They didn't want to concern themselves with people like me.

I don't have a job. The way I get my money depends on the weather. I might be going creeping – that's when you go round the offices. You find the building and you go into an office and you creep about for chequebooks and cheque cards. When someone goes out of their office, you dive in there and take the chequebook, card and the cash. I leave the bag, so they don't even notice they're gone. Then I'd go home and clean the card and the chequebook. Now, when these new kind of chequebooks started with a calendar in the back, we used to buy some special transparent paper. It cost about a tenner for five pages. You cut it out so that it would fit exactly round the outside lines of the calendar. So, what we used to do was go in the bank and write out 'Pay cash', with whatever name it was. Always wear a nice suit, a tie. Pull out a wallet, pull the card out separate. Never look too well dressed; try to look like a clerk, you don't want to be too flash. Anyway, they used to put a cross on the date at the back when they give you the money. So when you come outside you just used to rub it out because you had it covered with the paper. You could do about eight or ten cheques like that.

If you didn't go out and get your own chequebooks, you had people that used to get their living just getting the chequebooks by creeping. The creepers sell you the book and the card for £7 a cheque. Then you might get two girls to work for you; you pay them £10 for each cheque they change. If they change twenty-five cheques a day, that's £250 a day, and they're happy. The rest is yours.

When you're doing the book and cards, you're travelling the whole country. Never work in London because there you've got cowboys looking out for it. The cashiers get rewards for spotting someone at it. We used to get up early and get out the house by seven o'clock. You'd get up to, say, Suffolk, by ten o'clock so you start going in the banks straight away. You take one girl with you and on the way up she's practising the signatures – practise, practise, practise. You get there, and you get her to sign the card you got in that name, and the other card you got in another name. Then she runs into one bank, and comes out with the book and card and fifty quid. Nearly every town's got four banks, so if she's been into Lloyd's, she then goes into the Midland with the other book and card with the other name. She comes back. By that time, you've cleaned the other book that she had and you give it back, and then she goes over the Natwest, and then Barclays. So, in that town with two books, you've done four cheques. You've got yourself £200. Then you drive on to the next town. You always have a map of the area you're going to work, and you work out all the little towns. You work out a route from where you come off the motorway and you work out the amount of banks in each town on a route that'll take you in a circle and bring you back to the motorway at the end of the day.

You've got three days to work a book you got in, say, the morning. You get it one day, you work it the next day, and then you work the next day up to twelve o'clock. That's when the hot list comes out and is in the banks; you never send them in after that.

So you have the girl, who's the worker; your driver; and you're the cleaner. The cleaner stays in the car, cleaning all the time. The driver will go in behind the girl and mind her. If the teller goes off, as long as he stays in sight, the girl stays. But if the teller goes out of sight, the driver gives her a tap and she goes back to the car. Then you leave that town.

Nine times out of ten, it's good, steady work. Say you have three books with an average of twenty cheques, you can make £3,000. You take out £10 for every cheque the girl's changed. Then you've paid £7 already for each cheque to buy them. Then you've got the petrol money, and you've got to feed the girl and the driver while they're out. You've got to pay the driver £10 a day, so in all, I end up with about £1,500. By the time the banks close at half three, you've got a nice few quid on you. The first thing you do then is find the best restaurant. You get in there, and you've still got a bit of plastic so you can eat the best meal you can have. You just give them the card. We used to have the best kind of steaks, the best wine, the best this, the best that. Every night. We tried all the Rothschild wines and all the different sauces. That's what you're working for.

Now they punch a hole on the calendars and you can't do any of this no more. I don't know how to get round the punching now. When they changed from stamps over to the calenders, nobody knew what to do for a while. We spent ages working out different methods and we come up with this. The only way now is to go abroad. Germany is still all right but

France is getting much too hot. What you do is you buy a birth certificate – a blank – and you fill in the name. Then you can get a passport, easy. You take two girls over, for a day or two days, and run them round every bank with the books and cards.

Why do I do it? There's something about it, the power. My power's in the achieving. And it ain't the 'Hee hee, I had that bank over.' It's not that. It's getting the money, the doing it, and it's the fact that you're capable of doing it. And you get a nice living out of it. You ain't hurting no one – it's only going on them insurance premiums. . . .

There's people that find burglary acceptable. They're called drummers. It's called drumming 'cause you go round knocking on the doors to make sure people are out. When they're not in, you get in quick by the window. I think it ain't nice to intrude on other people's houses. But I got to be honest – I have done it. I used to do all the country work at one time. You never rob a house in the East End. Never, because it's a working-class person. You never ever rob your own.

When you're drumming, you get up very early and you drive out to the country. You pick the area you're going to work. You never pick Virginia Water, 'cause that's been worked so many times. I worked there many years ago and got away with it but I wouldn't do it now. But if you're going to go for something, go where you're going to get the most; get the big ones who've got it and are insured. I mean, this sort of house, you couldn't go round this sort of house. [We were sitting in the north London home of two writers.] How could you come into this house and rob someone like this? Or someone like you? People see your face on the telly and then they think, you must have bundles. But you're only a working person, when you get down to it. What you've got you've grafted for, and that's something to be admired – know what I mean? You ain't one of these who've had it slapped on yer. Good luck to yer. What you got, you grafted for. That won't stop a lot of people; it just depends on how you are. If you're going to go for something, go for where you're going to get the most. It's no good coming up to people in the street and taking their Cartier watch or gold chain from round their neck; that's not going to pay me rent or feed the kids. And if would just get you a lot of bird, it's needless.

The worst time when you're nicked is being in police custody for three days. They've got to charge you after three days. You're took to court on the third morning. If you get your bail, you get out, if you don't, you go to Brixton. In Brixton the doors are unlocked all day. You can have your food sent in, and you're allowed half a bottle of wine or two cans of beer. And you get a visit every day. When you're actually inside, say, at Wandsworth, it's twenty-three hours bang-up, normally. You're locked up twenty-three hours a day, and you get one hour a day exercise. But when you get shifted to the actual prisons where you're going to do your sentence, you work all day. They have workshops where you put things together – components, making toys, little games, painting soldiers, machining clothes. It's all things like that. If you work all week, like, you get up at half-six, into breakfast at seven, back to clean up your cell, then into work by eight. Half-eleven, back to dinner, then locked in your cell till one. Out your cell, back at work till half-three when you have your tea. Then you're locked up, and it's the end of the day. You get into the routine. . . .

You get these young mugs who might be sixteen, seventeen, who go out and do a post office – shoot some old lady and then get twenty years. And they think they're right clever for doing it. They might have only got £500. But then you might get someone who'd been going out with a book and card year after year, earning thousands, and they never hurt nobody in their life. And these young people get a long sentence and they'll be crying their eyes out. But the man who does it for a living, he knows his risks. If you can't do the time, don't do the crime – that's the saying. It's obvious that I'll be put inside again some time. It's on the cards. It's a fact of life, a percentage, isn't it? Unless I found something I could do that paid me the money and I was happy doing it. But what could I do? What is there? I'm ignorant; I'm not bright. All I've got is common old street knowledge. I find corners where I can get a few quid out of something but that's no good, is it? What can I do? I'm not working for no one else, ever. If I'm going to work,

211

it's going to be for me. I'm not going to make someone else rich.

What is, and what is not, work is socially defined; it is not a quality inherent in any particular act, as we have just seen. Certain jobs give people a valued status in society in other people's eyes and therefore also in their own eyes: equally if work is reduced to an unsatisfying chore, then the image of the worker is diminished, both to himself and to others, alienating him still further from the job. Some of those I met loved their tasks, others accepted their daily stint with equanimity, while many barely tolerated the boredom and frustration. Rewards came from doing a job well, from a sense of individual fulfilment and status gained; from the friendships formed, the feel of belonging; and from material recompense

Les, now fifty-six, achieved every small boy's dream and became an engine driver on a diesel train but he looks back to the old days of steam with a much greater sense of fulfilment. Sometimes a job can be a source of great satisfaction to an individual, even though others look down on it

The transition from the steam locomotive to diesel was an exciting adventure in the early days. That happened in my part of the country the north-east, in 1965–6. I feel that if you were to interview a hundred drivers who had done both, most will say, 'Give me the steam locomotive every time.

I was promoted fireman in March 1947, something like five years after I started on the railways in the cleaning shed. I progressed up the scale as I became a better fireman on to the main line Darlington to King's Cross trains, but I started work between the collieries – Newport, Leeds, Durham and Northumberland coalfields.

I had very little passenger work then. You must bear in mind that on a steam locomotive you could shift up to thirty tons of coal on a journey easy

In them days with the steam locomotive, you had the engine in front of you and behind your running tender. You got the draught in any event and could keep quite nice and cool, despite the firebox, and if you had inclement weather, you put up an old sack or a side sheet to stop the wind or the rain. You could make your own comfort on a steam locomotive.

A steam locomotive to a fireman and a driver was a challenge. You had a steam gauge there, and unless the fireman kept a head of steam up the driver was in trouble and, equally, the driver had to coordinate with his fireman.

The worst thing that could happen was to have no water in your boiler; the lead plug gives way and your boiler collapses – total catastrophe. There's nothing you can do then. There's only one thing you are going to get, that's your cards and off the job. I never dropped a lead plug, thank God, or I wouldn't be here today. But there were leaks often enough, and whilst they don't stop you, they made your job one hellish lot harder, because you were fighting against leaking water dropping into your firebox, and lashing fire round the boiler making the difficulty of getting a head of steam much greater.

There were far more challenges than on diesels. I think it's a real sadness that jobs in this industry have made men become a bit of a robot, a human robot. Then so much was based on judgement – can I do this, can I get that, what can I achieve? You could make a good journey or a bad journey, but often a good fireman and a good driver went together – one man made the other.

If you were to say to me, 'Would you like to set the clock back?', I would not hesitate to choose steam, and I don't think much of that is sentimentality with me. I could go home in them days and say, 'Well, I've done a damn good day's work', and I could say to me dad, 'Well, I will get the spade out and do two or three hours in the garden', which I did because I like gardening. But today, on a diesel locomotive, you are sat in one position, and. . . . although you are going at substantially higher speeds, there is no real involvement. You are contained in a cab with two or three levers to take you on your journey. Quite honestly, when you get off at the end of your shift, you just want to creep home and sit down and put your head back and do nothing. Of course, there's been progress to the extent that trains go between point A and point B much faster than they did in my early days.   it's progress, but progress at what cost?

There were drivers who were so looking forward to being in a nice comfortable cab with no steam to worry about, no fireman to worry about – they would have done it for nothing. But the unions were not far-sighted enough to see what would ultimately happen to our jobs, and the people in them I think the unions should be more concerned about whether jobs are interesting. This must be the starting-point Of course the money is important – it's essential – but I no longer find my job 100 per cent satisfying like I used to. If you put the clock back I would not be an engine driver I would try to be a lawyer

Anthony, aged thirty-four, a television producer who might be termed a workaholic, also understood the plea-sures to be obtained from work – not only satisfaction in success and monetary reward but also from doing a job which was well thought of by others

I wake up and watch television I think breakfast television in this country stinks, but I watch it I watch it in bed, most of it goes through me. I like the news, and I channel hop

I normally get to the office at nine-thirty – that·s because most people in television don't start till ten anyway If Ameri cans are in town, we have breakfast at their hotel I talk to Australia first in the morning – we have an office there now Often by the time people call me back it s the evening and I'm at home. I talk on the phone at home I talk to Los Angeles almost every day, and I talk to New York once a week I travel quite a bit, go to LA once a month usually for about a week I couldn't do business without the phone I hardly ever write letters. I find paper work a waste of my time I don t do any administration at all Someone does it for us.

I have my own company We do two things – we market programme ideas to independent television companies and we make programmes and sell them. I'm investigating the opportunities for co-production ventures in Australia and developing formats suitable for the market over there. I do know I'm different from any other producer in this country because I'm a salesman.

I sell an idea by adapting it to the needs of the buyer. If he wants an American character, he can have one; a European location, he can have it. But he's getting what he wants. Or you sell a show because it's tied to a host who is saleable. I don't know how I learnt to do it. It certainly was not in the independent companies I've worked for – there we were just live producers. I work out what's needed – our intelligence about what the different companies and the network are looking for is very good. I don't treat it any differently from any other sort of sale. So, you know that there is a need for a four-door hatchback car, and that's what you make.

My biggest success was sold because I knew this particular company and ITV needed something on a particular night to put against the BBC, to see it off, once and for all. We are now successful enough to be asked by a company to fill a space. They literally say, 'Seven-thirty on a Friday, we have got to make twenty-six in a period of twelve days in the studio, non-reward show, and a budget of this. Now deliver the show.' That defines it absolutely. You can't give away a car, because they already have three shows giving away a car. So you've got to make it what we call 'non-reward', which is usually a video machine. You can define it just like that. They may want celebrities – we'll book them. So then you go to the shelf upstairs, pull out four celebrity lists, and you go to the file and you pull out four formats, and then you say these are the sort of formats where you don't have to give big prizes, simple enough, it's Friday night, it's got men and women, it's got this, it's got that. These are the programmes you could show. We show them and they say 'Yes' or 'No'. . . .

Companies can't afford to employ someone like me. It would cost them £50,000 a year, and they might never come up with an idea. Financial security for me would probably mean a million quid. There's the house, a nice house, I'd buy it outright. I think to work for someone else now I'd need a

215

salary of well over £100,000 a year, because of the tax problems. . . .

I used to think the best job in television was the controller at an ITV station, a big one. Now, I think I've gone past that. It would be a backward move for me to be a controller of a major ITV station, both financially and creatively. Financially, I earn more than they earn.

I'm a great believer in the ratings. I'm not ashamed to say that I'm a producer of games shows. It is a glamorous world and I can't stand the inverted snobs in television who complain about it.

I think television in this country has gone off. You can never really put your finger on it, but I watch a lot less TV in the evening than I used to. I used to watch everything. I still keep the television on during dinner if there is something I want to watch, but turn the sound down. I recently met a director who said he didn't have a TV set and never watched television. Well, I think he should get out of it.

The people I get on best with in television are the stars who like being stars. . . . The truth is it's dead easy, it's good fun and it's unbelievably well paid. It's not a tough or aggressive world, as some might think. I find it very friendly   My personal guidelines are that I'm scrupulously honest, I'm not really aggressive, I don't get depressed, I've learnt not to worry about anything. My tactic with employees and colleagues is to tell them the absolute truth when it can really embarrass them. I'll tell them other people on the show thought they were lousy, and I'll say, 'I thought you were appalling', but I'll tell them what they did well. I do say a lot of things I don't mean. I feel paternalistic. I like doing all this on my own. I know how to do it, naturally and easily, and that's just years of experience. .

In this country people resent you for being successful too young. But I don't flaunt it; people that flaunt it are even more unpopular. I drive a Porsche, but it's a dark one. I suppose I bought that, not so much as a status symbol, but because I wanted it. I resent other people resenting success.

My work is the most important thing in my life I think my wife certainly knew that when she married me It s not that

216

I'm not there, but I'm somewhat one-directional. My wife does complain about my enthusiasm for the business, and bears the brunt of bringing up the children. During a run I can be in America a lot; it's a bit tough on the kids, I think. But it helps that she's been in the business too. Of course, the material rewards weigh that up. She is off on holiday with the children next week. Off to the sun. I can't go, unfortunately. I'm too busy. But last summer I took the whole family to California for a month. It's not a bad life. . . .

All my friends are in television. I don't think I have any outside, which is frightening. But if we have an evening with other people, non-television people, I'm bored rigid. I feel I'm there as the token television producer, to have a go at.

When it was my birthday last year, we had two shows on the air, and three shows that weekend, so we set out the entire house with video recorders. Wherever you went, if you shut the toilet door, a machine came on and you had to watch one of the programmes back again. We invited everyone and you had to come dressed as your favourite television programme. It was a great success. I came as a pilot. I said to everyone, 'I was going to come as a television series but we never got it made.' It was so simple. It was wonderful.

I only have one other interest, and that's horseracing. It's a day out in the fresh air in the middle of the week. It's the fun of bunking off from the office – that's sinful. I always go with people in the business, and we talk about TV. We had a box at Cheltenham for three days this year, and it was all TV people. I suppose television's an obsession with me: here's something I can be good at, so I'll carry on doing it until I'm *very* good at it.

To be so successful, to have achieved so much, Anthony must have worked very hard and have been extremely ambitious. What drives men to want more than the ordinary everyday rewards which satisfy their colleagues?

Toby, a management trainee of twenty-three, longed for power over others.

217

I haven't set my sights on anything in particular, but I know the type of position I eventually want to be in. I know that I want to be in a position of authority. I want to be recognized as an expert in whatever I'm doing. I want to be respected. I think everyone wants that. If I become famous in the process, fair enough, but that's not what I want. I don't want to be famous, I want to be in control of people – but not in a nasty sense. I've always been leader in anything I've done, and I think it's because I have definite ideas. If I think somebody else is talking sense, then I'm prepared to listen to what they say and perhaps change my ideas. I dislike the hierarchical system that operates where just because somebody's older than you then it automatically follows that they're wiser.

Some wanted to do better than their fathers, whom they described as 'rather hopeless', 'weak', 'had given up trying' or 'a disappointment for my mother'. Fifty-one-year-old oil company executive Mike had a grandfather who was an army officer; as a small child he was dressed up in a drummer boy's uniform to be photographed standing beside the old man. He then felt, as he grew older, a terrible fear engendered by his family's ambition for him; he had to escape the assumption that he would go into the army.

It starts by other people setting expectations for you that are not your own, and which may seem too difficult to reach. You then take these over, and to achieve anything less than that seems to be running away; you never want to lower your expectations, because that means failure. I did not want to go into the army – I did not think I would make a good general – and so I decided to go into industry, to escape if you like. But the ambition was still there, not mine but 'expected'. I used to think I could become managing director; I don't any longer. And I look on that as being real maturity. To turn round and say, 'Look I don't want to be managing director, because (a) I can't be, and (b) if by some awful circumstance I was, I wouldn't be a very good one. Because it's not me. It's not a role which I would do well', that takes some doing.

Others were not affected by family pressures but set themselves realistic ambitions, which were attainable without too much difficulty so that, as forty-eight-year-old James discovered, they could relax and enjoy life.

I've been here for nearly twenty-nine years and in that time I've had a variety of jobs. I've never been in one job for more than five years and the average is around three or four years. I'm basically responsible for the company's international marine business – it's a major international group. I'm glad to say I'm one of those very lucky people who have got tremendous satisfaction out of the job I've been doing. I've often asked myself if I could have been an entrepreneur if things had been different; I don't know the answer except that I've been very happy being the corporate man. I've never really felt any great urge to break out and run my own company. I've never had those feelings of being trapped, though I'm sure there are a lot of men who do. If you're on the outside looking in, this company is a monolith, yes. But when you're looking at the inside you realize that it is, in fact, not only several hundred different companies, but several hundred different businesses.

I get into the office soon after eight and I leave about a quarter to six. Seldom do I actually have to take work home, but I do often spend weekends away on company business, and do quite a lot of travelling. It's important to me to feel I've made a mark on life in some way. To be honest, I get a considerable degree of personal satisfaction out of having reached the level I have in the company.

Some men explained ambition as pure selfishness. The definition was given in a mock-apologetic way, which justified the need to be obsessed by work in order to succeed. Bank manager Edward at forty-eight was now acutely aware of the passing of time, that life was short, and that he still had to climb a few rungs further up the ladder for his own satisfaction.

It's a funny thing, ambition – it's in you, there. It isn't necessarily because of your family and the need to provide. It's something deeper than that. It's a selfish thing; you do it for yourself. I've always had to provide at home, and I've always managed to, but I haven't worked that much harder for the family. I've worked harder for myself, because I'm reaching up all the time. There has been a conflict between my family and my work, and my family has lost because I'm ambitious; and given the chance I think I'd do the same again.

In one way or another, a great many men from a variety of backgrounds seemed to be saying that if you are a man, you've got to prove yourself in some way, and the most obvious way to do that is through work. Part of this 'proving yourself' was the urge to get up the ladder of promotion, and some men found that if they found the job they wanted at a low rung on the ladder, it gave them a slightly bitter feeling when others less talented than themselves went up past them. They also said that other men seemed to think less of them because of their lack of ambition.

But those who stay on the intermediate rungs of the ladder for twenty-odd years or so, doing the same job happily and well, are the lifeblood of any organization; sustaining motivation and nurturing those who are not too ambitious is what management is all about. The art is to make every rung of the ladder important to someone, as Basil, a Midlands security officer who is about to retire, recognizes.

I've enjoyed my job here – it's been over fifty years. I know this is being a bit naughty, but you've got a little bit of power over some of these jumped-up bosses – Mr This and Mr That. But Mr This and Mr That has to do what he's told by me, because I've got my orders, I've got my instructions. And I can carry those rules out. It's naughty to say it, but I love it.

Occasionally however change occurs in an organisation or a man reaches the end of his tether and becomes appalled at the thought of carrying out the same task over and over again for the next twenty years. This happened to Maurice who works for a television company, and who in his late forties realized that his creative and influential professional life was over. He had been in charge of a successful regular programme, but someone younger from outside the company was promoted over him. Since then he has been given a prestigious new title without a proper job attached to it.

Frankly, I don't care any more; this organization has changed beyond all recognition. In the old days, everything was much smaller and to my mind much better here. Growth has not improved it. The programmes are not as good – more technical, yes, but not as good – and the atmosphere's not the same. I think I fulfilled my ambition in a way by editing a very successful programme for a number of years. I have what they call a planning job now: I'm supposed to sit here and think about the future. I shall retire as early as possible, and get on with the garden. What I resent is being put in a corner out of the way. I've got a lot of experience that is just going to waste. I see them making mistakes time and again. It's possible after years in a job that one gets a bit stale, even a bit lazy, and you lose the edge.

Being pushed aside was an ever present fear for many men as they grew older. Loving their jobs, being filled with ambition, revelling in power, battling for the top, many men were lost in a world of work. They stayed late at the office, travelled, gave up their weekends and their free time to the furtherance of their careers. Such enthusiasm for their jobs could make wives and children jealous and constant absences were a source of considerable irritation to their families. James decided to involve his wife in his work when he realized that his frequent trips abroad were putting too great a strain on his marriage.

When the children were small I was gallivanting about all over the world, away for weeks on end. Then my wife was content to look after the family, but she became increasingly threatened by my absences, as she had more time on her hands. It would have been very strange if she hadn't. *She* felt there was a threat, even though I can say that there wasn't. Also she felt I was having the more interesting life. So in the last few years she has been able to travel with me quite a lot. I mean, she now sees travel for what it is – not just a gin-and-tonic-sodden binge. She's come home exhausted, with me. She sees the people I work with both inside and outside the company; it's helped her understand the job, the people and the frustrations. This is often the problem with husband and wife – 'Oh, you don't understand, and you can't understand'. It's literally true because there is an enormous wall between what the husband does in the office and what the wife knows about it.

Some men expressed both a sense of guilt and a direct conflict of interests in the way that their career affected their wife and children, like this recently elevated bishop.

My wife had an extremely good job – she's a doctor. She had to give it up and it was another two years before she found another one, not quite as good. She minded terribly; she wasn't cross about it – we made the decision together. She had been given the impression that it wouldn't be too difficult getting a job around here, but it was just when the cuts were beginning and it turned out to be much more difficult than she was led to believe. Being very good at what she does, she's found it very hard that her work has been secondary to mine at times. But then there have been times when I've refused to be moved because of family needs.

Few allowed their wives' careers to take priority over their own because, they would argue, she was more responsible for the day-to-day bringing up of children; such a reason was the accepted traditional way of look-ing at the relative importance of husbands' work versus wives' work. Those rare individuals who were happy to encourage their wives' careers to flourish, even when it led to dramatic reappraisals of their own ambitions, recount their experiences in Chapter 16.

Despite the fact that work assumed such an important role in the lives of almost every man interviewed, many explained that there had been a surprising element of luck in their manner of choosing a job or career. Sometimes it all hinged on one chance conversation. Certainly men under thirty seemed to have had the benefit at school of some sort of career advice, though few seemed to have taken it; nevertheless, the choice of career for most men seemed a haphazard affair unrelated to their talents, needs or interests. Many started the vague search for 'something to do' by asking their parents' advice. Fathers often wanted sons to follow in their footsteps, though there were some notable exceptions, for instance in mining districts where men often wanted something cleaner and less dangerous for their sons. Some men started out on an unsatisfactory tack trying to please their parents in their choice of job, and their success in a later career of their own choice could be based on the strength of character and purpose it took to turn against parental wishes. Those men who were forced or persuaded into jobs by their parents not surprisingly ended by disliking the work.

Some men said they hadn't any idea at school what they wanted to do, and had set off in entirely the wrong direction for them. Others had jobs, mainly unskilled or only semi-skilled, which were so grindingly monotonous that they only served to provide the money to finance the rest of their life. Heavy manual work, however, at least provided the right 'macho' image for boys who were least successful at school. Gerald, who had worked for years on the Ford production line at Dagenham, said his job had required such little thought that he had spent his time devising ways either to pass the time or to do less work than the production line required:

I went to work in the press shop, stamping out the actual bodies, the doors, the bonnets, the panels – imagine doing the same repetitive move 125 times an hour for eight hours a day, five days a week, fifty-two weeks of the year! You live in a fantasy world really. It destroys people's minds working in there. It's a bloody hell of a place to go to work. I can remember clearly what I used to do. I'd work out my wages that I had to come; I'd work it out in pounds, then in pennies, then in halfpennies, just for something to do. That's what I found myself doing. When you're on the production line, you start when the hooter blows and you stop when it blows, and you don't leave until you're actually told to leave. In that place, the management only lays out its manufacturing line on the basis of the production of the greatest number of commodities, and the human element, the human factor, is the last thing taken into consideration.

Some men felt their lives were a continuous performance of roles for which they were ill cast, though perhaps the one that sat easiest was the role they played at work. If they worked in a hierarchy, they all knew exactly where they stood, down to the more subtle nuances in some organizations of whose office you went into for a friendly chat and whose you avoided.

Titles for tasks, subtle variations between offices in an endless delicate gradation, a personal secretary, a meal in the right canteen, often mattered out of all proportion to their utilitarian value, for they were visible symbols of achievement, the enviable signs of career advancement. Matthew, a local government officer, recognized the need for such perks.

There are a lot of status symbols around in departmental offices – fitted carpets, clocks. You have to remember that office life depends entirely on the social culture, so it's different here from America or in Japan. What happens in a British office reflects British society. It is a class-ridden society. When you've climbed near the top of the ladder, it's easy to say the whole thing's petty, but when you're trying to get your first foot on the rung all these things are important and they help to keep the system going.

But what was it that men enjoyed about their work? The one most consistent reason given was, 'I'm never bored.' It didn't matter at what level they were working: what mattered was how each job could be made interesting. Shop steward Godfrey, aged sixty-two, was well aware of this.

Some years ago we tried an experiment. It was a joint management/union suggestion; to be fair to the company, I think they initiated it. The lines were laid out so that instead of staring at someone's neck all the time, people were put to face each other, so they could work and talk to each other. It was not often that people made mistakes, as the job was so repetitive. Previously the only chance of a conversation was if they stopped work and turned round, and spent a few minutes talking, which took one away from the job, or you had to wait for the tea break. I think those were the best days of the company when people put in a jolly good day's work and, in fact, were more agreeable during the day. Management showed an interest in helping them get over some of the sheer boredom that's attached to assembly work.

Not being bored often included the idea of doing something new, such things as helping mastermind a green field project, setting up a new part of the organization abroad, moving to a country never visited before, dealing with a new client or patient, selling a new line in a shop, or as coalminer Tom put it:

The mine fascinates me. It's a love-hate thing, you know. You hate it and there's something fascinating about it. I just can't explain. It's breaking into new ground; you don't know what's in front. It's exposing something that's been there millions of years not touched. It's fascinating.

The pleasure of a job with no responsibility could be as great for some as all the power in the world. At twenty-four Keith had tried a number of jobs but ended up as a labourer digging foundations for a new development in Halifax.

I enjoy the job – it suits me, and I've got my body into fantastic shape. I start early and then go down the road for some bacon and eggs. I enjoy the feeling of physical labour and being out of doors, though it's bloody cold in winter. I have no worries except to decide whether to do a bit of overtime or not. Just stopping and sitting down at the end of the day is fantastic. I like going home and just sitting. It's wonderful.

Many working-class men, who had little responsibility for their work except to do it in as short a time as possible, talked of the pleasures of working as a group or gang. Kevin, a thirty-five-year-old London dustman, could see many other advantages too.

This job is well paid. You do get good money on it. This week, it's £97 take home. That's not bad for a single bloke. You get perks as well. It's surprising what people throw away. One chap bought a brand-new electricsander – cost him £65 – but he couldn't get on with it, so he offered it to me. I said, 'Do you mind giving me a letter stating that you've freely given it to me?'
It's six blokes working together, and you've just got to have a laugh when you're working. You're always taking the mickey out of each other. It's hard work physically, hard especially in the hot weather. But you work for yourself more or less, you've got a task, and the harder you work the earlier you get home.

Men of all classes said they enjoyed a feeling of responsibility, of other people relying on them in some way. One of these was Andrew, a GP with a large rural practice in East Anglia, who had spent twenty years in the same community. The aspect of his work he liked the most was delivering babies, particularly in people's own homes.

It's the one occasion when you share something with a family that you can't really put into words. It's the satisfaction of giving

226

and having people relying on you at a moment in their lives they're never going to forget.

There were others who said they enjoyed the freedom to use their own judgement, like sixty-four-year-old bookie Ben.

It's a very exciting world. The excitement for me is pitting my sort of knowledge or ability against the punter. When I'm wrong, I pay and pay heavily. When I'm right, I win, and there's always an element of luck. You get a photo finish – some for you, some against you. If I were lucky all the time, I'd be rich as Onassis, or I could go out of business and be skint, but basically I've done very well. I'm happy when I've only lost a little when I should have lost a lot.

Self-employment seems to offer many of the advantages already mentioned that men were looking for – independence, responsibility, variety, freedom from hierarchy and from younger men leapfrogging over one's head. However, those who worked for themselves have had to learn to keep going through the tough times on sheer willpower and self-discipline, always motivating themselves until it becomes automatic. James works from his home.

My life as a writer has been exceedingly important. I don't even need to make myself get on with it any more. I've got into the position where research and writing is a drug, and I do it because I must, I'm tied to it, I've got to get through the next book. It's not just the deadlines – I want to get on to the book after.

Obsessional self-driving can create in some men inner tensions which lead to stress and breakdown, while others thrive under the pressure of enormous self-imposed workloads. Stress enables some people to accomplish more, it arouses and excites them, impelling them to greater heights than ever before. When they feel the pressure is excessive a few are able to shift it by delegation, choice of priorities, by abandoning certain projects, or by working even harder. But many men suffer from unrealistic deadlines and unrealistic budgets, set not by themselves but arrived at sometimes logically, sometimes not, by their company. One in four men die of coronaries – many of them because they have not learnt to cope with stress. The system of hierarchical promotion that affects most men at work means that if they wish to achieve success they are forced to take jobs higher up the scale, jobs which may not suit their temperament or skills. This system does not allow a man to continue to be rewarded for his competence at the level which both suits him and in which he is most valuable to his organization. All too often the wrong man gets pushed up the ladder into fields he does not enjoy, where he is less competent and so under greater stress. Yet, if he stays where he is, he may find his wife berates him for not getting the expected increases in salary, which are the reward for promotion, and his colleagues may think less of him for his lack of ambition.

Nick, a police sergeant of thirty-nine, should according to his age and peers have been a chief inspector by now, but he felt such strong ties to the slum district where he works that not only has he not had time to study for the necessary exams, but felt disinclined to move on.

Yes, it has got me into trouble, and I resent it sometimes. I never feel bad in the community here because there's so much work to do and I love it. It's more when I go on duty to a big demonstration and some young fellow I used to know comes up and he's a chief inspector; I can see him eyeing me in a funny way. Perhaps I didn't think much of him before, but it brings it all home to me then. The biggest difference my wife and I ever have is over money – she worries about whether we've got enough to pay the bills. I know we have, but I can never prove it to her. She may hold it against me that I've not pushed for promotion.

There was one drawback to promotion that I hadn't considered until the bishop pointed it out.

For the first time in my life, I now have a full-time secretary. It's the business of having someone who knows where you are all the time. I find that a bit constricting. It's partly, I suppose, this business of being brought up to behave well, and having a job in which you're expected to behave well. There's something in me that doesn't want to behave well. I think this sudden lack of privacy, which has just hit me, will get worse. It's very difficult to commit indiscretions, and I find that quite a problem now.

Men engaged at every level of work, longed for feedback on their performance. As Fred pointed out, being noticed made a great deal of difference.

I think dustmen are the type of thing some people take for granted – you throw your rubbish out and you expect it to be collected – you don't really notice it till they stop doing it. Some of them are so bloody-minded they think all dustmen do is pick up crap, and because they pick up crap, they're crap themselves. But some people think a hell of a lot of dustmen. There's people in these streets I've made friends with – personal friends now – they're more than just people I empty bins for. It's not necessarily a class thing, some of the middle classes and some of what you might call the high-class people is just as good as some of the normal working people; it's just whether they appreciate someone is doing something for them.

Again at all levels, men complained that the things that they did well often went unnoticed, whereas the things that they did badly were over-criticized. Getting feedback might not always be positive and helpful, but at least it was a start. Robert, a prison governor of fifty, sees his prime responsibility as creating an atmosphere in the prison in which all people (staff and inmates) can relate to each other in an open and undamaging fashion, but many of his staff had had no practice at this kind of openness.

You do come across plenty of intransigent types on the staff, yes, but if they're outspoken you can deal with it. If they are passive knife-in-the-back people you can't. But then at every meeting you go on about how you'd prefer to be faced. If the

229

place is bad, it's the staff's responsibility just as much as mine, and they should bring it out openly and not talk about it in the tea-room or at the gate.

When discussing women at work there was often an ambivalence voiced on the one hand as admiration for the effort women were willing to put into their jobs and on the other as suspicion that most women would end up putting the family first. One general manager of a well-known High Street chain store said they had no women directors, as the most qualified and talented had refused final promotion, but also admitted that their training programme might not yet be adequate. A few men were resentful that women had jobs when many men were unemployed, but no one said he feared female competition would oust him from his job. Edward, the bank manager, revealed an ambivalence about working with women common to many of my informants.

I don't think women have such a driving ambition as men. There are going to be more women bankers, though, they're coming through now. Within the last ten years, say, there has been a dramatic change. It's been forced upon large companies because ability is a scarce commodity. But this place cannot run without people with good practical, sound common sense and technical ability. In other words, they've got to have the brains. They've got to have a certain presence about them as well – it's a package deal, banking. And there aren't enough of them about. I run this place, and I've always run any place, on equality. I don't care whether you wear a skirt or trousers or whether you're black, white, yellow or green. And age doesn't matter either. It really can't, today. From working closely with girls and women, the only problem you have is once a month. And when they are going through that little six-day period or so, with three days either side of it, they can be very, very difficult. And their decision-making is impaired. I don't care what you women say, it's just three days either side of the peak. And in my experience, men don't have moods as much as women. There are men who are very moody, but in the main I think women are more emotional. Those three days either side, it affects women's judgements. I just think a woman can take the wrong decision. But I wouldn't mind working for a woman boss at all, so long as I respected her ability.

Some men said women had always wanted it both ways. They wanted equal pay and all the perks the unions had fought for but wouldn't work nights, wanted special concessions for looking after families and could not do demanding physical work. Other men in dangerous jobs said if women worked alongside them, they would feel responsible for their safety.

But men from a number of different worlds, some of them traditionally all-male preserves, were anxious that women should join them in equal status. They felt aggrieved that women should find it harder to get promoted or be taken seriously at management level, and thought the presence of more women could improve the atmosphere, and perhaps make male colleagues relax and become less competitive. Jeff, a thirty-five-year-old university lecturer in history, has grown out of the conviction that women are there purely to look after men.

I think it would be a great relief if there were more women in jobs that carried a high status. Women are still excluded in all sorts of ways – this is a brute fact. Out of fifty teachers in this faculty, only seven or eight are women, and I am always conscious of their exclusion. I am conscious of their anger and their bitterness at their treatment.

Work dominated most men's lives: they talked about the stresses and strains it brought, the rewards and pleasures, the miseries and the heartache of failure. Men were happy to work long hours for themselves, if their job was rewarding in a way that suited them, but complained that too many of their jobs were dull, repetitive and out of their control. Some men's jobs were so ill-defined that they could never stop working without a sense of guilt or inadequacy at not having accomplished their work satis-factorily. Chance played a large part in the work that many ended up doing, which, when they considered how important it was in their life, surprised them.

Few men were willing to give up boring jobs, because of the fear of redundancy and its effects on them and their family. Their fears, particularly in areas of high unemployment, were often based on the experience of what it had done to other men, near neighbours and their families. Some men were on a treadmill and painfully aware of it. They felt they were only working to finance the family and they dreamed about getting rid of the constant burden of being the breadwinner. But there were others, mainly working class, for whom it was a matter of pride that their wives did not work and stayed at home in their proper place with the children. They felt it just and fitting that they were the sole supporters of the family unit.

The majority of men interviewed across a whole range of backgrounds with jobs requiring a wide variety of skills expressed a sense of powerlessness at work: an inability to affect the way they were required to do a particular job, the hours they started and finished, and the way their jobs could be changed without consultation. There was a sharp contrast between the commitment of those men who controlled their own work, and those who got on with what they were told to do. Those involved in union work or who had management positions dealing with personnel were well aware that vast and productive changes in human terms could be made in the area of job planning, but felt that shifting the system was a near impossibility.

Chapter Twelve

UNEMPLOYMENT, REDUNDANCY AND RETIREMENT

Men are getting used to the idea that there may not always be a job for them. But it is the most threatening and undermining notion they have ever had to face. Men dream about what they would do if they won the pools and could give up work for a life of idle luxury, but the problem of unemployment, without the cash to make it pleasurable, is the harsh reality of millions. There are few aspects of unemployment that can be turned to a man's advantage: he loses face, he loses status in the eyes of others, he loses the reason for getting up in the morning, and he may well lose his wife. An ever-increasing number of unemployed men are driven to suicide. The problems of unemployment for the individual go far beyond any easily available solutions.

Men spoke of the sense of being broken, shattered and lost by this experience. It is not uncommon for men to find the shock of being fired so great that they are unable to admit it to their wives: they continue to travel to work, filling in the rest of the day as best they can sitting around in parks or railway stations, existing on a pittance.

There is a pattern to the behaviour of most men who have been sacked, such as Bert who was laid off when the Lancashire textile mill he worked for closed down.

At first it's just a shock, even though you might have been expecting it. You can't say before how you're going to feel. I had a bit of redundancy money due to me, so the wife and I went off to Morecambe for a few days. I'm forty-five and not likely to find a job again easily. Other men were laid off too, but it were mostly women in the factory. I'd say it's definitely the worst thing that's ever happened to me. I've always worked . . . and worked hard.

It happened two years ago. At first I was busy enough. I did all the jobs round the house that I'd always promised the wife I'd get round to. I got an allotment and planted it up with some vegetables. I was looking for jobs all the time, I'd signed on at the Job Centre, and I'd talked to everyone I knew who might be able to help, but it's desperate round here, and there's so many out of work, there's no point in looking. . . . Gradually things got worse. I knew I wouldn't get a job – I just lost all sense of purpose. It's hard to keep cheerful.

The wife has a part-time job in a canteen which takes her out. I sometimes wake up and the hardest thing is to get out of bed – there's no reason to get up and nowhere to go when I do. I do go out of the house at least once a day. Usually in the morning I just ride around on my bike. My wife can get on with the housework and I'm not under her feet . . . the days seem very long . . . being unemployed is the most degrading thing that could happen to a man.

The forty-nine-year-old Liverpudlian Jo, whose comments open Chapter 2, had been made redundant several times in his life through no fault of his own. He had a successful brother with whom he had always compared himself unfavourably, but he was a chemist down south and unable to help in the search for a job.

I know five times sounds a lot, but it's the sort of thing that can happen to you here in Liverpool with everything closing down as it has over the last few years. There's been shut-downs everywhere. I'm not skilled, I've been a van driver and delivery man most of my life, but there've been times when I've taken what's going.

I have had some bad bouts of depression in the last three years and had treatment for them; there's a downhill slope towards complete demoralization when you're out of work.

There've been times when I've had to take a firm hand on myself to stop wondering whether it was worth going on at all. If it wasn't for my wife and daughter, I think I might have done something drastic. There was a time I found it hard to bother with washing or shaving, but I try now to keep myself neat and tidy. . . . It goes against the grain that my wife goes out to work and I stay at home; it's not how a man expects to live.

On a grey, cold and blustery day in August I was stuck in a slow procession of heavy lorries through twenty miles of semi-built-up wasteland in the Midlands – flat, industrially smudged countryside. I had an appointment at a centre for the unemployed, and my directions said it was opposite the dustcart depot. There I met Gilbert, a gentle, slight man of thirty-three, who spoke very quietly while looking at the floor.

I wasn't brought up with me brothers and sisters. They was taken away from me mother when I was little because she neglected them. Me mum had a mental breakdown. Me father was away in the army so we squatted in an old army camp but I had a good childhood, it was a happy time. I used to get everything I wanted: me mother spoiled me because she didn't want to lose me, I suppose.

I wasn't too good at school, but mind you, I wasn't there half the time. I was a bit backward. Maybe if I'd been there a bit more often, perhaps I would've done a bit better. I left school when I was fifteen. I didn't have any qualifications at all and I went straight into a factory, sanding down cabinets – sink units, I was doing. It was a job. I didn't earn a lot. About £6, I think.

At first I didn't like the work but after a few years I think I did. You get frustrated and might lark about a bit, you know, have a joke with a friend and things, like, to pass the day away, if it's a boring job. I had an unskilled job in a factory when I was made redundant four years ago. It was a bit of a shock, but expected since there were so many round here that were unemployed. The worst things about being unemployed is not having money to spend on things what you want, like we really need a fridge and a carpet, things like that. Course, I'd like a colour television. We had one but I had to get rid of it. We couldn't afford it, so we had to go back to black and white.

I do get depressed about the boredom, but I just have to put up with it. Staying indoors is the worst thing you can do. Coming to the unemployment centre does help a bit but even coming here you feel depressed at times. Some days you don't feel like really doing anything. It can get like you just stay in bed in the mornings, but I've found it best to try and get up, if you can. You can start lying about and sort of give up. I get up about eight or nine.

I don't smoke but I do drink. That's about the only thing I do. . . .

I live with my father. He's retired. Since my mother died last year he doesn't like being left on his own at night, so it does make it a bit awkward. He thinks something's going to happen to him. He thinks he's being haunted by her, he keeps on about it.

I get £47 a fortnight. Me father's a householder, so I get less because I'm living with him. I do need some new clothes; I can't remember the last time I had a new shirt. I would be better off if I left home but my father needs me there, really. Otherwise he'd have to go in an old people's home. He's nearly seventy-nine. He's still quite fit but he's been in hospital, he had an operation. Me brother comes to see him now; we never used to see him before my mother died. He's getting on a bit now, he's nearly fifty. I like him but we're different. He's more talkative than me, he's happy you know, jolly. He's a carpenter. But he wouldn't have my father to live with him.

My father gets on my nerves. It's not so much his habits but I think he's a bit selfish, like, because he wants to stay in. But I can't blame him, and I get on with him quite well, really. About the only thing we do together is go down the pub. He's got his pension, but it's not really enough. I don't think he's got much, 'cause he has to spend some of his savings if he wants to get out and have a drink. So he ain't much better off

236

than me. He's a bit better off in some sense because pensioners can have trips out.

In the winter I don't manage to get out at all at nights without him. I generally get out on my own about once a week in the summer when it's light, but once it gets dark he doesn't want me to leave him. Lately I've stayed at home in the evenings and watched television.

I'm not even looking for a job all the time but I still go to the job centre. I haven't given up completely, but round this area, I don't think there's much here. I put myself on for mainly factory work. I'm unskilled, so that gives you less chance. You've got to have some sort of skill to have a better chance.

Not all my friends are unemployed, just one or two, I would think. If you're unemployed for a long time it affects your will. You lose your confidence. You become depressed; you lose your point to live. At times it does cross your mind to steal but I think, hang on, it ain't going to do me any good if I do.

I couldn't emigrate because of my father. Well, I could, but I couldn't very well leave him. I think that bothers me. That's the trouble, you see, if it was just me on my own, perhaps I would try somewhere else in this country, but basically I just couldn't leave him. . . .

My dad's a bit old-fashioned sometimes, you know. I couldn't take a girlfriend home for the night. He thinks that's wrong. But he was born in a Victorian age, wasn't he? So he still thinks that way.

I suppose the best thing in my life is my painting. I don't know anyone else who paints. I started when I used to get comic books, and that. I used to do little drawings. Used to copy Mickey Mouse. I think I would quite like to have gone to classes, improved my painting. . . .

Younger men, who had never known work, seemed less demoralized but just as bored. They had never had the label of a job to attach to themselves as an identity. Their identity was found in their group on the street corner, and in pop culture. Charlie is nineteen, has never worked, and lives at home in Stretford, Manchester. His father, also unemployed, seemed to Charlie to be out of touch.

My dad's on the dole. He used to have a job in a factory. He's always talking about how the Labour movement has let him down. He had a boring, futile job in a factory and he'd rather do that than be on the dole. I just avoid politics altogether, it has no relevance to people of my age. I'd like a job, yeah, but summat a bit better than he did. I might join the army, at least they'll train you for a skilled job. I don't mind not having a job, not really. You shouldn't really mind, you know, because you worry too much and crack up, I suppose. Weekly I think I get £25. It's not much – I give some to my mum. She keeps nagging me every minute to give her money. . . . I don't go out a lot – I can't afford to. I've got some friends in work and I have a drink with them occasionally, and go to football.

Winston is twenty-two, unemployed, black and born in London. His parents come from Jamaica.

One thing I've learnt over the years and being on the dole, you have to be patient, you can't rush things. You have to just keep calm in all situations. And I've kind of refined it to an art with me. My dad tells me it's not worth thinking ahead yet. You have to take a day as it comes. It's just not worth planning the future because it might not never turn out like that. Like, today's Thursday, I like to think about Saturday; I never like to go further than that.

Today I got up about half past eight to catch the postman. The Giro comes to me. It's Social Security. I get £47. It's all right for my needs, but I ain't a big spender. I give £12 to my mum. That's all she wants; the rest is mine. On a Thursday, when I have my money, I don't have nothing much for breakfast – all I have is a cup of tea or a cup of coffee and a sandwich, or just two slices of bread. I wait until the Post Office is open, about half past nine. I cash the Giro. I buy my newspaper, my *Voice* and my *Echoes*, and I buy a box of cigarettes – Benson and Hedges. Then I come home. I put down my money for my mum and I sort out my money, what I think I'm going to do with that money. Then about half past eleven I listen to the radio, look out the window and watch people. I live in a maisonette. So by that time, I'm just getting totally bored. Then about twelve o'clock, I play my tape of reggae music for about an hour and a half. By the time my tape's finished, it's about half one. So I've got one hour to kill before I come up here to the club, which opens at half past two and finishes at five. So I go out and walk around, anywhere. My mum doesn't ask me to do jobs around the house. She's given up on that idea now because I can't be bothered to do it. I say I'll do it, but I just don't get round to doing it. My dad helps in the house. Now he's unemployed, he cooks the dinner.

When you've got money, you find out the day goes quick. But when your dole cheque's finished, you think the day's like a month. I spend most of my money on food. I get hungry very quick. Like, if I have my dinner at home at six o'clock, half an hour later I'm hungry again and I have to get some money to buy something to eat. I don't drink a lot of spirits, I just drink a lot of beer. I like vodka and lime, but I drink that only when it's my birthday. I smoke weed, but other than that nothing else. I'm tempted. Sometimes I lie on my bed and think about what if I sniff cocaine or smoke opium, but I never tried it.

Black people are put at the bottom of the scale. They get all the dirty jobs to do, like cleaning the streets, doing the sewers – all the dirty jobs that white people don't want to do.

Some white people are now finding out what it's like to be on the dole. Before it was just black people on the dole. Now white people know how blacks feel. I think that makes them closer together. Because before when they used to walk the streets, they used to see black kids, of my age, standing round at corners, at cafés, and they thought, 'Nah, I'm never going to be like that.' Then when they get unemployed, they find themselves out on the street corner with their friends, at a café. And then they realize how hard it is to get a job after that.

Being black and unemployed creates other problems too, as Ray found:

I've worked, sort of, for two and a half years. I was an electrician for a theatre company. I lost the job because I had a fight with some other boy. He kept his job and I lost mine. . . .

I was the only black person there. I felt a bit funny, you know.

I've been for quite a few jobs. . . . One job was working in a wine store and I went to try and do that, and the bloke said to me that I had the job, so I've to phone him tomorrow to tell him my ex-workplace phone number. But when I phoned him the next day, he said, 'Sorry, mate, we've already found somebody.' And that really sort of got me angry. And like a fool, I went down to the shop and had an argument with him. I shouldn't really have done that. I ain't too sure if I was turned down 'cause I'm black.

Many men choose voluntary redundancy today when they know the chop is coming. The primary advantage is the payment they get, but for some it is also the time to seek professional advice, and plan another career.

Some men, afraid to admit redundancy to their wives, had been surprised how supportive she had been. For the first time the wives thought they had a real job to do – helping to be practical, to plan the next job, suggesting ways of cutting down on expenses, and remaining cheerful despite being avoided by their neighbours. Neighbours and friends apparently often go out of their way to avoid the newly redundant man and his family. Like bereavement, it caused people the embarrassment of not knowing what to say, or how to behave. The more successful the man, the more hard-hit his wife and family as a result of the dramatic change in lifestyle.

Arnold, aged fifty, had been operations director for a retail furnishing company with branches throughout the Home Counties when he was made redundant in 1982.

One or two of my friends have been embarrassed, I think. That's a fairly common reaction. They haven't stopped seeing me, because I think I learned that you don't go around with a long face and say you've been made redundant. I've said to a few people – slightly tongue in cheek – I'm having a sabbatical, I'm out of the rat race. That's putting the best possible face on it. I'm tough with myself. I'm less tough with other people at times, and sometimes I should be. It's one thing I've learned, I hope, to be a little tougher in situations which may require it.

My wife was shaken and surprised, to say the least. Her attitude is actually very different from mine. She was very angry at the way I'd been treated. She could go and strangle the lot. Fortunately I've got a very good marriage. We've been married twenty-four years. She works, but only briefly – ten hours a week at the local school. You see, her anger – resentment – is greater than mine. I don't think I have any, really. I accept it.

We've had to cut our costs just in case we needed the money. We said we couldn't afford to have a holiday, and we've said we'll cut down a bit on this, and cut down a bit on that, perhaps on the paper bill – but if you've been reading *Punch* for years you can't give that up, can you?

The children have tried to cut down, and they've understood, and they've been told pretty well what's going on. At that age you don't fool them. One is at college, and the other's working in a bank quite close by. The elder one is supporting herself and making a small contribution to the household. We're still supporting the younger one and will continue to do so until she finishes college. But what all this has done is unite us, rather. They're past the worst of their teenage years, it seems to me. The relationships have been improving all the time. That's partly because they're getting older and more mature and understanding, and the uncertainty of my life over the past year has tended to bring us together as a unit. I think my situation has enhanced the relationship with my wife. I don't think she thought less of me for losing my job, no.

Stanley, aged fifty-two, was personnel director for a group of companies with a labour force of nearly a thousand people. The atmosphere changed when a new managing director was appointed.

He called me into his office and he said, 'I want to talk about reorganization. Unfortunately, it's bad news, as there's no position for you. You are redundant. . . .' It came as a shock because I'd always been a company man, I've put in a long time, and I've always earned my keep. On the flip-side, I was relieved in a way to be out of that atmosphere. Quite frankly, under this particular man, I think I was destined to have a position of reduced authority in time, or be removed. I think he would have done exceptionally well in the Mafia – there was a terrible atmosphere there.

I went home and said to my wife, 'It's happened. He's fired me.' I think the reality didn't hit my wife then. And unfortunately the next day we had a letter from the hospital saying, basically, that she might have cancer.

We sat down very methodically and analysed the situation. And my wife said, 'Well, we will continue in our social life. We will go out exactly the same. You have nothing to be ashamed of.' And quite a lot of people have said that as well – it was just the circumstances.

They did pay me enough redundancy money for me not to worry for the time being, because they knew full well it was unfair dismissal.

You oscillate between different emotions, but there are times when the reality really hits you. You suddenly think, Good God, what's happened to me? I haven't got a pension. My wife did not work then. She had to have an operation, but thankfully has recovered. I set her up in a business – I'm better at finding her a job than myself. I've also got her a part-time job in the mornings, and it ticks over.

I don't really feel less of myself, no, because on balance I think it was the relief of being away from that awful environment and not having to work in this Mafia type of thing.

The worst thing about being made redundant is, having reached a reasonable position in life, virtually from nothing, seeing all your life knocked from under your feet and having your life destroyed, in a sense. And I felt in the initial stages that I'd let the family down – and I thought, maybe I should have been a 'yes man' at work, maybe I should have agreed with things that I knew were wrong or were not going the right way, in order to protect my family. But my wife didn't want me to do that.

Hopefully I'll get another job. We've gone through all the various spiels of where do I go now. Do I go and run a pub or do I open a post office? Do I go back to consultancy – quite a number of avenues. But what I've decided upon is finding an executive position.

A lot of nice things came out of the redundancy, a lot of nice things. Quite a lot of the lads off the shop floor still come up to my house or phone me up and ask for advice, or just come for a talk. And one of the old boys off the shop floor out of the factory met me about a week afterwards, and he said, 'We're awfully sorry what they've done to you. There was no need for that at all. There's nothing I can do about it, but I've talked to my wife, and what we've decided to do is when we go to church on Sunday, we're going to say a special prayer for you and your family.'

Using redundancy to make the change in career direction a man has always wanted can be positive and successful, but the majority of managers and executives work in large companies because they are team people and not good at working by themselves. The office fulfils many of their needs for social life, companionship and motivation. Setting up a business on their own is probably impossible for many of them; the psychological barriers are too great. But the older man who's been operating at a very senior level in a large company may find that voluntary redundancy coincides with his own wish, and the wish of his family, that he should ease up a bit, despite the damage to his pension rights.

Gary was fifty with five children. He worked for an international oil corporation as a personnel training manager. When the opportunity arose in October 1983 for voluntary redundancy on advantageous terms, he decided to take it.

For the last six years at work I travelled extensively in Europe and went to a lot of out-of-the-way places like Finland. I spent a great deal of time in the Middle East and worked all over the United States – New York, Dallas, to the West Coast. I always travelled first class, lived on expenses and stayed in nice hotels.

For a short time it was marvellous, but then came the reality of spending my life hanging around at airports, the discomfort of twelve-hour plane journeys and the constant disruption of family life. For the last four years I didn't even know what continent I was going to be living in in twelve months' time; what country was just a minor detail. Someone else was in charge of my destiny.

I was successful at what I did and enjoyed it. If I had stayed with the company, several things could have happened. At worst, the contraction in the industry could have led to compulsory redundancy. I could have been moved to another part of the organization and given a different kind of job, or I could have been promoted, but that was very unlikely as in my specialized field there were only two more jobs higher than mine and I might have had to wait a long time for this promotion.

The alternative was either to get a job with another major company in a fixed position where I would not move around so much or to work for myself. So I decided that I would set up my own company. Some years ago, before I joined the oil corporation, I had run an antiques business for a year. I found that an invaluable experience in business and in being on my own. I now have my own training consultancy where I specialize in rapid development and training of managers – quick promotion to better and more senior jobs. . . .

Starting up on my own at fifty was not too frightening. I know I can do the job and meet those challenges. The challenge is more one of how do I do it, not can I do it. My apprehension is, will enough people want me and my skills?

My aims in the short term are to earn enough to live comfortably without undue worry and to enjoy what I am doing, and long term, to live a wider life than I was able to before, to spend more time with my family and have the epitaph, 'A gentleman, a scholar, and a rare judge of whisky.'

I enjoy the flexibility of my new life which has greater variety and is much more stimulating. I now have an office at the management school and a secretary one and a half miles away, but it means I can work irregularly; I am no longer hooked to a nine-to-five routine. I work in short concentrated spasms and then relax. I have more time for my outside interests and for my family.

But Gary was unusual. Most executives found the going a good deal tougher. Arnold did everything he could to get another job, including going to a company that specializes in finding jobs for unemployed executives. In fact, an interview with them is part of the severance deal that some companies now offer.

I'm an optimist by nature, and pretty resilient, and when it comes to the crunch, a fighter. And I knew what I had to do and I was bloody well going to do it, come Hell or high water – which was to maintain the family stability, to maintain as high a standard of living as I possibly could – and it's hard to change now, really. And the work I'm doing now is of a freelance nature.

I think I'm going to be offered a job on Monday – my third time to see them – and it's a company quite close to me. It's a pretty attractive job and I think I'm going to get it. So the end is near, or so I hope.

You don't say you were made redundant, you say you left. The story is that I left to set up my own business. You have to have a cover story because it keeps you out of the bog. You see, what a possible employer will explore most deeply is why you left your last job. You know, did you chase the office girls, or were you incompetent? It's a presumption that there must be something wrong if you left and you didn't want to. So one of the things you learn from this employment consultant is how to cope with that without telling them lies, outright lies, which are fairly easily detected by anyone with any sense. But I left to form a business – a very good reason for leaving, that.

The effect of retirement can be much the same as that of redundancy, and it comes as a shock to many men. Those who seem busiest and most successful in their jobs are the ones who often said they spent least time planning for retirement. They often had no idea of what

245

they were going to do or where they would live, and admitted that the idea frightened them. Some professional men coped by taking up even more demanding jobs: they took directorships or chaired commissions, like Raymond, who retired from the civil service in 1946, aged fifty-six, and has only really stopped working in his nineties.

Since I retired I've had various jobs – I took a trade mission to Brazil, for one thing. That was rather fun. I was given financial and trade experts to come with me, and I embarked on these negotiations. I've done a number of jobs for the government, and just kept busy. I had to give up my job, but I don't think I could have given up working.

The biggest problem that faces those who retire is loneliness. They miss the companionship of their fellow workers; chatting to neighbours and friends is not the same. Because of the cost, many retired couples are forced to give up their car which makes them feel even more cut off, particularly where local transport is unreliable or non-existent.

Many said they felt very poor despite their savings and, having looked forward to old age, were finding it rather a miserable time. Winter was worst because there were so few things to do then that didn't cost money. For some men Saturday shopping was an event they looked forward to. Unlike their wives, who preferred to buy during the week when the shops were empty, they chose to go when they would meet a crowd, in the hope of bumping into an old friend or two.

Some men choose to retire early· if their company offers them the option. But at fifty, with fifteen years to wait for the state pension, it could be more of a struggle than they had expected. Panic assailed them at the realization that they might possibly have 'nothing to do' for the next twenty years. Men who had been competent and meticulous planners at work found it impossible to approach the problem of retirement with the same calm professionalism.

Many had dreams of immersing themselves in the peace and quiet of village life. Those who had acted upon such fantasies, like Robert, a retired commercial traveller of fifty-four, to escape the grim life of the anonymous hotel or boarding house, thought it had been a mistake.

We moved here from London – my family originally came from Devon, and my wife always fancied a cottage here. We thought we'd buy a house we could afford to run easily, and I'd get a job helping out locally, in a store or taking the visitors out fishing. But we've found at our age that you miss your friends, it's not easy to make new ones, and you're definitely an outsider – a foreigner – until you've been here for at least twenty years. We do feel out of things, the locals aren't easy to get to know. . . . My wife misses the grandchildren. Where we were before they were just round the corner

This sort of tale is all too common, and much worse if either partner dies before they have properly settled in.

'What do you do?' It's an everyday question put to strangers. If the man is unemployed, redundant or retired, he often feels ashamed, unwanted and without identity when he has to answer: 'Nothing.' Such an answer also makes the questioner feel awkward and embarrassed because he does not know where to place a non-worker in society's pecking order. As a result he probably lumps him in with failures, has-beens, the old and the ill. But as more and more people experience bouts of not working, such attitudes will have to change. As Winston, the Jamaican, pointed out: 'Now white people know how blacks feel. I think that makes them closer together.'

There were individuals who had taken care to plan, with their wives, their voluntary redundancy or their retirement with the precision of a military campaign, but they were the exception. For the rest there is nothing but the gloomy prospect of life without work, because work has become obsessively central to men's lives, and few men have learnt to judge their value as human beings other than through their work.

Chapter Thirteen

MEN AND THEIR FEELINGS

The subject that men found most troublesome to put into words, and which caused the longest and most strained pauses for thought, was the world of their emotions and their feelings. The range of emotions which they experienced seemed, according to them, rather limited; it was not something they were used to talking about nor had they, in many cases, given the subject much thought. Although some had shown intense love or hate when talking about their parents and great anxiety and concern when talking about their children, it was not immediately clear whether this was the tip of an emotional iceberg, or all they had to show. Did they possess a submerged emotional life which they were not practised at talking about, or had these hidden feelings been stifled and killed off at an early age?

It did emerge from many conversations that it was in this area of their lives that men felt under most threat, were at their most vulnerable and indeed felt so surrounded by potential traps and pitfalls that, like a dangerous mineshaft, they had sealed this section of themselves off. Sealed it off in particular from women, because women are the intrepid explorers in this subterranean world and men, who had revealed themselves as being essentially creatures of habit, could not cope with being too heavily challenged in this area.

It also becomes clear that, for traditional men, talking

about or revealing the existence of this whole world of the emotions is thought to be unmanly, irrational and if given too much rein, likely to get out of control. From early childhood on, men are chided, laughed at and derided if they are detected exposing their emotions and so they learn to hide their feelings.

One of the great battlegrounds between men and women today lies in the world of misunderstood feelings. In such arguments men often cannot understand what women are going on about, and women seethe with the frustration of not being able to make themselves understood in what seems to them perfectly plain language. Colin, a sales executive of fifty-five, said his wife irritated him by always talking about the difference in their 'perception' of their life together. She always wanted to know exactly what he was thinking and longed to talk things out if she thought they were going wrong while he didn't 'raise issues because I've no wish to stir things up if I think they'll blow over'. He agreed that he never asked his wife what *she* was feeling.

The world of men's emotions is a difficult one for a woman to enter or to understand. Because women are used to responding with their feelings and certainly used to talking about them, they have a much greater opportunity to learn about the effect of their behaviour on others, and to put themselves in someone else's shoes. Empathy was not something which men seemed to practise: many of the informants seemed to have no experience of seeing things from another's point of view.

When talking about emotions many men compared themselves unfavourably with women, whom they envied for their much wider repertoire of feelings. Tony, a thirty-year-old solicitor, summed up that feeling.

I don't think men are devious, but they are incapable of talking about some of the things women want to talk about. In fact, I think men are always wondering what it is that women know about that they don't. Men are just bad at taking responsibility for other people, for other people's feelings. They feel threatened when someone – and it's usually a feminist or a woman – tries to force them to take into account another human being *all the time*. Women do this naturally. Men feel it's an inadequacy, but it is also painful, having recognized this, to try to change yourself and your way of thinking.

Men are remarkably good at avoiding confrontation in areas of personal relations they would rather leave untouched. Men are successfully self-deluding in their behaviour towards others, and often lack the ability to empathize with even those closest to them.

But just as they couldn't predict how someone else might feel, some men couldn't even work out what their own most significant feelings were. Having dug around inside themselves, and thought for a while, they still had nothing to say. Others said they needed more time and would like to have another conversation later. Many had become so practised at bottling up their emotions that they were no longer aware of their reason for doing so nor of the effect it was having on them. Those men who were anxious about the repression of their feelings thought it might in the long run do them some harm.

But there were some who leapt at the opportunity to discuss what they felt. It was as though they'd been given permission, at last, to explore a taboo. Their answers were surprising. They talked openly about the release of aggression, of courage and self-control, but were nervous about expressing tenderness or gentleness. One exceptional man, a septuagenarian, spoke about his role as comforter of others and displayed, without embarrassment, qualities of compassion and sympathy. Alec, whose family have been funeral directors for several generations, has seen a great deal of heartache, having nursed his wife through a long terminal illness, and is an expert in helping people to grapple with their sense of grief and loss.

I think, on balance, I would say that emotions are better let out. I certainly would advise never to fight nature over this. And this applies to men as well as women. I think it's very sad that men are not supposed to cry as much as women. Men and women cope with bereavement in different ways, though I don't know if anybody really copes with bereavement. There's a lot of talk about time being a healer, but I don't think that that's really correct. Time will form a scab over the wound without healing it. Life does go on but differently. Life can never be the same again after death. Professionally we're funeral directors, but we're amateur psychologists, doctors, ministers; the advice we give people varies according to them.

All I try to do is to react to people's needs. But the only real help out of bereavement comes from inside one. Quite a number of people will turn away from religion in bereavement. They'll say, 'If there is a God, why did He let this happen?' The feelings are so mixed, the feelings of anger, guilt, shame. Sometimes we have to act as an emotional sponge. They're not really angry with us at all; they're angry with the world. But if anybody wants to vent their spleen on the world through me, I'm here. People often want to come back to talk after the funeral is over.

It was significant how many informants equated any reference to emotion simply with crying. It seemed all they were able to talk about, and they judged themselves as emotional or not on the basis of how often, and on what occasions, they thought it permissible for a man to cry.

Bill, a fifty-five-year-old furniture.removal man, said, like the majority of men I spoke to, that he had been taught not to cry:

I find it difficult to cry, and that's because of my upbringing; I was always brought up to believe that it's effeminate to cry. I can only recall crying about twice in my lifetime – as a man. I think I'm more emotional now than I ever was. I'm moved by things very easily; I often get tears coming to my eyes, although I don't cry very easily about other things. For example, Chrissie Evert losing at Wimbledon – a girl that I admire very much – it touched me a little bit. I got the same kind of feeling watching the marriage of Prince Charles and Lady Diana on TV. It made my eyes water. I get that kind of feeling about being British, too, at times. The Falklands War affected me a lot. I got that kind of feeling when it was going on. In some respects, it's a pride, I suppose. It's a pride in one's own race, if you like.

Many men like this latched on to crying as though it were the *only* emotion they could feel. And their own examples of being proud to be emotional were often descriptions of the times when crying would be automatic, the response to music or the emotion of a crowd, or a sentimental film. Automatic and, I suspect, not very deeply felt.

That need to block off their deeper feelings common to so many men was summed up by this cabinet minister who, like Bill, suffers the sad dilemma of weeping freely at the theatre or moments of great national sentiment, but skilfully forgets and puts behind him any emotional matters of deeper significance; his contradictory feelings mirrored those of other men:

Men control their emotions much more strictly than women, even though they might be boiling with fury, terribly sad or depressed: I see a lot of that in this business. I think women are much more sensible; they let it all show. For men, it's partly that you must never show your true self to the people you're working with. It's a tradition. It's passed on for years. As a man, I'm really rather shocked when the PM loses her temper with senior colleagues, as she does from time to time.

I'm terrible at any emotional things in the theatre or the cinema. I weep when they play 'God Save the Queen'. I wept at the wedding . . . tears ran down my face. . . . But I'm very bad at expressing myself. I bottle up my feelings very much.

I've developed a self-discipline so that when things don't go exactly right, I say, Right, that's finished, let's forget it. One doesn't altogether forget it, but I don't want to let it go on nagging at me.

The gentler feeling men admitted to were reserved for home or for the presence of women. Very few men said they were ever expected to show sympathy in the context of their work, except for example to a secretary who had lost a boyfriend. Richard found that being expected to show sympathy to another man was simply embarrassing.

I think I'm more likely to break down with a woman. Say I cried, which is a frightfully shaming thing for a man to do. I've certainly been brought up with a horror of bursting into tears. I've only done it twice since school, I think. The last time I did it my ex-wife was round here smashing the place up and screaming abuse, and I suddenly felt very terribly sorry.

But I've certainly never done that with a man. I was very embarrassed when a friend of mine suddenly cried. I couldn't put my arm out to console him. I froze with embarrassment. If a woman cries, there's a great gathering impulse. I mean, you can't bear it when a woman cries, but you can do something about it. With a man you just don't do that. Stiff upper lip and all that. I should think it's at an enormous cost.

So if men only permit themselves to show emotion of a shallow and meaningless kind, what happens when there's really something to cry about?

Ron, a senior foreman in a large factory and a keen amateur gardener, had recently been told his wife was dying. It would be understandable if he'd broken down completely but he clearly thinks – as a man – that it's better to hold back your feelings than give in to them:

I think generally men are better at handling emotions than women. I've been pretty emotional myself over the last few months, but that's only natural. Quite often down in that greenhouse I've felt all choked up, and sometimes wished I

254

was back at work. But generally men are better at controlling their feelings. I wouldn't think less of a man if I saw him crying, because my father's a bit emotional. We both had a little sob on Christmas morning when we was up in the hospital seeing my wife.

Here the greenhouse, but more often the garden shed, seemed to many men, whose houses provide no opportunity for privacy, to be the only place where they could cry loudly and in private with no inhibitions.

But many men saw crying as a sign of lack of self-control and reliability. It is so hard traditionally for men to show what they feel, and several GPS I spoke to said if a man broke down and cried he probably needed serious attention. And Andrew, a doctor with a country practice in East Anglia, confirmed this view though he thought it was therapeutic for either sex to let their emotions go.

As a doctor I should take a weeping male much more seriously than a weeping woman. But there are other ways of showing emotion apart from the negative ones. Showing love and affection is probably more important. And some men find this very difficult.

There were a number of informants of all classes who knew this to be true and they were often the ones who spoke of themselves as being a 'man's man'. Plumber Sid, aged thirty-seven, is almost ashamed to show either his natural affection for his young daughter, or sorrow when a member of the family died. And it's what other men think that worries him.

I do have a gentler side to my character. My wife and I will sit down at home and watch the telly in the evening. Our youngest daughter will sometimes lay across us. I mean I wouldn't do that in front of another man. I could imagine another man seeing that and thinking, 'Geez, he's some sort of weirdo.' I last cried when my grandmother died about three years ago. I was terribly sad about that, but I tried to suppress that for the sake of the wife, 'cause I thought that she'd obviously break down. As it was I cried and she didn't. I was quite relieved afterwards.

The idea that men were not to be depended on as colleagues if they showed outward signs of emotion was confirmed by those I spoke to in the armed forces, in industry, the fire service, the police and in business. As one army officer put it,

Men are supposed to be relied on as the people to count on. Men are the stronger sex. We shouldn't be seen to cry. Women will never be successful senior officers because they have this weakness; all women cry. They cry openly in situations in which a man wouldn't.

These men are trained to deal with fear by facing it head on and to fight, if necessary, a flying picket, a raging fire or an enemy sniper. The unacceptable action was to flee or to show cowardice. Even though in certain circumstances it might show good sense, such behaviour would bring the condemnation of peer group and superiors alike and leave the fleer full of shame and guilt. But though men were trained for bravery and toughness in so many aspects of their world, there were sometimes things they had to face which needed just the same amount of guts but for which they had received no preparation. The tough and successful company executive, James, said:

The worst moment of my life, which will always remain with me, is when my wife was very ill in 1964 and she was on the danger list for four days. I saw her at the end of the first day and I was convinced that she would be dead in the morning. I remember it vividly. I was staying at my mother's at the time with the two boys. I remember going to bed that night and arranging my clothes so that when the phone rang – when, not if – I could dress in a flash. You suddenly realize at a moment like that that something is about to happen which would destroy everything. On the other hand, there is a benefit there, because it makes you appreciate what you've got. At the end of it, you say, my God, I nearly lost that, and you suddenly become intensely more aware of what benefits you've got. So like all things, there's a good and a bad.

Don, a GP who spends his life looking after the needs and anxieties of others, was also quite unprepared for his wife's recent and sudden death.

My wife died at the relatively young age of fifty. The children were by then almost grown up. We'd been married for twenty-seven years. . . . I suddenly realized that she did absolutely everything for me. I can't cook, I have no idea about shopping or running a household. She was the financial wizard of the house and looked after all that side of things. I felt as though a large piece of myself was missing, a piece that could never be replaced. . . . I did think of killing myself, easy enough in my business, but there were the children – I think that's what ultimately stopped me. The greatest shock was finding out what an insufficient human being I was. I'd always thought of myself as a self-sufficient sort of fellow, able to cope with most things pretty effectively.

There are men of course who can both show their feelings and recognize the advantages of so doing, and who said they would not look down on another man who did so. A few men, like Bob, aged seventy-four, a retired gynaecologist, said how unfair it was that they were not permitted, sometimes by women, to expose their feelings openly.

I find expectations placed on men very annoying. I want to cry, frequently, on all kinds of occasions, sometimes just for emotion. Somebody can say something which is neither sad nor demanding of sympathy but which suddenly seems to me to reflect huge areas of conflict and tragedy, and it just makes me want to cry. I'm enormously ashamed of it when I do cry, and try to hide it. Music often makes me cry. But why should I feel ashamed? Except crying makes one look very ugly. Crying is not a pretty thing. My whole upbringing was from a father who pushed masculine attitudes that men, boys, don't cry. 'Stop it! You're just a blubberer.'

Those whose marriages had ended unhappily looked back with guilt and shame, regretting past actions, particularly the hotel manager Clive who, though he could feel regret, expressed in almost the same breath his fear that he could not feel love.

My wife and I married when we were still in our teens; I was married for seven years and we had two children. I enjoyed married life very much but I don't know why I married so young, and it was my idea not hers. We came from the same sort of background, but it just didn't last. My interest waned ... I'm a little like that with the people I've loved. I'm definitely not going to find someone whom I can go on caring about, I'm incapable of love, I think. . . . I left my marriage because I wanted to change my life, I was having affairs, fooling around a little. When I left my wife I gave her everything I owned – our home, the bank account – because I was wrong. The worst thing I ever did was leave my wife. She was very badly hurt, it was awful, I'd have given anything to have prevented that, I do regret it. When I left home I asked her what she wanted for the children, for me to see them regularly or just to send presents at Christmas. Well, I saw them for a time and then she changed her mind, she was going out with someone else and thought it would ruin his relationship with the children. So I agreed and didn't contact her. Three years later I called the home I'd left her, and they said it was sold. I don't know where she is. I try not to think about seeing the children now, I deliberately don't think about them . . . it's my biggest regret.

Richard, now forty-four, had a similar experience and feels the same sense of remorse at an earlier hardness of heart.

I was terribly spoilt when I was young, I had a lot of money and if I wanted something I usually got it. I wanted this girl, I married her. We were both very young, we had a son. The marriage lasted about three years; I walked out on them. It was ghastly. I couldn't walk out like that now. I can still see her now, watching me leave and crying. I couldn't do that now. I left because I was in love with somebody else.

Very few of the interviewees said they had ever felt real hatred for anyone, although they did voice strong dislike and bitterness if they thought they had been treated badly. There was sometimes a strong feeling of self-righteousness and self-justification from men who had broken the rules in some way, been found out and punished: men like Lionel who is forty and serving a two-year sentence for company fraud;

I didn't really expect to go to prison, it was a shock. I started from scratch in the metal business ten years ago, and was sent to prison for a technical fraud, in my view. Prison is hell. I shouldn't be here – there are a lot of other people who should, mind you. This time here hasn't taught me anything. It's been a complete waste. The only thing you learn is hatred, that's all. Hatred for people, though mainly for the officers. It's no punishment for the back-street johnnies in here, they live better than they do outside. But for me it's a big punishment. I find it very hard here.

The same sense of unfairness was voiced by Brian, who murdered his wife because she was having an affair with a neighbour. He felt tremendous indignation when he was treated in prison as anything other than a man of high principle, an ordinary man who'd just been pushed beyond the bounds of self-control. Why should he be locked up with the likes of Charlie Richardson and some of the Kray gang?

That's not fair on me bringing me in with these kind of men. They're such men that would stab you in the back as soon as look at you. They're very violent. For the rest of us it's a spur of the moment thing. I mean even the padre, he said, 'I could be you.'

The feelings that give rise to violent behaviour are common to both men and women, but it is much more likely for a man to be involved in physical violence than a woman. I talked to some men who lived in a world where violence was an accepted form of behaviour, and others who had surprised themselves and others by one single act of extreme violence which seemed out of character. Even in those communities where violence was a way of life behaviour was controlled by a strict code of ethics. Johnnie, who had earned his living by crime for the last twenty years, but had spent very few of them in jail, said he'd never used violence in burglary or on any of his other jobs, but sometimes thought it quite legitimate.

Violence is only used for cash. You have to do what you have to do. The security guard is told not to resist., You pull a gun on them and they're told to hand it over. They're only getting £80 a week, it ain't their money. If they just hand it over, the insurance will lose and there'll be no one hurt. A lot of guys like me, if they get a decent amount of money, might go into a little business and never go at it again. Down the pub they'll be the quietest people and the politest people. They can't afford to get drunk, they might say something out of turn. The only people you find with the big mouths are the young kids who are going round bashing old people over the head. They're the sort of people that most of us have contempt for, they get no respect.

Another East Ender of fifty in prison with his two sons, all serving life sentences for the murder of a local man, said that in his view there were different sorts of killings.

There's what I call a decent killing: you've had a few drinks in a pub, someone insults you and you hit him, he falls down, hits his head, and he's dead. That's a decent killing. But in here [the lifers' wing of a large prison] they have done such rotten nasty murders. They're really shocking. Some of the guys in here are decent, but the kind I hate most are the 'noncers': those guys that have sexually assaulted children and then killed them. I'd bring back hanging, I'd castrate them.

Men do get into fights, you can't help it – I'd smack a guy in the mouth if he'd insulted me. Every man's got to look after his own little bit of honour. It's natural too for a man to protect his wife, his family, his children. You don't learn that, you grow up with it like a dog grows claws. No man likes to be belittled in front of anyone. Now if a woman insulted me in front of others, I wouldn't punch her but I'd give her a nasty slap.

Another violent prisoner Francis, convicted of sixteen rapes and attacks on women, explained that his humiliation by the police in a previous case, and the strip searching he had suffered in prison, had led him to seek revenge by a campaign of attacks on women that the police would find hard to solve. He explained that he was basically a very private person and that he regarded human bodies as private, especially his own when he suffered the indignity of a naked strip search.

My whole campaign was against the police, their methods of detection. I used to get a buzz knowing they didn't have a clue. I don't have a sexual problem, my enjoyment was in getting back at the police. How can you enjoy it [rape] when you're a loving person? It was a physical mechanical act of aggression. The first thing my wife said to me right after the trial was, 'Was it anything to do with me?' She was relieved when I said, 'No'.

Though some men bitterly regretted their violent outbursts, there were others like this chairman of a chain of High Street shops who thought that anger could be a useful weapon.

I can show anger openly and I'm also able to use temper deliberately. It's very good for you and you can stop it when you want, you can turn it off. I've lost my temper uncontrollably in rows with the opposite sex.

However, a young Conservative politician saw that

such behaviour could be double-edged. In this world it did not pay to show feelings. There were so many potential rivals and enemies about that any sign of strong feeling might be used against you or seen as a chink in your armour. He often found he had to pretend to like people more than he did in order to remain their political allies.

I spend my days talking to and working with people I don't like. I have to come to some agreement with them, some mutually agreeable meeting-ground. This can never be done if there's open hostility. I feel I cannot afford to show my dislike for anyone – my career might depend on them in the future. One learns not to take these feelings too seriously.

Friendship was approached by many men of all ages with a clear and quite deliberate sense of caution. They rarely had women who were really close friends, although they said they preferred their company to that of men. This seemed to mean that spending leisure time with women rather than with men was less threatening for them, but that they never really allowed anyone to get too close.

A cabinet minister put the view that there are just certain things a man cannot talk about even to his friends.

I'm not quick at making friends. I don't believe I've got a dozen friends. Acquaintances I have many, but friends very few. If things are going wrong at home, if there was a crisis, I might go to my oldest friend, but men hardly ever talk to each other about these things. I suppose, if I had a business crisis, I might look around for someone whose judgement I could trust – it might be someone I normally don't see much of.

Clive, the manager of a large hotel, spends much of his leisure time with women, perhaps because he too finds relaxation with men, beyond a certain point, rather threatening.

Men don't open up to each other. If they do it's in a bragging sense, the bragging of their exploits, or whatever, in work or pleasure. I think men are very frightened of being exposed, whatever their weaknesses are.

Dan, a TUC regional organizer and member of the Communist Party, does not find trusting people, even his wife, very easy:

Most of my friends are political activists, probably within the Communist Party. By the nature of what I do and by the nature of my political activities, my circle of friends is very limited. It's limited by the time I put into doing what I do, but I don't actively encourage friends, I suppose, or gather them to me. But then, what is a friend? I would never tell *everything* to anybody at all. There's always a secret. That's just the way I am. That's the way that gives me the security of my life. There are things my wife doesn't know about me. I don't know if she minds not knowing – I've never asked her. Though naturally within a marriage relationship your wife would know virtually everything about you anyhow, because you live with her. There are just certain things that I never really divulge to anybody. I keep it to myself. They're generally just thoughts about a situation or how you see a situation. I don't know – a person once said to me, 'Dan, the trouble with you is you're always looking to see everybody's handle. You can't accept anybody on the face value of what they are.' And that, I think, is true. I always want to enter any situation on my own terms, and I never really totally trust any individual.

A great deal has been written about the effect that a public school education can have on a man later in life. Men who attended such schools were aware that they had been trained from an early age to stifle their emotions, and although that might be of some value in the business world, it could be a decided drawback if you wanted a happy home life. James, a company executive, had been educated at a top public school.

A typical British boarding school education can drive people's emotions deep into them so that they feel they have to conceal them, and they lose that trick of rapport with people which you need in a family. In other words, a public boarding school is an artificial society and can breed artificial relationships in the home society.

We men are not supposed to have emotions, are we? To some degree at school one felt it was not the done thing to show emotion, that the right thing was to have a slightly blasé, cynical and aloof expression on one's face most of the time. I think the disadvantage of this is that it sometimes then makes it very difficult to show emotion or to bring emotion into your conversations or discussions or relationships – where it does matter.

From time to time I'm told that the children find me difficult to approach on some things. They would say that I was frightening; I'd say it's because I've got my head in the paper, or something like that. If you're just back from the office, you don't want suddenly to have a whole string of problems thrown at you. That's what you deal with all day.

A bishop said he could not bear to send his children away to school because of the effect that going away to school had had on him.

I think having been sent away like that from such an early age was damaging. It's made me – like a lot of other people – quite warm and affectionate up to a point, but there is a point. It's the price of survival. I'm better than I was.

You become deep down very reluctant to trust yourself absolutely to anybody; there's a kind of interior self-sufficiency. It's very difficult to say to somebody, even your wife, 'I love you', because you're giving so much away.

But, as James points out, there is a plus side to this early training.

If you are a businessman, you've got to keep your emotions well under control and be able to keep a deadpan expression, and not get too closely identified with an interest, which is valuable.

I was once told that the most effective method of negotiation was never to say a word. You just sit there with your arms folded and stare straight into the other person's eyes, and you do not let a flicker of expression cross your face. He will be embarrassed, he won't know what to do, he'll feel he wants to keep the conversation going. And gradually he will deploy his whole case in front of you, without you having asked a question or said a word. I try to use that technique; I try, but it's not easy.

Dan was not worried about controlling his emotions at work. He had learnt to suppress them for practical reasons.

I fancy I don't show emotion that much, because I prefer not to. It could make you vulnerable. You have to see me as an individual that's been active in trade unions with shop stewards for fifteen years, and when you're playing the game of politics on the shop floor, or dealing with an individual across the table, right from day one you have to play around in your own mind with elementary psychology.

That doesn't mean to say that I'm not an emotional person. Within I am. And suppressing emotion takes its toll, yes, I think it does. You're training your mind not to respond to normal situations. You're acting out a certain role, you don't want to give away anything. I represent the shop floor and have their interests at heart. It becomes a question of willpowers. You have to destabilize the other person, that's the way I see it. In doing that, I don't wish to show any form of emotion that could be looked upon as a weakness, whether it's vanity, conceit or emotional instability.

And it is easy to see why men have to hide their feelings at work when many react as James did.

I am likely to listen to people with problems. I don't know why, but I do. A few men at work do come to me with their problems. It's difficult for male friends to come to the director of the division with their problems, because that's seen as a weakness – but one or two do. Then I have to say, in all frankness, if people have emotional problems, you worry about the next stage up in terms of promotion. If I saw a man crying at work I'd assume he was having a nervous breakdown. That is very unfair, since some people are better at hiding their problems than others, and those that are perhaps less honest get away with it. But it is a fact.

But I found some men struggling against this tide of belief, trying to build up a system where emotions could be used positively at work. Robert, the governor of a large men's maximum-security prison, stressed the important role which feelings played in his work.

When I first started in the prison service, I was struck by how like it was to the army world I had come from.

I do very little administration work. I think there are more important things. The real work is creating a society inside these walls which is progressively improving. The ideal society would be where people help each other, so there's genuine emotional communication. You never get that, at least very rarely, but you work towards it.

But you gradually improve things so that the laughter is more pleasant, there's a more relaxed atmosphere, people talk better. Listening to staff and talking to staff, relating to staff, it sets an example of not paternalism, but an equality, that recognizes you've got different jobs and experiences, and you care not *for* people but *about* people, so that they in turn care about each other. There's no doubt about it, it works. I know it works. It takes a lot of time and an immense amount of patience. It's not what you say that counts, it's the way you behave. I mean, you can call someone stupid but you can still get across the fact that you respect them. And you realize that one third will be with you enthusiastically, one third will go whatever way the wind blows, and one third will be against you.

There was one prison officer in another prison I used to work in, who said it was all a lot of complete rubbish. He said it was utter tripe. And all he was there for was to control people, and he wasn't going to have anything to do with these personal relationships. Yet on his landing, he had the best personal relationships there. He was good at it, but he wouldn't admit to himself that he was anything but tough. If he comforted someone who was crying, it wasn't to give him comfort, it was because the blasted noise was coming through the wall and keeping people awake.

Men seem very romantic at heart. They confess that they fall in love dramatically and some quite easily. And yet on the question of love itself, they are a great deal more reticent. Many men talked with great feeling of the love they felt for their children, but seemed embarrassed to speak of the love they had for their wife. Some clearly felt less for their wives than for their children. Even men such as doctors, clergymen, psychiatrists and community workers, used to counselling and helping others, sometimes admitted that they found their own emotional life in a mess: Robin is forty-six.

If you deal with a lot of human suffering, as I do as a priest, you do need to keep things at a distance. I feel the feminine side of me is more emotional than the male part. There's a difference between the emotional self-control I need for my work and my own awareness of feelings and pain. If you hold your own feelings down too much, or for too long, you may be paying for it. I'm sometimes afraid that I cut off my feelings so effectively that they aren't there any more. There are occasions when I know I should be feeling something, and I'm not. I think the pain of life can be so great that you sometimes need to defend yourself by not feeling.

My wife and I have had our problems like any other couple and I think she would tell you that I'm rather hard to live with. I defend myself from her emotional demands by burying myself in my work. I think it's an excuse that many clergymen use. In fact, I think many of the clergy have pretty odd marriages. I'm conscious that my wife has to put up with quite a lot that's wrong. I think she, like many wives, is the more mature emotionally.

One man, Mike, finally decided that at fifty-one, blocking off all his inner feelings was a grave mistake.

His wife had recognized that there was something wrong with their relationship and persuaded him to come with her on a Marriage Encounter weekend run by the Roman Catholic Church, of which they were both members. He said that his wife thought that

she was not married to a *person*, that I was always just relating to her expectations and a set of rules. And she was right. She had a problem and I didn't know I had a problem. The rules were a defence, a defence against my own image of myself, which was reinforced by a lot of people, including my mother, my grandmother, my grandfather.

During the weekend fifteen couples were encouraged to open up to each other, privately as individual couples, and communicate as they had never done before.

I found it an amazing experience. It actually made the last step that I needed in the sense of releasing myself, although it was very painful. I realized after twenty years of marriage that my wife was a *separate* person from me. Now I think I accept that fact, which is another rather important point. I think it's only fair to say that now I'm no longer frightened of my wife. You see, I was frightened of her *feelings* more than anything else, her expression of feeling, and my having to respond to it. I was frightened of my own feelings, and of hers. In other words, I was frightened of what was coming at me and frightened of responding, because it was quite contrary to all my training and upbringing. I feel free now from a continuing series of voices, editorials, saying, 'You oughtn't to do that, it's not right.' I can banish them. They may come back but I now feel I've got the power to banish them. And I've learned to be more honest about my feelings, I suppose.

All my life, I've been told, 'You must not cry', which I've taken to mean the same as 'You must not feel sad'. So feeling sad was a *bad* feeling. And that made me feel guilty, which is also a bad feeling, you see. You've got this whole build-up. There was no way to express feelings acceptably, because they were very frightening things. People got run all over by feelings. I remember my mother crying, which I felt was a most unfair weapon. She was crying because she was miserable. She cried because she felt I'd been unkind to her. And that was quite right, I had been. And when I used to come back for the holidays I never fulfilled her expectations. She was very ill. My father and she had split up during the war, and so there was always this clash of expectation, producing guilt, producing defiance from me and from her the accusation that I didn't love her.

For a time I had been to a psychotherapist to try and release my feelings and myself. I had a sense that it was chipping away a sort of hard case, and as it fell away I realized it was *me*. I was chipping away at *me*, until I'd got a very thin coating, which made me very sensitive. At that point I didn't want to go any further because it was too painful, bad enough as it is. Then I arranged to go on this Marriage Encounter weekend. I was very unsettled about it because in my thin-cased incarnation I was feeling it might not be very enjoyable.

My wife and I told each other of our feelings about so many things over the weekend. I had changed so much. I was looking back to a former self, though this was just the beginning. At one point I had to tell my wife what I felt about our marriage and about myself. All I know is, by this time I'd gone up to my room by myself, and I suddenly could take it no more. I simply burst into tears – I just couldn't go on. I felt I was being burnt alive. It was the most agonizing thing, but with a sense of relief. It was the first time I had been absolutely forced to be myself. It was as if a final bit of the hard casing had been removed . . . it was like chipping through a rock and water flowing. At the beginning of the weekend I had found it exceptionally difficult to say anything nice about myself and now I had finally broken through to myself and I found I was OK in spite of the bad bits . . . By normal standards you would have said we were a perfectly happy, well-integrated married couple . . . but at one point I had to tell my wife how much I loved her and to express everything I felt for her. I thought – I can't. I haven't done anything like that for my wife for ages. But somehow once I started there seemed so much to say. I have learned that if you want to hold your marriage together and make it a really living relationship, you have to tell each other of your deepest feelings every day if possible and make time to listen to each other.

I think the experience has given me a sense of joy. That's different to happiness. Happiness is a bubbly sort of thing; joy is a much deeper, calmer thing. I feel competent now. I feel I have a centre which is worthwhile and which I'm competent to express to the outside world which, to some extent, I didn't before.

So that weekend experience has certainly changed my way of appraising myself and that makes a very big difference in the way I see other people. I think it's going to affect my work very considerably indeed. I think that it's going to make it much much easier for me to communicate with people. And I think the key to making a big company like this work is for men to learn to express their feelings. But to do that would require quite an investment. They would have to do some basic things, like bringing in, on an absolutely equal basis, men and women, because that's the only way you're going to break through the conditioning that makes us believe that women are *feeling* and men are *rational*. That, in a sense, is absolute rubbish. I think both men and women are a mixture. And there may be many men with a much more feeling component, and many women with a much more rational component. For example Margaret Thatcher comes across to me as a very rational person, and I am upset by this because I suppose deep down I think of women as more feeling than rational. And it upsets me even more because I find that I'm actually much more feeling than rational and my 'messages' tell me that men should be the other way round. There shouldn't be tensions of this sort . . . we are all individuals and we shouldn't try to force ourselves into stereotypes: 'Me Tarzan, you Jane'.

I think my colleagues would find it difficult to handle if I started showing my feelings more – and, incidentally, I should be very foolish if I became a stereotype convert and went overboard, and said, 'Right, it's all feelings, chaps, and watch your body language.' They'd shrink away, I should think.

Like so many men quoted in this chapter, Mike was brought up not to cry but to grit his teeth and hide his

270

tears. But this meant hiding other feelings and emotions which welled up, too. Self-control became of paramount importance, so that love and affection, pleasure, enthusiasm and joy became equally hard to demonstrate. Genuine emotional communication becomes warped.

Like other men I spoke to, Chris, a bank clerk, found that he was only brought closer to other men by a joint involvement in sport.

I've just joined a squash club and go several nights a week. Quite a lot of the men at the bank play it. I'm not as competitive as some of the others – it can be a very aggressive game. One thing does come over very strongly, and it's a new experience for me. I'm conscious of a new friendship – comradeship – I mean; sometimes you will see blokes standing in the shower chatting for ten minutes or so. It's obvious they're not just having a shower. There's more to it than that; they're having a conversation that perhaps they couldn't have anywhere else.

But it is mothers as much as fathers who teach little boys not to open up. Schools reinforce this message, as do workmates, friends, colleagues and the traditions of our society, so it is no wonder that men feel inhibited about expressing their emotions. There is a price to pay for such self-control, 'an enormous cost', as Richard said. Is it worth the price?

Chapter Fourteen

AGEING AND APPEARANCE

Although most men disliked the idea of getting older and were concerned in varying degrees about ageing, many felt that loss of looks was a greater disaster for women. They thought that women must suffer agonies with each approaching wrinkle, which is an interesting reflection on the value that men put on women's looks (and does not necessarily reflect what many women feel). As Victor, a comprehensive school teacher of thirty-one, explained:

It is a truism, I think, that men tend to grow old more gracefully than women, without having to try. Men on the whole age better. I think perhaps it adds to their character. After a certain age women really do have to try to keep up appearances. Most women, that is. My mother's not really very old, early fifties, but she's let herself go – my father dying and other strains she's had to cope with. For a man that wouldn't be old.

The major worry for a great many men to whom I spoke, and one which was always expressed in an offhand, joking fashion, was the fear of being unattractive to the opposite sex. Richard put it like this:

In my experience the only sex problem – and this is never discussed on television or radio – the only male sex problem that I've ever come across in conversation is that a man isn't Warren Beatty. He dreams miserably of the ladies he'd like to sleep with if only he were Mick Jagger, say. The average man finds that he's revolting to 98 per cent of the opposite sex, if not more. And that's a fairly reasonable figure. Most men are unattractive to the opposite sex. I mean there's somebody for everybody, but on the whole men get used to the idea that they are unattractive to women, in a way that women don't. If you said to most men. 'Would you like to be Mick Jagger?' they'd say, 'Yes.' If you said to most women, 'Would you like to be Jerry Hall?' they wouldn't know what you were talking about.

That is a view with which a few men may agree.

The physical attributes that many men valued were height, build, hair and a slim waist, and for those who were losing their hair a little self-delusion had to be practised.

Giles is an affluent insurance broker in his mid forties, with thinning hair. He loves his job, thinks it is all a game that should not be taken too seriously, says he is happily married, and is obviously popular with his male colleagues. But he has problems.

I do worry about getting older. I'm not so worried about my hair because I've got this wonderful feeling that in a fortnight's time it's all going to be all right. I'm just going through a phase at the moment of getting a great big stomach and losing my hair, and all that. I feel that in a fortnight's time my hair will grow again. I'm not worried about getting old, I don't think. I'm worried about being unattractive, actually. I mean, when I was thirty I went down to Taunton with a client of mine. Anyway, we had our meetings and had a very good dinner, then we went on to a disco. There was an absolutely divine eighteen-year-old in velvet hot pants. I thought, this is tremendous, I *must* go and dance with her. So I walked across the floor looking frightfully cool – I thought – and she turned round and said, 'Piss off, Grandad!' That was tremendous – I mean it wasn't good. I don't think I've ever consciously been to bed with anyone younger than my daughter – oh, I have, in fact, yes.

Twenty-five-year-old homosexual Barry takes himself much more seriously.

If I find myself attractive then I think I'm probably attractive to other people. I'm obsessed by my appearance, by my clothes, by my skin, and it just goes on and on and on. I don't really know why it is – I suppose it was coming to London where I met lots of people and started to go out to clubs, and to dinner and the theatre. I realized that appearance is quite important.

I've started going to a beautician – on the surface I treat it as a joke, but underneath I'm quite serious about it. I mean, what the Hell, you see all these people walking about with spotty faces and they really don't have skin problems – they can do something about it. I've just finished a three-week diet to clean my system out – leeks and grapes – and I take it seriously. I feel better, I feel I've achieved something.

I wear make-up, but only foundation. I take about two hours to get ready every time I go out – I think it's important. I don't consider myself an effeminate person, but I certainly have effeminate traits. All my male friends treat it as a joke – they don't really want to know if I go on for hours and hours about skin and things.

But it is not just homosexuals who think of beauticians and of improving their looks. Signs of ageing were of significance to men in business, who thought looking young and healthy was an advantage. A man of forty who dyes his hair does so because he does not think the signs of greying make him look distinguished, as they are supposed to, but just old. Loss of hair made men feel old, unattractive and less masculine. Paul, an actor, is in his mid forties. He wears a toupee and feels naked without it.

My girlfriend keeps urging me to throw it away – I suppose she sees me often enough without it. I don't think I've got the nerve to arrive at work one day without it. I do think about it, and in many ways it would be a relief. It does make me look younger, I think.

Hair was talked about rather a lot in these discussions about ageing. Bob, who is in his seventies, often wondered if he would rather have been a woman.

And on the whole, I think I would. The reasons are totally trivial. One is that most women keep their hair. I mind *terribly* about that. Not having hair gives one a feeling of inferiority – you just feel that you haven't got something which you enormously admire, for one thing. Hair is an absolute passion for me; I notice people's hair more than I notice a lot of other things. To a lot of men, I think this is terrifically important. One feels it's a loss of attraction. And however much people say that others don't notice, one doesn't believe it, of course. I once seriously thought of committing suicide because I was going bald.

We all know men both in and out of public life who comb long strands of hair over their bald pate to cover it up. If the strands get blown about, they detach themselves from the scalp and wave about in the air. I asked Alex, a university lecturer, why he thought it improved his looks. He smiled rather sheepishly.

Well, there was a bit more hair there to begin with, and the spot I was covering was rather small. I just didn't like the idea of going bald. It started rather young with me, and it made me look so – well – old. And in my job I was surrounded by pretty girls whom I fancied like mad. I'd rather use my own hair than have a wig. I suppose I don't really mind as much now I'm fifty and the rest of me's beginning to fall apart too.

Perhaps not surprisingly, men under forty were much more likely to experiment with dress and, wherever they could get away with it, to have eschewed a formal suit for work. In many occupations, even in offices at a senior level, men now work in jeans and casual sweaters. Men of all ages were happy to admit they used aftershave and deodorants, had their hair blow-dried at the hairdresser and had even learnt to do it for themselves at home. For other men the regular use of sunbeds was just part of wanting to look their best. Norman, a Yorkshire coalminer aged thirty-nine, a tough Rugby League player with such a good tan he looked as though he had just returned from the tropics, said, 'It's a special offer down at the local sunbed centre, twelve sessions, half price. No I don't mind what people think.'

The manager of a first division football team said he encouraged his boys to use a sunbed before they played abroad, it made them feel good and they didn't risk getting burnt if they were off to a hot country. He certainly used one himself. But he had noticed a difference over the last few years in footballers' attitudes to their appearance. So many of them were now offered modelling jobs in their spare time, which they enjoyed doing, that they ended up being given all sorts of fancy things free. He had no objection to this extra-curricular work if it didn't go over the top or bring the club into disrepute.

Lots of our lads have a perm now, and no one would think of teasing them about it, and I don't object to them wearing jewellery as long as it's not too ostentatious. Chains and bracelets are all right but if a lad wanted to join this club wearing earrings I'd be inclined to say, 'You can get rid of them first'. Well, I think that's unacceptable, they're for women and gypsies. Some of our lads will come in for a match wearing a leather suit that's cost a few hundred pounds. Well, they can afford it on their pay.

The gap between how old men felt inside and the features that faced them in the mirror each morning could pose a problem. George, a CID officer in his mid thirties, did not seem to care for reality.

I still tend to see myself as a twenty-five-year-old. I don't like the thought of getting older. I hate the thought of losing my hair or my teeth. But perhaps when I'm not attractive to women any longer I'll just stop worrying about it. I like to think I can still go out and pull the birds – it does one's ego good every now and again.

Thirteen years older, James was more conscious of the ticking of the clock.

I don't think one's noticed growing older because each day just follows the day before. I suppose there are shattering moments when one looks back and thinks, My God, twenty-five years married, that's a lifetime. But it doesn't seem like twenty-five years. And twenty-seven years with the company, though I haven't been doing one job in that time – it's been compartmentalized into a series of jobs. I'm obviously not twenty-one any more. I don't feel older. I think that one regrets it because one sees life passing by and I wonder if I'll have the time to do other things. What other things I don't know, but if I had more time I'm sure I'd find some.

Ralph, the owner of a multi-million-pound company, sees his seventies as a time for taking stock. A man of immense drive and energy, he still works harder now than many men half his age.

I mind getting older and I don't want to become a burden and deteriorate. I enjoy every moment. I think I shall look back on my life with pleasure. I think, on balance, that I've made a contribution. I was more constructive than destructive. Today I look with horror at what the world, society, is doing to itself. And the inability of mankind to progress – I don't mean technologically – but in human terms. I think we've made no progress in many thousands of years from a human point of view, of course. Many argue with me, saying we're more caring, but we talk about blasting ourselves out of existence.

Some men denied the importance of their looks and clothes entirely, although I fear they were not without a certain vanity. That is not a criticism, but it made me wonder why men, particularly those of the old school, are rather ashamed to admit that they have thought about their appearance. It is, perhaps, surprising when one of the hallmarks of the English gentleman is his perfectly understated and never-too-new attire. I use the word 'vanity' because these particular men so often chose their clothes with an attention to colour, arrangement and material that could not have been achieved without some thought. I overheard a middle-aged man at a boat-race party explaining away his Garrick-Club tie. A woman had remarked how pretty his colours were – faded pink shirt, soft green knitted jersey, old lovat tweed jacket. He looked horrified.

My God, please don't call me pretty. This tie, if you recognize it, is only like this because the Committee were choosing a club tie over tea, and in desperation over the colour were suddenly inspired by the sandwiches they were eating. Cucumber and salmon.

It does seem that men either feel embarrassed, or think they should act embarrassed, if they are complimented on their clothes. A few men to whom I spoke still let their wives buy all their clothes. Allan, an artist in his seventies, says that his wife even buys all his shoes without him being there. 'She knows my size by now.' As far as clothes were concerned, 'Anything that covers me is all right – it's mostly my wife's taste. I suppose it is nice if somebody says how nice I look.' A few professed no interest in clothes at all. One admitted that on promotion to a rather prestigious job, at the age of forty-three, he had gone to Moss Bros and bought every conceivable sort of clothing he might need, including sportswear, and that he did not intend to have to bother about clothes ever again. Some men were embarrassed when their younger wives started to buy them colourful casual designer clothes. They were prepared to wear them on holiday (just) and if they went abroad, but drew the line at turning up at the local club in them.

There was a sharp division between those who approved of male jewellery and those who did not. The latter usually got more enraged by this than almost anything else they spoke about. Security officer Dennis:

I hate men with perms, and with earrings. My daughter's first boyfriend had an earring. I ejected him from the house. I opened the front door and threw him out. I lost my temper. My daughter was upset, yes. My wife was, too. She said my eyes stood out like a maniac. And I threw this bloke out. I've regretted it. I've never apologized for it. I was so incensed – old-fashioned.

Men who do not wear jewellery are scathing about those who do. Bracelets and medallions came in for much ridicule, particularly from older men. Younger men were rather more tolerant about this than their elders. Andrew, a thirty-eight-year-old hospital orderly who wore a wedding ring but no other jewellery, said he would not have done it but it meant a lot to his wife. She had been on holiday on the continent and was impressed by how many men wore wedding rings: 'She seemed to think I really meant it if I wore a ring.'

Sexual and marital problems connected with ageing have been mentioned in their appropriate chapters, but another dismay common to men concerned lessening physical prowess, particularly for games players. Each sport makes different demands – some are mainly for the supple, while others, like sailing or golf, can be carried on for decades. Unfortunately Albert, an auditor, had chosen one of the more energetic ways of taking exercise:

Sport is paramount to me and doctors would probably argue that you're past your peak around twenty-seven, twenty-eight. I'm past that. It's a terrible thought, but I play first team rugby at the moment and I've got to make the choice in a year or two either to move over and let younger players in, or call it a day. I can't imagine how it's going to feel – I can't imagine not playing rugby. I suppose I will go on playing, but I'll just have to accept that I'm a lot slower.

Piers, a dentist, might be able to keep up his enthusiasm a while longer, but already a certain frantic tone could be heard.

I worry a lot about putting on weight, so at the moment I'm reasonably conscious of what I eat and how much I eat. I play hockey every week, and squash regularly. I do enjoy playing squash. I think I put on weight very, very easily, even though I use up a lot of energy.

Apprehension about encroaching age mounts on birthdays, each individual having his own least popular age. I was surprised how many young men in their twenties had an overbearing feeling of getting old too fast, though Henry, a commodity broker, does inhabit a world where the young work incredibly hard and then hope to get out.

I feel young; I like people to call me 'boy', but I've got the feeling I'm becoming a man fairly fast. I used to look about three or four years younger than I was, but suddenly now people ask me what I am and they think, Well, yes, you are twenty-five. Exactly bang on. I think, God! Perhaps the pendulum's swinging the other way.

Children were seen as a compensation for age in two distinct ways. On the one hand is the view of Ron, a factory foreman aged forty-eight.

I thought forty was just like any other birthday. I thought it went quickly. I remember when I was thirty, I said to somebody, 'Crikey, that went quick, from twenty to thirty like', and he said to me, 'It'll go even quicker from thirty to forty.' I would like to go back to being thirty or forty. I'd like to go back then because I had no aches. It was nice. The kids were young and it's a nice time when they are going to school, and we'd go and see their bits at school. I wouldn't have minded more children, another two.

And on the other, Edward, a bank manager who is also forty-eight, told me:

If growing older is seeing one's own children grow to maturity and start off on their own careers as relatively well-adjusted human beings, then its's good. I certainly wouldn't like to go back to raising young children.

Cautious about admitting how much they care about their appearance in the first place, men can get away with seeming to mind less about the depressing aspects of ageing. But when pressed, their candid use of such terms as 'a great big stomach', 'losing my hair' and 'overweight' shows how conscious they really are of the effects of time. Most of all they seem to mind being 'past it', past being able to kick or hit a ball with dexterity, past being looked at themselves with interest and past being able to pick up the pretty girls. But it was 'Piss off, Grandad,' which really hurt.

Chapter Fifteen

TRADITIONAL MAN

When men were asked to say what it was like to be a man they most often replied that it meant you could be selfish. Men, they said, had the freedom to do what they wanted to do, and could avoid the things they didn't want to do. They could see that women were different from them, and on the whole they were entirely unenvious of the female role, though they thought women had many strengths that they did not have. Men thought that men should ideally be strong, both physically and mentally, and though physically stronger than women, agreed that for sheer endurance women could outlast them in a number of ways. For most, however, just being a man was better.

Men talked about the need to be the hunter, to go out into the world and provide for their family, about the need to prove themselves, with all of which thirty-seven-year-old plumber Sid heartily agreed: 'If you're going to be a man, you've got to prove yourself in some way, and the most obvious way to do that is through your work.' But men also have to prove themselves by competing and winning; by being masculine and responsible, by being sexually dominant even though they might prefer to be passive, and by being aggressive.

Here are some of the things they said – first, John:

The business executive role is the role of the hunter. I love it. It's twenty-five hours a day and the canines drool and you're in there; it's masculine and macho, the whole damn bit.

Naval officer Neil said:

Men like other men to know in the most subtle way that they're OK. Professional ability gives you a higher rating with other men, but if you've got a guy who's exceptionally good, other men can only usually look at the few faults that he has.

Another member of the forces, Gavin, a captain in the Royal Hussars, expressed his ideas in a more concrete form.

The man is the chap who's meant to deal with the burglars; and you hope when it's raining will get out and change the puncture.

School teacher Victor said:

I think modesty can be a very dangerous little number, really. For a man it's quite a dangerous thing to do yourself down, at work or anywhere else. Often if I say, 'I'm not particularly good at this', you find that suddenly it gets reported back that you're hopeless at that. It's very bad news, really. I think twice now, particularly in things connected with my job.

It happens in rugby, too. I can remember when I first joined the team I'm with now. I hadn't played rugby for a while because I'd cracked my skull and I was advised not to play for a few years. When I went back, they asked me if I was any good. I said, 'Not particularly', and as a result I wallowed in the fourth team for about a season. I'm afraid I then put myself forward, boasted a bit, and people began to notice me more. I now play for the first team.

Men do not like the power women have over them, particularly sexual power, as forty-year-old carpet layer Eddie observed:

Men like sex better than women, but a man must rely on what affection his wife doles out to him, because women are the only legalized dispensers of affection in our society. Women must be surprised and delighted at what men will do for affection.

283

Men suffer from a number of anxieties, one of the greatest of which is fear of failure, a point on which local government officer Matthew, commented:

I know a lot of men in their forties who had dreams when they were young, but their dreams didn't come true and they have no real life any more. At forty they plod along with an uneasy sense of failure but no new goals. I think women of forty are very different from men. They seem only recently to have discovered their dreams – everything is good and it's all in the future.

Men who decided that success is not for them have to be prepared for the consequences, as Ronald, a VAT inspector, told me:

I suppose I have already decided that I have no great ambitions to go to the top – I'm not really interested enough. I think I became bored and frustrated at the sacrifices that had to be made. I think if you want to be a 'success', and I mean in other people's eyes, you have to work so damn hard at it, and that doesn't appeal to me. I haven't got two pennies to scratch together, and I don't really care. I have a wonderful life, I do all the things I enjoy doing and I don't want to do much more than that at the moment. . . . I'm aware that some people probably think less of me because of it.

I think men suffer from feelings of inadequacy in their careers. I would think there are few men who had never thought to themselves, 'I'm just not going to make it; this job is going nowhere. If I lose this job, I won't get another. Everything could tumble about my ears.'

Factory foreman Ron thought that 'As a man you're not trained to think about the role of man – you just are.' Many men found it difficult to be really close to anyone, male or female, and difficult to have the kind of friendships that they saw their wives involved in. They often spent time with other men pursuing similar interests, but rarely were the barriers down. Men, though good at apparently everything else, remain hopelessly shored up behind the mask of successful manhood. Matthew again:

It's difficult for a man to be alone with another man, just left together doing nothing. What can they talk about except very superficial things? Men are not trained to have feelings in relation to other men, and find it hard to have a simple friendship outside their job, or when not enjoying doing something together.

Men fear social disapproval, which makes them on the whole rather conventional; they fear public disgrace, and have anxieties about public embarrassment. Men are preoccupied with their status, at home, in the hierarchy of work, and in society as a whole. Where men feel free to break the rules at home, at work it can be a different and more serious matter. This policeman was happy to admit he had had affairs, because the opportunity arose, but felt conscience-striken about being dishonest at work.

The worst thing I've ever done is tell lies in a magistrates' court. I was convinced that the man was guilty, and he was. He was a villain, and he was cocking a snook at me. I was a young man then and I told lies. He got three months. It worried me terribly for months and months and I spoke to him afterwards. He said, 'I was guilty.' That eased my conscience, but that was the first and only time that I've ever done it.

Men dare not look inwards at their feelings in case they become too aware of their shortcomings. Part of being a man is, after all, not showing weakness. As no one is secure or strong all the time, a man must hide all indications of self-doubt or weakness. But some men are aware of their contradictory position. They know that releasing feelings, talking about them and dealing with them, does some good, but to do so may endanger not only their status as a man but their professional standing also.

If men are supposed to be strong, they are also expected to be tall. Victor told me:

I think it is an advantage to be big in male society. . . . I definitely know a number of small men who suffer from not being tall. It's the archetypal thing where they tend to be a bit pushy. Small men seem to feel the need to assert themselves much more than others. You often find the most aggressive rugby player is the smallest.

Derek, a travelling salesman of thirty, corroborated this and expanded on it:

I am five foot two and this has affected me profoundly all my life. I have noticed short men have two ways of dealing with it; they compensate by being aggressive and pushy, or they become sensitive, develop a good sense of humour about themselves, and fight the putdowns by saying, 'Those people must be dimwits and I am more intelligent.' . . .

Recently I went to buy a new tennis racquet. The sales assistant was very young and cheeky, and he said, 'Do you want a child's racquet?' I just thought to myself: You're an idiot.

I often see other men looking at me as if I am strange, but it is something women rarely comment on. Being short has helped me approach women. You know what it is like to be looked down on as women are. I am much more comfortable with women.

Men are confused in their relationships with women. As long as men persist in thinking that it is all right to refer to women as girls, they will maintain their built-in prejudice against equality. TUC organizer Dan said:

Men have got to learn to understand their own confusions about women. They must learn to criticize women in a normal way and not in a sexist way; to stop saying, 'You are a bitch', but to be able to say, 'You are wrong.'

Mick, who works in the film industry, explained:

Men are often confused about sexism and sexuality. Women are opposed to sexism – the building-site leer – but not opposed to sexuality, the normal appreciation of physical beauty.

Many men are afraid to display what they think of as feminine characteristics; one of their greatest fears is to be thought of as homosexual. Security officer Dennis told me:

What's unfair about being a man, and a big man like me, is I like pretty things – I like women's dresses. My wife does dressmaking; I love material, soft material. What would a psychiatrist make of that! But I only do it in private with my wife, and I look at things in shops. I'm frightened to show that I like women's things, pretty dresses and pretty things. I like flowers. But I don't want to show people that I like pretty flowers in case they thought that I was, not homosexual, but a little bit effeminate.

Men are expected to compete, as a cabinet minister explained:

Men are so competitive. From the moment that they start, even at public school with exams, they're beginning to compete at being the top boy, or the captain of the house, or captain of the eleven. State schools are exactly the same. The competition takes the fun out of it, even in sport. Sport's so commercial now, it's so well paid. I don't think Test matches are much fun any more. But life is tremendously competitive, from the moment that you put on your white collar – or, I'm sure, when you first go into a factory.

Men like joining clubs and spending time together, as Lord Eastbourne told me:

I go to a club. I enjoy it and use it when I'm alone. I think the men's dining club appeals to me because you get the same sort of conversation that you get after dinner when the girls have gone. It's normally politics, but it needn't be.

Kevin, a dustman, spoke of a very similar institution at the other end of the social spectrum:

I usually go down the pub Friday lunchtimes, Saturdays, Sundays and a couple of times during the week if I've got the money. All depends. There'll be about half a dozen mates there. I never buy a round of drinks because I drink shorts. All me mates drink beer, so it's a bit awkward if you're drinking shorts. We talk about all sorts of things; sex – fantasies, mostly. If you see a nice girl walk past, or a nice girl in the pub, you talk under your breath – 'Oh, yeah.' But it's all talk most of the time. Some of them talk about horse-racing, football, boxing. We only talk about politics when an election comes up. The film that was on the telly the night before. But we mostly talk about sports, and that sort of thing.

A fireman talked of his club, in practice just as much an all-male preserve as any in St James's:

I think I'm a man's man. I spend a lot of time working with men, and the one regular social gathering I go to is all-male. That's a model railway club. I've been working on my own model railway for a long, long time. I keep it up in the loft. The club's all-male. A woman could belong, certainly – it's just that they don't seem to come along.

Men are supposed to be brave, as Harold, a diplomat, confirmed:

I was born in 1890. The Great War came just about my last year at Oxford, and a great many of my friends were wiped out. I was committed to the Indian Service and working for the Secretary of State for India, so I wasn't allowed to join up. I was presented with white feathers, which was an accusation of cowardice. They were given by women, mostly young women who thought they were doing the patriotic thing driving their menfolk into war. I minded the white feathers.

Men are supposed to behave like men – something that a factory buyer had cause to complain about:

I went into a pub in Brentford with my wife and sister-in-law and I went up to the counter and got some beer. Everybody was in the way and I said, 'Excuse me, please', as I would normally say it. Then some fella, big fella, said, 'Oh, sweet-talking fella.' I think it's a shame that people are like that. There's so much room for niceness, I think.

Their sons are also supposed to behave like men, as miner Tom assured me:

I've never encouraged kissing in the boy. I want him to be a man. This is why I don't mind him having a motorcycle and doing the things that boys should do. My son wanted an earring, one of these sleeper things. I said, 'No', and that's as far as it goes. I don't want him to be one of these poofs. Everyone's got their role to play and the man's got to be the man, and let the woman sort of wear the make-up and be very attractive. The man can obviously be attractive on his own, or be very smart, but I don't see why men wear make-up and carry bags.

Men are supposed to be successful in sex, Victor explained:

I've noticed when the chaps at the rugby club are talking about sex, they're always telling what she did to him, but never what he did to her. The public image is that of conqueror . . . but privately I've often felt inadequate. When I've had sexual relationships with women, the first few times are an absolute disaster.

Few men like being alone according to Richard, who works in the theatre.

Men are supposed to be self-sufficient, aren't they, and yet they never live on their own. Men who long to leave their wives are deterred by it. The one thing they can't face is living on their own. I have a friend who's just returned to his wife – they're terribly unhappy, they shouldn't be together. But he went to live in a flat for three months and he couldn't bear it. Men go into relationships looking for support, because they feel inadequate, but they can't recognize it. I wouldn't choose to live on my own ever. I did it once, but I wouldn't do it again.

Many men are lonely, Bill, the manager of a firm, told me:

I don't have many male friends. That's one of the problems of being in the situation I'm in as a manager; I tend to be a bit of a loner. I don't often associate with colleagues with whom I work. They get too close and then you lose your sense of leadership, if you like. You're regarded as one of them rather than being in charge. The other problem I've had is that I've been moved around a lot. I've devoted much of my time to my business, and I've found it difficult to have any close relationships.

Taxi-driver Fred said that men learn early to be interested in what money can do:

I was born in Bethnal Green, a poor family. When I was about fifteen a friend of my father's said, 'I'm going to take you out this evening', and he took me to the dogs. It was a beautiful sunny evening and I always remember it. I saw the bookmakers and all the rushing and excitement, and I had half a crown on me. And I can even remember the name of the dog. It was called Lady Perr. I went up and put my half a crown on, and lo and behold, the worst thing that could ever happen to me, it won – at eight to one. There was no tax or anything at that time. I had £1 2s 6d, and with this I had my eye on a very nice girl. She was about six foot two, I think, and when I went dancing with her I was able to kiss her on the knee. She used to work in a pickle factory. Very, very attractive. When she knew that I was in the money, I took her out for a week on the £1 2s 6d. I took her out . . . we had spaghetti on toast twice in Italiano Peppa, and of course at the end of the week the bird had flown. But that gave me an inkling of what money could do.

John explained what he thought men liked about being a man:

The nicest thing about being a man is just a sense of being masculine. I like decisiveness, aggressiveness, humorousness in anybody – male or female. I don't think there are any bad things about being a man. I just like the whole thing. Christ, yes, I wouldn't change. I've never wanted any girl children because I think little girls, like big girls, are far too smart for me.

If these thoughts on being a man and these traditional descriptions of the male role seem to lack a certain breadth and depth, it may well be because men are rarely required to be self-reflective. But some have tried. They have looked about them in the 1980s; they have seen what their wives and girlfriends are doing and thinking, and they have taken action.

Chapter Sixteen

MAN AND MODERN WOMAN

The rise of feminism and the rebellion against the traditional feminine role, the use of the pill and the increase in the number of working women are some of the things which have influenced the lives and minds of a great many women over the last twenty-five years. But the evidence seems to be that the average man has been very little affected by feminism, and when he has, he feels varying degrees of antagonism. *If* he has changed, to take the cynical view of Sydney, a retired further education lecturer, it's only because women have forced him to.

In my lifetime men have changed. In my opinion the change has been forced on them by women. Women have changed. Women have a so much bigger say in everything that goes on. I think men were quite happy to go on as they were – being the boss cat and doing everything they wanted to. But now, the poor devils, so many of them don't have a chance. I don't believe that women should have authority because we've seen what they've done with authority. Men are being cowed and subjected to all sorts of trauma, I think. There'll never be a balance between men and women, like there'll never be a perfect society. Women were unhappy, but they didn't make a big to do about it. Now if they're unhappy, they form a society or an organization or a commune. I think that's a lot of balls. They're unhappy, so they're unhappy. They've got to learn to live with it. That's what I think. I know it sounds terribly reactionary.

Though he did represent the feelings of a handful of men I met, his was not a typical view. I asked men generally what they thought about feminism, whether they felt they knew what women were getting at, and where they had come across feminists, if at all. The general consensus of opinion was that feminism was all right as long as it did not go too far. Matthew, who did not like to be thought 'chauvinistic in any way', said:

They seem to be shoving it down people's throats, because they think that's the only way they're going to be noticed, so they think the end justifies the means. That kind of over-aggressiveness is very unappealing. And it does make men defensive, yes.

Asking for equal pay was fair and accepted by the majority of men interviewed, but there were aspects of feminism which upset men, and left them feeling confused. Time and again men talked of sympathy with women wanting to get to the top in their job, but sadness if this meant them losing their femininity. Terry, a young agricultural worker, spoke for many when he used the word 'fanatic'; I heard it again and again in this context.

Sometimes I think women's libbers go a bit too far. They have all these committees and refer to each other as chairperson, and all this silly thing, and not calling themselves a housewife, but a houseperson. I think it's ridiculous. Whatever they feel about themselves, they're still a female, a woman. I won't say all of them, but it seems that some of them, as with all these sort of movements, you get sort of fanatics who take things to an extreme.

Hugh, a thirty-five-year-old married solicitor from Essex, voiced the same opinion using an equally vehement vocabulary.

Occasionally I come across women's libbers, but I don't like them. I think they're anti-male, usually. I think they're strident, I think they're often humourless, I think they're intolerant, and that's basically what I find unattractive about them.

Tom, a Lancashire coalminer, waxed biological.

These Germaine Greers aren't really women, they're throwbacks, you know. I think people like the Germaine Greers of this world tend to cause trouble and to divide. I have met the emancipated woman. I wasn't very impressed. I think it's got to be down to the hormone thing – you know, they're one short or they're one too many.

He too would prefer women to be feminine rather than feminist and, as far as his work was concerned, thought there were good practical reasons why women should not go down the mines.

I like a woman to be a woman. I like to see a woman nicely dressed. I would never ask my old woman, any woman, to go down the mines. A woman could work on the controls and do an electrician's job to a certain extent. I wouldn't ask them to go to the far end, to the production district. It would be impossible for men to work in the same way, or behave in the same way if women were down the mines. I mean the sanitary conditions are incredible down there – there are *no* toilets. Your nearest toilet is at the pit bottom.

Other men in traditionally masculine jobs, such as Douglas, a thirty-seven-year-old fireman, did not want women working alongside them because they would be a liability. He also resented the inhibitions which he thought women would impose on him and his friends at work.

I have mixed feelings about women on the team. The brigade is a great all-male preserve. You can relax, you can be yourself, you know. When I say be yourself, you can be typically male chauvinist, if you like. You can make jokes about women, you can swear, you can do what you like. You can walk about half naked, come out the shower, you haven't got to worry. And you're talking to guys who've all got the same sort of interests. It must be very similar to being in the services, in the army or something like that. I think that, of course, that part of it, would have to go out the window, because regardless of how liberated or how friendly a couple of women were who were going on the team, you still would be prevented from asserting yourself in the same way.

Forty-eight-year-old factory foreman Ron was cautious but more positive. He thought that from his limited experience, women *had* advanced their cause in the last twenty years.

I haven't really come across any aggressive women's libbers. I mainly deal with males here. I think women should get equal money for equal work, and equal opportunities. But it's like fashion, isn't it – if they go to the extremes, then I'm not so keen. But as long as a woman keeps feminine, that's all right. I believe in education for women – I believe just as much that my daughter should be as well educated as my son, because in later life her children are going to benefit from her education. I agree with all that sort of thing, but I don't agree with these girls that are marching and burning their bras, and all that business. I just like them to be a little bit feminine, and for there to be a gradual change. And I think gradually it is. Even if you look back to, say, twenty years ago, I think that girls have got a lot more say and are a lot better educated and are treated more as equals. I can only go from my limited little nest, I suppose.

The constant equation of bra-burning with feminism became too repetitive to have any meaning. It seemed a convenient symbol which men had grasped at for want of a clear idea of what the women's liberation movement was all about. Changes in women's needs and desires affected them in different ways, depending on their jobs, on where they lived, the pubs they frequented, their leisure pursuits and the attitudes of their wives. Most would rather not have thought about the whole issue, preferring to turn their backs in self-defence on something they feared. Ron was not, however, the only one to look for laudable elements in the greater emancipation of women. This thirsty thirty-nine-year-old Yorkshire miner did too.

I just play it by ear with the women I meet. You can usually tell within the first few minutes if she's willing to buy a drink, and I wouldn't be offended if a woman offered to buy me a drink, no.

George, a CID officer of thirty-five, married to a wife who does not work, voiced a feeling common amongst men who preferred their wives to stay at home: he was concerned that if women became more liberated children would suffer.

I haven't really come across any women's libbers. They always give me the impression of being a little bit butch. I hope you're not a woman's libber, are you? I certainly don't find you as being butch at all. [Laughs, embarrassed] I don't really know what they're trying to prove, really.

Since Adam and Eve, it was always the man that's got to take the lead and be the leader of the family or the breadwinner, or whatever. I'm all for women going out to work, but I think it should be the man still that leads. I think it'll be a sad day if ever women do become completely liberated. I mean, somebody has got to look after the children, it's not really that a man can breast-feed a child. That's got to be down to the woman, hasn't it? Discipline has got to be down to the father.

The confusion caused in men by the problems of coming to terms with feminism is illustrated by Barry, a gay musician of twenty-five, who had been working as a temporary secretary. He feels women are intimidated by their experiences, but it is their own fault for not hitting back at male exploitation. On the other hand, he detests the sort of feminists who do stand up and fight for their rights, and finds their attitude offensive.

A lot of women are just bored with their existence. They're just child-bearers, cleaners and cooks with no power at all. I don't know whose fault it is, because the women let the men do that to them and so the men take advantage of it. I've got a friend who's quite liberated, she's quite intelligent, and yet if she goes home to her boyfriend, if she arrives at home at eleven o'clock at night-time because she's had a drink with me or something, he'll absolutely flip, while it's quite acceptable for him to be in the pub with his mates until eleven and reel in very drunk. And I certainly don't think that's reasonable.

Of all the typecasts of people in this world that there are, the people that I hate the most are feminists. I detest feminists. Not because of what they're saying but because of the way they say it, and their whole attitude. For instance, if I was on the tube and there was a woman standing and I was sitting, I would not give up my seat for her any more, because I just feel, well, there's a small sector of you lot that says, 'We're women, we've got equal rights', and I just feel, 'Well, have your equal rights.' I don't like strident feminists, yet I have immense respect for women who succeed in their own careers. I think it's very sad that most women just leave school, do their typing training, go and get married, go and live in the suburbs and settle down. That's something I found when I was doing secretarial work. I mean, what sort of life is that?

Lord Eastbourne was equally tangled in his approach.

I certainly don't think that it's a man's world or that it should be a man's world. I think there really should be equal opportunity in everything that takes place. I don't think there can ever be, quite. The physical make-up or mental make-up of a woman is such that she's not prepared, when she's had a child, to leave it as much as a man is. I don't think you can help it, however much one would want to. And this is obviously very restricting.

But for the most part I found that men from all classes, ages and backgrounds were willing to fight powerful rearguard actions to defend the traditional male and female roles. A young army officer, Gavin, was most precise about where he stood and what women did.

I still think, you know, that we should revert to our stage in society where there's males and females. I mean, this equality thing where you have to advertise for a daily person, or something – I'm no more going to employ a man to clean my house out than anything else, specially as I'm a bachelor. If there's one thing you need in the house, it's a bird, because they know how to run houses. You get a bird to come in; she puts flowers on the table and generally sharpens the thing up.

Advancing with the women were one or two men: I spoke to a few who were totally in favour of women throwing off the shackles of a male-dominated society. I did not find them easily. The first, Arthur, is a highly experienced journalist, now seventy-two years old.

I am all in favour of women's liberation. I consider the equality of women a perfectly natural condition. What surprises me is that they've put up with the other condition for so long. Of course they still haven't achieved what they want, quite. I am perfectly well aware of the disadvantages that women have had to put up with, I'm surprised there haven't been more Mrs Pankhursts. I suppose there are certain physiological reasons why they can't be exactly the same as men. But isn't it rather an exceptional man who doesn't understand their point of view? Is it true even now that there are men who don't want women to be freely equal?

I'm surprised women say they find discrimination in the media, I'd have thought it was the one realm where you wouldn't have found it. It's difficult for us men because of course you've got to be a woman to have experienced it.

This point was often made and understood by gays and blacks. Mick, who works in the film industry, thought to be gay by those in his office simply because he did not proposition the production assistants all the time, thought he could see a change in his own attitude as he had grown up.

I think men probably do need to go through some sort of revolution. I think they need to become more honest. I think a lot of their bad behaviour towards women is only superficial – a lot of it is what I call 'building-site leering'. It's the way other men expect them to behave. The way they want to be seen to behave. And the fear of being thought pansy or homosexual is very strong. I certainly remember behaving like that, but I grew out of that fairly quickly. I certainly remember leering at women in public places.

I remember one occasion very strongly. I was about eighteen, I suppose, a student in London, sitting in a restaurant leering at a woman and her coming over to me and saying, 'What are you staring at?' And being absolutely lost for words, instead of saying, 'I think you're very attractive.' Being absolutely lost for words, because that was the norm that was expected of me – that's what men did. I was frightened out of my wits when she came over to me.

My feeling about feminists is that they ought to be bringing people together and talking about how men can be involved in their problems. I think the women's movement is too engaged in the struggle of separateness. They seem to be saying, we want women to do this, women to do that. In television at the moment, there are little units making programmes presented by women, directed by women, and researched by women, for women, when surely it's all about involving men? They've got to talk to men about it, and most intelligent men find it [the treatment of women] obnoxious. You talk to the really intelligent perceptive men, they hate it. I can't understand the way men, superficially anyway, want to relate to women. I can't understand this boys together stuff, 'She's a bit of all right.' I cannot. It's obnoxious.

Some active trade unionists said they'd been educated by the women around them, after long and heated arguments, and now felt they understood some of the complexities of the feminist point of view. Men like Godfrey, who has been a left-wing shop steward in the engineering industry, tended to be more sympathetic than other men to any analysis of women's place in society in political and class terms, and were ready to see that women as a group had been oppressed in a male-dominated society.

I think there's tremendous confusion developed at the moment by the feminist movement. It's a very complex question which needs to be discussed and argued out properly. I try and see it clearly and sharply in political terms. I recognize the oppression of women in society, and ours is a capitalist society with a class system. As a working man in that society, and a craftsman on the shop floor, I would look down and see below me – in class terms – the craftsman's mate. He would look down and see below him the labourers. They would look down and see below them the immigrants – blacks, Asians, or whichever. And the whole lot of us as males would probably look down and see women.

So we men are exploited at work, and subject to various pressures. Because we live in a patriarchal society, we carry that back home. And the wife drops into her stereotype position, and becomes our slave, our whichever. But I definitely understand women's resentment, I fully accept all their arguments, but where I extend it and take the argument on is, if we just argue simplistically for women's emancipation and liberation without taking to task the actual causes and effects of their suppression, it won't necessarily bring about the liberation, or change society in any fashion.

Men and women are more alike in my opinion than what we are led to believe by the normal accepted sterotype roles. For instance what we require is more women managers, employers, to prove equality. It wouldn't bother me to work for a woman. I like to see women exercise their individuality and butt the system, including me.

I'm known as something of a sexist as a matter of fact. Me and my wife we fell into the stereotype roles. She stays at home and I go out to work.

In fact, a number of the men interviewed who said they were supporters of women's lib also said, like Godfrey, that they had not managed to work out the details in their own lives. They admitted it was hard for them to change a way of life and thought which was not only ingrained but also to their obvious advantage.

Bob put the popular male view that men need women to look after them; how else could they accomplish their work?

Although many men in theory are ardent supporters of women's lib, in practice it's very difficult. In my case, thinking about it, I can always quote the wife of William Blake, the painter, who was totally and completely devoted to her husband's career, or so one was told. She was the complete slave. Well, that I disapprove of, but had she not been that, it's quite likely that Blake wouldn't have been the considerable creator that he was. And so there's always this suspicion that my full creative ability has been, so to speak, held back because of this theoretical belief in women's lib. I don't think it's led to enormous complications in my case – it's always tempting to say that one could have done better than one has done, but there are other reasons for this in my case. But I think I know of cases where this has happened, where men's careers have been positively interrupted and not borne fruit because of this. Marriage, or a relationship with another person, obviously has its positive value in one's life. But the fact is that marriage leads to all kinds of things, like property, like children. If the wife demands so much freedom that gradually she unloads more and more of the practical work in the house, for instance, on to the husband, then the husband is held back in his world.

Ronald, a VAT inspector, thought that the right reaction to feminism, to which he was moderately sympathetic, was to learn which girls in the office were particularly sensitive to the whole question and to take care not to offend them.

You're perhaps not so selfish as you were, with things like nude calendars about the place. But here in this office we're discriminatory because the women have soft toilet paper and the men have hard. The civil service itself has improved because when I first started working, if a girl got married she had to resign from her job, and hope she'd be re-employed. It's altered now and there is equality.

George had trained women for the police; he saw them as complex and devious characters who already had a great deal of power over men in getting their own way, and thought they had much to lose by becoming token men.

I think women's lib was a good thing. I thought it had to be done, because I think that women have so much to offer, but not in straight competition with men. Women are trying to be so much more than they are. If a woman comes into this job, she immediately is competing with men, therefore she feels she's got to be a little bit masculine. When I used to be at training school, I said we're losing these women because we're turning them into big hulking stormtroopers. We mustn't do that. Instead of giving them drill, we should be teaching them how to use make-up, use their feminine sort of wiles and all the rest of it. And use what God has given them in the best possible way.

For some men role reversal was the norm – they had done for years the jobs normally relegated to women. Alec, the funeral director, ran the family company and did all the housework when his wife, who died recently, became bedridden.

I'm not sure that I'm the right person to ask about feminism. Looking at it from the other point of view, I've done all the housework and cooking – the feminine side of life I've coped with for so many years that I've no difficulty about it. I think the lunatic fringe of feminism is worrying. I get annoyed when I see the word 'chairman' avoided. To me, 'man' is mankind, and I don't mind if you have a man chairman or a woman chairman, at all. But I think chairperson and spokesperson is ridiculous and that the people who perpetrate this are doing their own cause harm. As far as we were concerned in our house, everything was joint. It never struck us otherwise. I'd like a penny for every nappy I've changed, both with children and grandchildren, but I know that up north that would be terrible. I didn't mind doing the housework as long as Pat was in sight, I could get on with anything as long as we were together. I can't say that I liked it – there's no soul about using a hoover, I suppose, but on the other hand, you are aiming for an improvement in the appearance.

Few men enjoyed women's chores. Cyril, a fashion designer in his mid-fifties, took this argument to its logical conclusion and encouraged his wife to leave the house and become more liberated. His comments about the problems brought on by women's lib seemed particularly apt.

I married very young an upper-class, convent-educated girl. She was very shy, reserved and proper. I suppose she appealed to me because she had led such a sheltered life – quite the opposite of mine. I'm afraid I got bored with that rather quickly, but we're still together.

I remember back in the sixties, way before women's lib, longing for her to work – to have an interest beyond the house, me and the kids. I positively pushed her into working for a photographer.

I have always been pretty sympathetic to women's lib. I like working with women; in fact, I prefer it. Being in the fashion business, of course, makes it much easier. Women are incredibly conscientious. They're marvellous sellers – they have no shame or embarrassment about business deals. They're like first-generation immigrants, they will do anything.

One thing I don't like about women and that is being attacked by them for what other men have done to them, or didn't allow them to do. They do have this annoying habit of lumping all men together. But, yes, I'm on their side.

I sometimes think that women have two voices: a soprano and a contralto in the same person; the one romantic, highly strung, sometimes 'difficult', and the other practical, realistic, sometimes quite 'hard'. I've always found it difficult with some women to know what the score is, as it were, Are we singing in the same opera? The trouble with feminism from a man's point of view is that the rules have changed. You are brought up by mothers and teachers to follow the rule book in life. I was brought up to be respectful to women. My role was to be the breadwinner, the hunter who went out and brought back the food. And then, wham, women started talking dirty at dinner parties and wanted you to share the household chores and resign from your club if women weren't allowed as members.

When our kids grew up, my wife had a strong women's lib line. She came out of her shell. I said I was prepared to do half the boring work if she was prepared to do half the bread-winning. There was part of me that longed to get out of the rat race. On every holiday I used to daydream about just staying on and never going back to the office. I don't think women always realize what a grind a man's life can be. I'm not sure if they really want the unpleasantness of working with a lot of hard-faced men. Most men's jobs are pretty grubby one way or another. It's quite a grind pulling in £25,000 a year as I do. I have to be polite to people I don't like, nice to the chairman, mind my Ps and Qs. Yes, sir, no, sir – all that bit.

In the mid 1970s my wife was doing very well as a photographer – she was earning a fair bit. But she got bored with it and suddenly decided to take up some university course. Now a man could never do that. It was a luxury – I envied her the freedom of choice. Sometimes I am a bit jealous of women. Perhaps I was for women's lib because I thought it would be a liberation for men too, but it hasn't really worked out like that, has it? I think women have won a few deserved victories but the recession has killed the whole thing. From what I see of younger girls in this business, they're not interested in liberation, it's not an issue.

Most of the men were not very sympathetic to women's complaints about female stereotypes in advertising or the media; they thought it unnecessary to complain about something so slight. Some of them thought this concentration on women's looks was flattering and said women would be the first to complain if men stopped noticing them. But Tony, a thirty-year-old solicitor with sympathy for women's hatred of stereo-typing, said:

Of course I can see why women become feminists and I think the only real solution is an economic revolution of some kind. I've got no objections whatever to pictures of women with beautiful bodies, or men with beautiful bodies. We ought to like ourselves as much as possible. What is so objectionable is the industrialization of that. A woman has become her hair colour; everywhere you look women are cut up into pieces. Look at the hoardings – it's like an anatomy lesson. Look at all the women's magazines – it's there on every page; the legs, the breasts, the hands, the eyes, the nose. It's an identikit. Men never experience themselves like that. The women used commercially like this have no identity whatever. It's the same with pornography. In the pornographic films the woman is just an image of sexual availability – she's not a person. And women who look at those films are being asked to identify with the subordinated women, the passive and beautiful object. The difference for men is that, although there are male sex symbols, they are a symbol of power and aggression; they have control over their own destiny, control of other people.

Jake, a painter aged thirty-two, charts the history of the feminist movement through its effect on his wife. In so doing he bears out the comments of Walter, the train driver, that such movements have a political basis.

My sense of women's lib has changed quite dramatically since those discussions in the mid seventies that exploded at every dinner table. The arguments then seemed to me to be more basic . . . to do with the oppression of marriage, and the economic argument then called the tune. It was all about jobs for women, women wanting to spend less time at home, how cooking and looking attractive were a trap. My wife was then going through a number of great changes. She was evolving all the time. First she was involved with the Labour Party, then moved on to the feminist wing of the Labour Party and the women's movement. She helped set up a women's centre and was struggling to get crèches provided for working mothers. She was in touch with the militant wing though always rather on the edges of that.

British feminism – unlike the American movement – is rooted in British socialism and Marxism. She was at odds with some feminists here because she believed in the wages for housework movement. But feminists had broadened their horizons into wider social questions and ecological concerns, and she had been going along that route without even knowing it. She became interested in the arguments about nuclear weapons, and all these things seemed like a violence done to the earth by men. So women had to try and preserve it. During this time she refused to get married because she saw it as a trap. In fact we broke up because we couldn't reconcile the differences between us. She had been married before and she had two children, but she didn't want traditional family life with all its patriarchal constraints.

There began to be a growing concern and talk about the family and children. In America it had all been seen rather differently. They felt that family life and bringing up children was difficult and rewarding, a very complicated business, but that it had been given a very low status. There are many women in their late thirties who now believe that not having children stands between them and happiness. Betty Friedan was right when she said that the women who had chosen to work and have children end up with facing the worst of all worlds. They have little time to spend with the kids and are working like mad to keep abreast of the competition at work.

A lot of the early ideas of women's lib were *reactive*: I'm not going to look beautiful, or be caught up in the home; then came the more complicated ideas of, for instance, childbearing as an idea of strength. According to the *New Statesman* the number of men who change nappies has risen in the last ten years by a colossal percentage.

I think a lot of these ideas found their way through magazines – all those issues that dealt with women's right to work and violence had a huge effect. For my wife and me it was a reactive time, very hard to be reconciled to the idea of marriage. For her, fathers and husbands were objects of mistrust. How could I place myself within all this? She had two children, which meant accepting family life. It became clear to women that a number of changes could and should be made. I think it's amazing that men have changed as much as they have.

Men have changed. Women's lib has opened up their lives in indirect ways. It's opened up the possibility for men to be fathers – unashamed of talking about their children. Even in those men who were hostile to it all, I've noticed changes – for instance in the politics of conversation; there's a new awareness among my friends of who's talking and who's listening and who's interrupting whom.

Unemployment and the recession have changed the situation and one can see what's almost a collusion between the feminists, who are now talking about the importance of family life, and that book [*The Subversive Family*] by Ferdie Mount, Mrs Thatcher's adviser, on the family as the defender of freedoms against the state.

During the 1970s I became very confused and could not see the world clearly any more. I couldn't see things except through the angry eyes of the feminists. Every little thing looked like an example of patriarchy and male dominance. Men hogged the conversation at dinner parties, they behaved in a condescending way to women, laughed at them, belittled them, trivialized their remarks. I became very obsessed. It's awful to be in the grip of a single idea like that. There were other polarities to that of men and women which I ignored, such as rich and poor, age and youth. I felt completely in its grip, it took everything else over. My work was affected. The problem seems to be that those on the left who wanted to make social changes on the basis of reason, could not comprehend that the self grows out of a number of perhaps undesirable psychological roots. They failed to understand that the self is formed by the very thing they were trying to destroy. Many feminists who grew up in the 1950s carry round in their head a strong image of their father. Their sexual fantasies may well be masochistic, and I would be in great trouble with the left for saying this, but it's not a contradiction for a feminist to have masochistic tendencies – those responses in her are automatic and uncontrollable. That's what she is, and no theory will change that. Patriarchy does shape people's eroticism, men's and women's. Just as many men want to dominate women, many women want to be overwhelmed by men. Patriarchy has made them this way. The fact is that the left is in disarray. The liberal consensus that dominated the talk of the intelligentsia in the mid 1970s has disintegrated. The inadequacy of the left is its inability to cope with the messiness of the human heart, and feelings.

So many women now go out to work that men have had to accept enormous changes. My earnings keep and pay for six people at the moment. I never found domestic work much of a problem – I'd lived on my own for years, I enjoy cooking and am fond of an ordered household. Recently we got married, which looks very conventional. My wife has just had a baby. We arrived at this point in a complicated, roundabout way and after many years. I work in her old flat, so that I can concentrate. She is at home, and no longer working for the time being. We have a cleaner and someone to help look after the children, so it all looks pretty conventional. She's said to me she now feels that the home is her source of strength, and that she doesn't find it demeaning to fulfil the role of wife and mother. She wants to run it well. It's a question of giving people their true status. We are lucky we can make our own timetable and arrange things as we like. In fact the household jobs get divided up in a pretty traditional way. I find I do the dirty, heavy chores, the dustbins, bits of carpentry, mending things; she organizes the food, cleaning and the children. If the baby cries in the night one of us gets up – usually whoever wakes first. It's taken us years to get to this point: we don't argue over who does what, we just accept that these things have to be done.

There is a major difference between men and women and it's concerned with work. Men *are* the jobs they do; it's an old cliché but it's true. Their work defines so much about them – without it many just disintegrate. For women being is more important than doing.

But we should celebrate the differences between us, work from our centres of competence. I'm not in favour of the androgynous approach. I don't want men and women to pretend they're the same.

The earthquake which has transformed the lives and horizons of so many women over the last twenty-five years has also opened up deep crevasses for men, leaving them shaken and confused. The old clearcut stereotypes of male and female are changing and for many men the answer is to close ranks in the old order that they understood, to defend themselves behind the armour of self-confessed male chauvinism. Some admit to feeling threatened but are unable to make any suggestions towards a new male role. A few admit that new attitudes and behaviour are called for but are uncertain what form they should take, and consider that such a conversion would be painful and probably impossible for the majority.

Cyril, a bookseller aged sixty-six, wryly observed that it might mean 'that men are on the way out. Women will learn to do perfectly well without them, and what then?'

Chapter Seventeen

CHANGE – THE NEW MEN?

Some men are beginning to voice their rejection of the male stereotype, for they are outgrowing the uncomfortable straitjacket of traditional masculinity, the pressure of hierarchical progression at work, the masculine preference for logical thought rather than feeling, the harsh competitive nature of their world, and the constant need to prove themselves, to do rather than to be. I don't believe all men want to change their lives, need to change them or are even capable of changing them, but there are many who could gain from a revolution in their lives, and that may mean a revolution for us all.

Some men have already experimented with a new style of life. These are not models that every man could copy, but they illustrate some of the advantages of change, from a a man's point of view, into what might be called 'The New Man'.

John and his wife are both in their thirties. They are both teachers, they have been married for over ten years and have a young son:

When we got married we drew up a contract, and got it signed and sealed by our solicitor. We wanted to try and define what our relationship should be and how we should conduct our life together. It was partly because of what was happening to our parents' marriages at the time and also those of other couples we knew. We agreed that we would re-read the contract every six months.

When I was single I was not particularly sympathetic to feminism until I met my wife. She believed in its practicalities very strongly, and she was the prime mover behind our contract. She felt women had much more to lose in marriage and long-term relationships than men, and she said quite clearly that she didn't want the traditional woman's role.

The first point in the contract was that she would keep her own name, and that everything in our life would be shared fifty-fifty. That not only included housework, but bringing up any children we might have, the decision on where we lived, and how and when we worked. This would allow both to have a career and neither would have automatic priority.

We decided to work in blocks of about three years, turn and turn about, and we are lucky to be in professions where this has been possible. This started with my wife teaching and freelancing, when I was doing a part-time higher degree and teaching part-time.

When our son was born my wife stayed at home for a year, and I went out to work.

We have divided the child rearing fifty-fifty as much as we can. We think it is important for our son and good for him not to see either of us as the sole breadwinner. We both cook, we both clean, we both do all the jobs in the house.

Under the agreement each person was allowed to lead their own independent life. They should be free to do what they wanted, as long as they let the other person know, and as long as it was not threatening to the other. For instance, at a simple level, as I am looking after our son at the moment, I need to know when she's coming home from work, and if she's away at a conference, how long it will be.

As far as sexual friendships are concerned, they are tolerated. We have always relied on honesty with each other, though we are both aware that an affair with someone else could lead to something bad. We would not have affairs with close friends, or people we work with. Certainly we would not discuss it before, but we might tell afterwards.

The block system has not worked absolutely on the three-year basis. One of the problems is that my wife is less able to re-enter her career at the senior level teaching her particular subject than I am. I teach English, and it's the sort of job I can dip in and out of and yet take up quite senior posts. We felt that my wife should build up her skills as much as possible so that they would be recognized as highly marketable, and she could go back into teaching at a higher point than is the rule at the moment.

Another point in our contract was that we would always keep talking to each other, and that we should try and grow parallel to each other rather than at a tangent, as can so easily happen. I am not the first to initiate it, but as we have kept talking to each other and have grown equally, when we do reach a crisis point, we find we are fairly near to each other anyway. And there are periodic crises. For instance, it's all very well laying out these roles on a fifty-fifty basis, but we have both already built up skills that we are good at. I am better at do-it-yourself and looking after the car than she is. Our childhood and growing up has given us these skills, and however much we wanted to, we found we couldn't transfer them. At one point I thought I was taking on more household work than I should be, so we have needed to sit down and work these things out in the best and fairest way.

We have both acquired new skills and there are some things, like looking after our child and cooking, which are entirely interchangeable. I don't feel I have lost any of my masculinity, and nobody has ever said that or hinted it to me, even close friends who are more traditional men, but I think I may seem less forceful. I certainly feel less confident than I did before. I have found the switch between teaching and being at home a difficult one. Being with a child all day is a very different world to the work of teaching.

I do sometimes get jobs abroad in the private language sector, and then our son goes to a child-minder, but I don't confess when I am working that I am a house parent. There's a strong belief that if a man is only working part-time he can't be as good. That's a lack of confidence because I can see mine is not yet an expected way to live. If people ask me about my life, I have to judge quickly whether they are the sort that will understand if I tell them.

If we have another child, my wife will stop work again and

be at home for a period of time. Though the more I spend at home, the less interested I am in being the breadwinner.

We do not talk about our contract to many close friends as I think they would find it threatening. When I look at other people of our age, I sometimes feel confused. They have got two cars and a double oven, and in one sense I would love the financial security they have got, but what I think is that they will never have the experience I am enjoying so much. I think it is an experience that twenty years ago would have been rather unexpected. It certainly differs from *my* family life and my own upbringing.

What is good about life for me at the moment is that I get a great deal of enjoyment out of working with my son. We do things around the house together. I take him to playgroup and often stay there and am now on the committee.

I see things more in terms of management roles. Although my wife is as well able to look after our son as I, her role at the moment is to earn the money and pursue her career. My job is the management of our child, to initiate everything that happens to him during the day, to organize his food and his play. In fact, my wife defers to me about what should happen to him. Whoever is out working baths him at night and gets him up in the morning; he wakes about 6.30 to 7.00. If I have been away at all, he turns to my wife rather than to me, and I do get pangs of envy if he goes to her. But he and I share so much together at the moment. There are fights and struggles, but I enjoy the life.

I have also got something that other men don't have, the chance to withdraw from the urge to succeed in whatever they are caught up in. Doing this job involves me in a depth of communication with my wife about understanding our son and of being able to listen to her problems at work which I would not have had if I hadn't been liberated from the pressures of having to succeed.

I can't compare this feeling with anything as I have never lived in any other way.

I am much more sensitive than I was. I have learnt more about women and respect them in a way I may not have before. Most of my new contacts are women. All my activities with my son bring me into contact with them. I can see that in meetings at the playgroup they defer to me as a man because they think I have skills different from theirs. This has affected the way I conduct myself; I am more silent in a group of women than I ever was before. I allow them to speak! I have learnt a lot from them – a good deal of common sense in child care. I meet mostly farmers' wives, and they have all been very welcoming to me. I think I know more about women and recognize skills in them more than I have ever done before.

John and his wife are trail-blazers, but others too had arrived at much the same position in their life, where sharing menial household tasks and bringing up the children jointly had become a natural part of life, though only often after a great personal struggle for the man. One of the reasons for this struggle is that mothers pattern in their sons a dependence on them as women, which most men cannot and will not escape. And what will happen to John's son? Will he combine masculine and feminine traits, strength and softness – will he become bewildered, or will he continue this new way of life?

Jeff is thirty-five and lectures at one of the new universities. His wife, who is doing post-graduate work, is forty, and their daughter is five.

I had no experience in childhood of the life I am leading now.

I became aware of what women were saying most actively through my wife, and I think it is rather important that it happened that way rather than just by my reading works by feminists, though I had done that too.

I didn't join a men's consciousness-raising group because of my sense that the changes necessary need to be part of everyday life, and there is the danger in such a group that the group activity can act as a substitute. Men's consciousness can be raised in one place and not in any other. I also thought men had enough ways of clubbing together, and there was the danger of getting hived off from women again. There's something rather protective about such a group, it's not risk-taking enough. I think it's significant that many of those groups did not last long.

At first there was a great struggle going on between us over the organization of domestic life and its relationship to professional life. I had to be browbeaten out of my deeply held assumption that came from my upbringing that women were there to look after me. I think childishness is a definite aspect of masculinity. When I was a student at Cambridge, although I had lived on my own, it tended to be communally, where women quite often did the domestic work. It was a difficult change for me to make, though now when I'm doing the housework, I can find it therapeutic. It helps me not to think for a while and it's part of your life, though it may stop you from doing other things you would like to do. I have been learning what it feels like to be a woman and helping with my daughter has been very important.

I was there at the birth and during labour and think that was very important to me. I would not depict life as a rosy ideal, there are still unsolved problems which centre round professional work and domestic work.

I am very sceptical of people who talk as though they have come through in a relationship, but I think I have learned that it is very easy for marriage to become bound by habit and habitual assumptions. If you live with a woman you need to be able to negotiate, to talk, and be conscious all the time of what is happening.

At first my wife always initiated conversations – now I feel that's changing, I feel as often as not it's me. Our daughter is brought up equally by both of us. She goes to playgroup, and on the odd occasion that we both need to be out, to a crèche. It's an enormous pleasure to me to watch her grow and change. I feel all sorts of love for her, though caring in this way can be difficult for a man to admit. It's certainly a bit risky in one's professional life to let it become evident. It makes you vulnerable. I suppose I fear that others might use my emotion as a weapon. At least small children don't come back at you. Because on this experience, there are things I can't talk to other people about. They will talk about it in a cryptic and

315

joking way, but not too many are interested in a full exploration of our experience. Perhaps they have more important things to think about. Although there must be a great many men in a similar situation to my own, I often find myself to be the only man in a group of women, and women seem to find it extremely difficult to talk to me about children. They don't regard it as something a man knows about.

The problem for me is that it leaves me feeling a bit isolated. I partly belong to a network of professional men and partly to a network of women. I think I know more about many things than a lot of men do, and I feel more independent as a result. As I care for our daughter, I feel better able to cope and care for myself. Other men might get into a panic. It's given me a strength that's difficult to communicate.

It sometimes irritates me that people talk to my wife about children and not me. It makes me angry because I feel I know as much.

One of the other things that happened is that my relationship with a few men has become very important to me. They understand this peculiar sense of loss I have experienced. I can only explain it by saying that previously I had a rather powerful complacency to the world of women. Women were there for men and not for themselves. Having learned that women are not at men's disposal has meant a sense of loss. There's a sense also of exclusion from feminist activities, exclusion on the grounds of my sex.

Feminists are now lots of things, but I have experienced that sort of attack women make on men and felt very guilty, and at a loss when women say men are to blame for everything. I don't feel that any more. There's a lot going on in my head; a revolt has occurred. I am a man and that I am not changing.

I do think women need to change, in that I hope the excess of hostility towards men felt by certain groups in the feminist movement will diminish. I hope women will be more able to trust men.

I am sure it is important for men to look into their feelings about their work, about family life and about the women they live with, and I'm sure from my experience men should be more involved in bringing up their children.

For those men who want to share the upbringing of the children, it *can* merely be a matter of choice and reorganization of their time. But inevitably it is spare time, out-of-work time, because as soon as that choice conflicts with the demands of their job then the problems posed are likely to be much more complex, and often beyond any individual man's control.

John is a barrister of thirty-four who has always been pretty left-wing. He has a love-hate relationship with his work because of its authoritarian overtones and because it is a very anti-woman profession. Women still find it hard to progress in such a hidebound world, and an aspiring male barrister needs a willing slave at home because his hours are so unpredictable.

If any change can happen for men, work is essential to that change because just as women are imprisoned in their homes, men are imprisoned in their work. You spend all your time as a man working to bring home money. It is mutually imprisoning. The only hope is that if women can escape, so can men. Man's social identity comes entirely from his work and not from being a man, but my problem, like many others, is that I can't escape from a job because of the problem of money. Very exceptional people can make that escape, or those who are forced to by unemployment. If it doesn't change, I think we are all on a treadmill to destruction. I see it as a choice between socialism and barbarism, men becoming agents of barbarism. Men are in the clutches of a great machine and on the treadmill of maintaining their standard of living. As they get richer and that standard increases then it gets worse. It is very hard for men to relate to children in this system. They don't ever have a proper relationship. You can do it, of course, if you are willing to be an unofficial football coach or a boy scout leader. Most kids are fatherless, most men are not fathers.

317

But *he* had to be both mother and father to his two small children for a time because his wife fell in love with another woman and went off to America with her. She had been going through a very experimental time and had taken the extreme lesbian position of rejecting all men, including her young male children.

My first reaction had to be to get the boys into a nursery, and this is much easier for a man. If you are a woman and you take your children to a nursery they say, Can you come back in six months' time when we will have a place, but if you are a bloke they take pity on you and they said, Do you want to leave them now or will you come back tomorrow?

For a time I gave up my job so that I could be around when they needed me. I already lived in a communal household where there were two other women who were partly surrogate mums, and that helped. Now I have a new relationship and the boys have a kid brother.

I had belonged briefly to a Men Against Sexism group – all those men down on their knees with Marx in one hand and a scrubbing brush in the other. We worked to provide crèche facilities when women met together, and men tried to regain their lost power by being nice to women. I objected in the end to the dishonesty of men who were not willing to specify *their* particular interests and made no attempt to see how if women gained power that would affect the power men had. Men will have to give up some privileges, but will gain in the whole richness of their experience. A lot of men in the group said, Oh God, we have behaved so badly to women. How can we make amends? But I am not into the politics of guilt. I can't look at the relationship between men and women theoretically or woodenly any more because of my experience. For most men it is still a theoretical question. They can't see it in everyday terms.

Many women are lucky enough to have a strong sense of their own identity, which some men seem to lack, and it is derived from their diverse relationships with other human beings – their children, their friends, and other women on whom they rely and with whom they share all their joys and troubles. Because of the many roles they are required to play, women have to learn and practise a number of skills, some very humdrum, that give them a daily sense of purpose and well-being. Many men, even the most successful in the world's eyes, do not have those experiences and lack that feeling of well-being. But though it would not suit all, some men have found it by swapping roles with their wives and becoming house-husbands.

Martin is thirty-four. He trained as a commercial horticulturalist, and worked for some time in the commercial glasshouse unit at an agricultural college. His wife is a barrister with chambers in London. They have two young children, and decided that they would bring them up without the help of nannies.

We waited some time to have children until my wife was well established in her chambers. I wasn't enjoying the job I had very much so I was happy at the prospect of staying at home and looking after our first son when he was nine months old. I had involved myself in his upbringing from the beginning, so it wasn't a shock. And we'd always taken everything in turns, so there were never any problems. I call myself a house-husband, I'm at home all the time, and I do everything a housewife would do. When we first got married it was obvious that my wife wasn't too good at housework, so if I wanted things kept to a certain standard it was common sense that I should help do them. I did have to learn how to cook – my wife is a very good cook and likes to take over the cooking at the weekends.

We are constantly up against the standard stereotyping. Recently we went to buy a washing machine and the sales girl was intent on explaining all its advantages to my wife even though I would be using it. When we paid, the man at the desk was keen to tell *me* of the six months' free credit. When he filled in the form and asked me what I did and I said house-husband, it obviously caused problems, and my wife had to fill in the form – I was nothing where credit was concerned. I don't mind at all that my wife earns the money. It all goes into a central fund, we both have cheque books and I spend what we need. It's no different from my having subsidized her when she was training. I suppose I'm different from a lot of other men, I've never been a man's man, and don't go to pubs with other men, I don't have a close male friend. We all go out together and are a very close-knit family unit. My wife isn't so dedicated to her career she has no time for family life. She works a very long day – anything from six in the morning until after seven at night, but her ambition is curbed by her love of the children. She spends most of her weekend with me looking after them.

It isn't possible that we should all be the same, but I know a lot of men who'd love to do what I do. I count myself very lucky. I talk to other fathers I've met through the playgroup I help at, and they're envious, but they can earn more than their wives and money must come first. I'm sure it's the financial aspect which prevents most men from doing what we've done. It may change but most men have no choice. Neither do most women for that matter, they are expected to produce and look after children, and they have no choice. I would imagine a lot of women do not want to be housewives or mothers. Some women would accept that they are not very good at looking after children – they're not interested. My wife admits that she could not cope with it. It is a strain at times: I always thought I was very calm, but children push you to the limit. There are times when I've had to leave the room to avoid hitting them. Most men don't realize what hell it can sometimes be for a woman.

I probably won't go back to full-time work even when they go to school – we both think there should be someone here to greet them from school. There are a lot of men around who have never even changed a nappy, but I wonder whether women may often be their own worst enemies by preventing men from sharing the children at a deeper level.

There were other men like this who had found new ambitions and satisfactions from questioning and changing their traditional roles, men who have left well-paid jobs with large companies and the world of men and joined the world of their family to take charge of their own lives at last; men who have grown tired of the demands of ambition and refused the promotion that would mark their worldly success, despite pressure from their bosses and the incredulity of their colleagues. There is yet a new generation of young men, some not yet in their twenties, who have stepped off the ladder at the bottom rung. Not just because theirs is the generation of despair and unemployment, but because they are men of talent and energy who wish to direct their lives in a less acquisitive, less competitive and less orthodox manner than their fathers. There are men who are not ashamed to be seen as gentle and caring, who realize that measuring themselves to every sphere of their lives in constant competition with other men is a futile and immature activity, which only helps to underline their insecurities. There are men who can form friendships with women undistorted by the idea of sexual conquest, and who are sympathetic to the needs of women to assert their own rights. These are men who value the positive and separate qualities in women and are not threatened by them.

Chapter Eighteen

CONCLUSION

I had always thought that, with a few obvious differences, man and woman were much alike, human beings with similar talents, anxieties, capacities and failings. What surprised me most about listening to so many men talking about themselves was how *completely* different they were from women in a number of significant ways. Men and women manage to grow up in the same society, and yet remain part of different subcultures.

My overall impression is that the world men inhabit, and from which we women are often excluded, is rather bleak. It is a world full of doubt and confusion, where vulnerability must be hidden, not shared; where competition, not co-operation, is the order of the day; where men sacrifice the possibility of knowing their own children and sharing in their upbringing, for the sake of a job they may have chosen by chance, which may not suit them and which in many cases dominates their lives to the exclusion of much else. As a woman, I was struck by the sense of detachment many men feel from those around them, and saddened by it. I am used to women practising the skills that break down these barriers, and know what pleasures this can bring; but many men see no use in trying to understand themselves or others better, because they believe human nature is unchanging. They also mistrust the exploration of feelings and see it as a time-wasting activity indulged in by over-talkative women.

Men have extraordinary intellectual, scientific and creative talents, but I felt sympathy for those who fumbled through life exhibiting clumsiness in the management of their social relations, sympathy for their families and colleagues who suffered at their hands, and sympathy for those who can't bring themselves to say 'I love you' because it is giving too much away. Intellectual giants are often emotional pygmies. As Koestler said, 'It's man who can leave the Earth and land on the Moon but cannot cross from East to West Berlin.' Many men simply lack the basic skills of communication in some important aspect of their lives, be it at work, at home, with others or with themselves.

Though men are constantly proving their bent for adaptation in the scientific field, they seem less flexible than women and far more threatened by the inevitable changes in their routine required by average family life, and coping with children. Men are often mystified by their wives' apparent need to feel closer and more intimate and are at a loss for a reply to such questions as 'what are you thinking', 'what are you feeling'. Many men interviewed seemed ambivalent about the need for dependence on, and intimacy with, one person, and found this expectation in their wives rather suffocating. It would seem that men spend less time thinking about their wives than their wives do about them, a fact which may be borne out by the difficulty many had in giving any sort of description of their wife, except in the vaguest of terms.

As far as children are concerned, equally shared parenthood is a reality in very few homes. The stereotypes handed on are still of mother, caring, warm and tender; and father, aggressive, competitive, and seeking achievement outside the home. These stereotypes are unlikely to change for some time to come, and although many fathers talk of the pleasure of time spent with their children, for them it is a part-time activity rather than an occupation.

Although often uncomfortable with their role, men certainly see themselves as 'top dog', and most want to keep it that way. This was justified more often than not by the theory that nature has made man the strong one, the hunter, the fighter and protector, and any change in this system would overthrow a natural and desirable balance. Many men were fixed on the idea that women are different because they have periods and babies. So, as there was no changing that, there was no point in trying to change anything else, either.

However, there often appeared to be a gap between man's dominant role in society and his constant personal fear that he had not come up to other people's expectations – had got it wrong with his wife, or been found out to be less able, less clever, less in command of his job than others thought. Many men feared that someone might see behind the game they were playing, the role they were so busily projecting. A successful advertising executive said he felt he had never done an honest day's work in his life, and wondered how soon it would be that others realized it too.

Some professional men admitted that they put on a certain persona with their city suit and, just as they would not wear sports clothes to the office, they camouflaged themselves to fit in with corporate life. Returning from Birmingham one day on the train I talked to an unusually candid civil servant from the Ministry of Defence. A northerner, with a good sense of humour and love of irreverence, he felt stifled by his fellow civil servants who on the whole, and no matter how senior, were at pains never to express a definite opinion that might be seen as taking sides. They lived, in his view, a timorous and carefully guarded professional life, of which he did not see the point.

I expected to find many more men than I did rebelling against the male role. But many had simply not considered their role as men, nor when they did think about it did they readily see that there was any alternative.

A lot of men mentioned that statistically men die five years younger than women and yet get their pensions later; this seemed an unfairness which should be corrected. They associated their earlier deaths with the stress of management or their jobs, and what some called the stress 'of being the other half'.

A few men were acutely tired of having to play the confident dominant role. In relationships, both young and old felt the fear of rejection, and some just wished women would book their tables in the restaurant, light their cigarettes and take over a bit sexually too. Some men said they were constantly being told, 'You're the man, you go and do it', and were beginning to wonder quite why it was always them.

When asked what it meant to be a man, I was surprised at the large and varied group who used the word 'selfish' when answering. With very few exceptions, all the men interviewed demonstrated a high degree of egocentricity that was tightly bound up with what they thought it was to be a man. Sometimes male selfishness was mentioned half apologetically and with overtones of guilt but it was often stated as a mere fact of maleness. 'I have to think about myself because I've got to get on in the world, and if I'm not selfish I'll be held back' is a paraphrase of what dozens of men said in explanation of their maleness.

Many of them seemed uneasy about aspects of their life in a way they found hard to put into words. Some said it was in the area of relationships with others, particularly with women and their wives, but the overall feeling was that they were confused about their role as a man. What was it they were supposed to be doing, thinking, and more often, feeling?

And if I give the impression that men, though in positions of power and control, have got everything organized to suit them, this is not so. Many men are aware that something is missing from their lives: an uneasy feeling that they may not be going in quite the right direction, that their lives can be full of too many regrets – regrets about not understanding the nature of close friendships; regrets at suppressing instead of developing the human qualities of tenderness, gentleness and empathy because their world does not reward such talents; surprise at a wife's bitterness when he announces that he is leaving her for someone else.

As a result some men *are* beginning to voice their rejection of the male stereotype, for they are outgrowing the uncomfortable straitjacket of traditional masculinity.

It was clear that many men feel that they do not understand women, and yet dare not get too close to other men. They will often admit that they prefer the company of women because they recognize that women are less competitive, but they are driven into the company of other men because they feel ill-equipped to deal with the emotional demands that women make on them. Men cannot live on their own, but they are lonely; they have allowed some of their deepest feelings to fossilize because to exhibit them is unmanly; they do not practise the art of loving because at best it makes them feel too vulnerable and at worst they know that to put someone else first means you have to come second, and few men enjoy doing that.

Women may be surprised by the sense of detachment men can exhibit in their sexual affairs, their ability to shut them off in sealed compartments. For many men marriage and married love become a routine that lacks secrecy, excitement or innovation, and they admit they enjoy the chase more than the certainty of capture. Once they know a woman is available they lose some, and sometimes all, interest in her. Their anxieties about sex were manifold, and often centred on one thing they had never been able to discuss with the person to whom it might matter most. Many had never felt able to talk to their wives about whether what they did in bed satisfied them. Some said they thought they were good lovers: 'had never had any complaints' and would think it 'bad-mannered for a woman to make a complaint'.

Understandably therefore, some men say they prefer sex with near strangers, because they have learned the anxieties associated with making love to one to whom they are committed. They also cannot always be bothered to have sex bound up in what they see as some complicated power struggle, nor with someone whose familiarity has bred both children and boredom.

It is clear that men do wish to impose stereotypes on women, by monitoring their looks, their behaviour, their choice to work, and even their involvement in conversation, but it seems to me they do so to try and impose on women the delicacy they themselves are not permitted. The majority of men did not want women to do hard manual labour, to swear or to compete with them in any of the accepted areas of masculine behaviour. The fact that so many women work physically hard all day at home, with children, out shopping and clearing up the mess men leave behind them seemed to escape their notice. Many men still accept the unfair principle of not bothering themselves about the mundane tasks of home and family. Men are not yet used to women arguing their corner, criticizing and holding unshakeable but opposite points of view from them. Hitherto these have been parts played by other men within a well-tried framework of male behaviour. Women who are supposed to be weak have become strong, and men who could once depend without question upon their woman's support and encouragement have found that times and the rules, are changing. However, I *was* surprised by the number of men who thought women more mature than men, more rounded human beings with a greater sense of their own worth. 'Women are too sensible to risk heart attacks for ambition, they're saner and they live longer,' said one. In fact some men seemed to have very little sense of their own value. They could laugh and brag in male company, keep up the appearance of self-confidence and self-importance, but behind the carefully maintained barrier was a fear and loneliness to be shared with no one. At best these feelings might be blurted out in drunkenness and then forgotten.

There are very few men whose lives and attitudes have so far been affected by feminism, though many made it clear they resented aspects of women's equality; and extreme feminism of any descriptiion was unanimously condemned. It seemed that for some their criticisms of feminism stemmed from the ability women have to make men feel inadequate.

There were a small minority of men, on the whole rather well educated, who were anxious that women should be given equal status at work because, they thought, the presence of more women at a senior level would improve the atmosphere and the success of their work-place. These men were entirely sympathetic to the problems facing women in their struggle to become independent persons and thought the unwillingness of the average male to accept the differentness of women was based on both fear and jealousy. Women were beginning to find a freedom and independence which many men feel they do not have. If women are becoming less dependent on men for their needs, then it changes the whole traditional balance of the relationship between them.

There were some men who were ardent supporters of women's lib in theory, but were weak practitioners. There was the man who said his own career had suffered as his increasingly 'liberated' wife had offloaded so much of the practical housework onto him: thus public feminism turned out quite often, men admitted, to be private chauvinism.

But there are changes taking place. There are men who feel that pure ambition which excludes all else is arid. There are men who have found a new closeness to their children, and have helped them keep pace with the inevitable changes in their own lives. Some have encouraged their wives' careers over their own, and are trying to escape the patriarchal and dominant role that fits them all too uneasily. There are men who can experience and understand any emotion a woman might feel, and be proud of it. There are men who want to make changes in their lives and not conform any longer to the expected male roles. Those who have tried have not lost their masculinity, they are not weaker than before though they may feel less confidence in their new life; they talk of unforeseen advantages and pleasures, of new intimatcies and strengths, and of a sense of being in control of their lives in a way they had not experienced before.

Nobody wants men to become women, or even more like women, but they should join women in trying to understand the effects of the dominant male assumptions which underlie our culture. For men are dominant but not free, and a re-evaluation of the masculine role would surely be as beneficial to some men as the feminist revolution has been to some women.

INDEX OF MEN INTERVIEWED

Albert (33; auditor), 279–80

Alec (70s; funeral director), 40–1, 86–7, 251–2, 302–3

Alex (52; university lecturer), 275

Alf (55; trade union official), 44–5, 70–1, 87–8

Allan (70s; artist), 278

Andrew (45; GP), 49–50, 226–7, 255

Andrew (38; hospital orderly), 164, 279

Anthony (34; television producer), 214–7

architect, 165

Arnold (50; redundant company director), 240–1, 245

Arthur (72; journalist), 298

Arthur (70; retired rural dean), 15, 19, 161–2

barrister, 262

Barry (25; musician), 21–2, 198, 274, 296–7

Basil (63; security officer), 89–90, 220

Ben (64; bookmaker), 112, 227

Bernard (72; retired MP), 41–2

Bert (45; unemployed), 233–4

Bill (49; company manager), 289–90

Bill (39; electrician), 106–7

Bill (55; removal man), 64–5, 111–2, 252–3

bishop, 222, 228–9, 264

Bob (58; prison officer), 36–40, 191

Bob (74; retired gynaecologist), 133, 181–5, 257–8, 275, 301

Brian (52; van driver), 117–20, 259

bus driver, 144

cabinet minister, 190, 253–4, 262, 287

chain store chairman, 261

chain store manager, 230

Charles (60; department store chairman), 71–2, 81

Charlie (19; unemployed), 237–8

Chris (25; bank clerk), 51–2, 67, 91, 271

Chris (35; tennis professional), 138–9

civil servant, 324

Clive (36; hotel manager), 137, 165–7, 258, 262–3

Clive (26; policeman), 56–7, 153–8

Colin (46; advertising copywriter), 16, 171–2

Colin (55; sales executive), 143, 250

company chairman, 51

Conservative backbencher, 140

Conservative politician, 261–2

Cyril (66; bookseller), 169, 309

Cyril (50s; fashion designer), 303–4

Dan (46; TUC organizer), 84–5, 92–3, 263, 265, 286

Daniel (30s; writer) 82–3

Danny (35; television retailer), 126–130

David (43; public school master), 83, 92

David (36; in television), 172
Dennis (59; security officer), 20, 55, 87, 165, 192, 279, 287
Derek (31; lecturer in a polytechnic), 173
Derek (30; travelling salesman), 286
Dick (26; milkman), 80
Dominic (44; company manager), 177
Don (56; GP), 80–1, 174–5, 257
Douglas (37; fireman), 59, 294–5

Eastbourne, Lord, 69, 103–6, 114, 287, 297
Eddie (40; carpet layer), 283
Edmund (69; retired school master), 196–8
Edward (48; bank manager), 19, 72–3, 219–20, 230–1, 281
Eric (37; engineering consultant), 108, 142

factory buyer, 288–9
fireman, 288
football manager, 276
Frank (62; professor), 136
Francis (38; convicted of rape), 261
Fred (40; dustman), 54, 89, 140, 158, 189–90, 229
Fred (55; taxi-driver), 84, 290

Gary (50; redundant manager), 243–5
Gavin (32; army officer), 145, 283, 298
Geoff (50; designer), 164
Geoffrey (48; violinist), 79–80, 132
George (35; CID officer), 66, 159–60, 192–3, 276–7, 296, 302
George (38; GP), 124–6
Gerald (49; factory worker), 223–4
Gilbert (33; unemployed), 235–7
Giles (44; insurance broker), 43–4, 90, 109–10, 273
Godfrey (62; shop steward), 225, 299–300

Graham (38; economist), 58, 175–6

Harold (94; retired diplomat), 27, 288
Harry (54; silversmith), 16–7, 170, 195
Henry (25; commodity broker), 280
Henry (50; hotel doorman), 139
Hugh (35; solicitor), 50, 53, 64, 173–4, 293–4

Ian (33; dentist), 15–6, 173

Jack (55; factory buyer), 56
Jack (43; farmer), 23–4, 29
Jack (43; trombone player), 146
Jake (32; painter), 305–9
James (48; company executive), 219, 221–2, 256–7, 263–4, 265–6, 277
James (68; writer and broadcaster), 138, 227
Jeff (35; university lecturer), 231, 314–7
Jeremy (29; estate agent), 29–32, 131–2, 162
Jeremy (29; photographer), 176–7
Jim (46; shopkeeper), 165
Jimmie (38; unemployed, part-time crook), 159
Jo (49; unemployed), 14, 29, 234–5
John (34; barrister), 317–8
John (45; management consultant), 41, 67–8, 77–8, 85, 145, 179, 194–5, 282–3, 290
John (30s; teacher), 310–4
Jonathan (49; sweet company chairman), 160–1
Johnnie (37; criminal), 207–12, 260
Julian (84; author), 138

Keith (24; labourer), 226
Ken (53; fireman), 45
Kevin (35; dustman), 20–1, 178, 226, 287–8

Larry (38; taxi-driver), 133–4
Les (56; engine driver), 212–4

Leslie (49; advertising executive), 27–8, 78–9

Lionel (40; company director), 134, 259

Malcolm (61; barrister), 42, 85

man at a boat race party, 278

Mark (40; car salesman), 82

Martin (34; horticulturalist/house-husband), 319–20

Matthew (45; local government officer), 158, 162–3, 224–5, 284, 285, 293

Maurice (54; in television), 221

member of the government, 143–4

member of the House of Lords, 193–4

Mick (40; in film industry), 15, 93–101, 171, 286–7, 298–9

Michael (44; BBC producer), 90

Mike (51; company executive), 16, 46–7, 73–5, 218, 267–70

murderer, 260

Neil (36; naval officer), 65, 191–2, 283

Nick (40; interior designer), 167–8

Nick (39; police sergeant), 45–6, 110–1, 228

Norman (39; Yorkshire coalminer), 276, 296

old Etonian, 193

Oliver (25; City broker), 137

Patrick (38; probation officer), 47–8, 61–2

Paul (40s; actor), 274

Paul (30s; teacher), 19–20, 175

peer, 141

Peter (52; engineer), 68–9, 163–4

Phil (20; pop singer), 172

Philip (50; tycoon), 168–9

Piers (34; dentist), 280

policeman, 285

Ralph (70s; tycoon), 140–1, 141–2, 277

Ray (19; unemployed), 136–7, 146–7, 239–40

Raymond (90s; retired civil servant), 246

Reginald (52; businessman), 126

Richard (40s; in theatre), 148, 161–2, 179–80, 185–6, 193, 254, 258–9, 272–3, 289

Robert (50; prison governor), 229–30, 266–7

Robert (54; retired commercial traveller), 247

Robin (48; insurance salesman), 35, 122–3

Robin (46; priest), 267

Rodney (42; army officer), 132–3

Roman Catholic monk, 186–7

Ron (48; foreman), 23, 41, 52–3, 62, 86, 189, 254–5, 280–1, 284, 295

Ronald (32; VAT inspector), 26, 91–2, 284, 301–2

Sam (43; wine bar manager), 115–7

Shane (25; male prostitute), 199–205

Sid (37; plumber), 255–6, 282

Simon (35; television commercial producer), 103

Stanley (52; redundant company director), 241–3

Steven (40s; RAF officer), 21, 25–6, 65–6, 77

Stuart (66; retired bank manager), 88, 147

Sydney (72; retired lecturer), 48–9, 137, 144, 147–8, 152–3, 158–9, 292

Terry (25; agricultural labourer), 88, 293

Terry (34; unemployed), 78

Tim (32; coalminer), 134

Tim (51; postman), 62

Toby (23; management trainee), 17–8, 217–8

Tom (44; coalminer), 64, 86, 135, 144, 225, 289, 294

Tony (30; solicitor), 151–2, 250–1, 305

Trevor (45; power station worker), 80

Victor (31; school teacher), 112–3, 205, 272, 283, 286, 289

Walter (54; train driver), 24–5, 28, 63, 135–6, 305

Wilf (36; caretaker), 50–1, 111

William (33; van driver), 53–4, 63, 114–5

Winston (22; unemployed), 238–9, 247

GENERAL INDEX

advertising, female stereotypes in, 304–5

affairs, *see* love affairs

ageing, 272–81

appearance, good looks
of men, 272–81, 286
of women, 145–7, 272, 286–7 305

arguments, *see* disagreements *under* marriage

armed forces, 256
homosexuality in, 191–2
see also Navy; RAF

BBC, 90

bisexuality, 181–5

blacks, 87, 166, 167, 239, 247

brothers and sisters, 14, 17, 23, 26, 29, 32, 236

Campaign for Justice in Divorce, 123

Canterbury, Archbishop of, 9

careers, *see* work

celibacy, 186–7

childhood, 14–27, 28–34, 36

children, 76–101
education of, 84–5, 264
fathers' love for, 267
fathers' role in upbringing, 21–2, 74, 76–84, 85–6, 92–101, 217, 306, 311–20, 323
as reason for marriage, 42
marriage problems due to, 173–4
and broken marriages, 72, 115, 121–30, 258
marriage saved by, 42, 109, 114–5
mothers devoted to, 77, 141
not to have any, 65, 90–1
pleasure in having, 42, 80–4, 280–1
and redundancy, unemployment, 240–2
relations with, difficulty over, 16, 22, 56, 72–3, 74, 76–81 92, 264
sexual behaviour of, 86–90
suicide prevented by, 257

City of London, 90

clothes, dress, of men, 275–8

clubs, 287–8

cooking, 52, 55, 70

crime, 207–12

daughters (*see also* children), 87, 88–9, 90

Deneuve, Catherine, 74

divorce, 21, 38–41, 72–3, 112, 121–30

dress, *see* clothes

education, *see* school

emotions, feelings, 57–8, 131, 139, 249–71, 285

employment, *see* work

Falklands War, 253

Families Need Fathers, 123

family, *see* children; name, family; parents; wives

fathers (*see also* parents), 17–23, 25, 27, 29–32, 56, 218, 236–7, 258

fathers, men as, *see under* children

feelings, *see* emotions

feminism, Women's Lib, 17, 169, 292–309, 311, 316, 329

Friedan, Betty, 306

friends, friendship, 263, 284–5, 289–90, 311
  wives as, 43–4

gays, *see* homosexuals

hair, 273, 274–5

hobbies, outside interests, 46, 47–8, 59, 288; *see also* sport

home, 43–4; *see also* housework

homosexuals, homosexuality (*see also* lesbians), 151–2, 155, 162, 189–205

housework, 53–7, 66, 68, 70

in-laws, 28, 70

interests, outside marriage, *see* hobbies

jewellery, for men, 89, 276, 279, 289

Jews, Jewishness, 29–32, 88

jobs, *see* work

Koestler, Arthur, 323

Laker, Sir Freddie, 9

lesbians, lesbianism, 167, 183, 318

living together, 46, 50, 87, 89

looks, *see* appearance

love, 40, 101, 267; *see also* emotions

love affairs
  of men, 43, 49–50, 61–2, 69, 100, 102–15, 120, 153–8, 163, 311
  of parents, 19, 21
  of wives, 43, 106, 111, 115–18, 174–5, 259, 311
  see also marriage, fidelity in

marriage, 35–60, 87
  disagreements, rows, 57–8, 71
  fear of, 22, 35

fidelity in, monogamy, 42–3, 49, 51, 165, 174; *see also* love affairs
  problems with, 28, 35–40, 45–60, 64–5, 69, 101, 149, 154, 163–4, 171, 173–6, 259, 268–71, 301, 327
  reasons for, advantages of, 35–44
  traditional patterns, changes in, 56–7, 310–17, 319–20
  wedding rings, 279
  see also divorce; living together; wives

media, female stereotypes in, 304–5

men
  different from women, 322
  feminine side of, 138
  good qualities, 12–3, 322–3
  creatures of habit, 249
  new role for, changing attitudes, 292, 297–309, 310–21, 322–9 *passim*
  traditional view of, 8, 249–50, 282–91, 297, 310–21 *passim*
  see also childhood; fathers; *also* clothes; jewellery; work *and other subjects; and under* appearance; love affairs; women

monarchy, royal family, 85, 253

money, 54–5, 228, 290

monogamy, fidelity in marriage, 42–3, 49, 51, 165, 174

mothers (*see also* parents), 14–9, 21–5, 27–33, 78, 238, 239

name, family, 77

nannies, 26–7

Navy, 65, 191–2; *see also* armed forces

opinion, differences of, *see* disagreements *under* marriage

parents (*see also* fathers; mothers), 14–34, 56–7, 76, 94, 223, 234–5, 268–9
  ageing, 27–8

pornography, 181, 183, 305
prostitutes, 161, 163, 185–6
   male, 198–205

RAF, 26, 65–6; see also armed forces
redundancy, see unemployment
Reed, Oliver, 9
religion, 74, 85
retirement, 245–8
rows, see disagreements under
   marriage
royal family, see monarchy

school, education, 26, 36, 84–5, 103,
   172, 182, 193, 264
secretaries, 229
sex, 151–88
   anxieties about, 170–1, 272–3,
      284, 289, 327
   difficulty in discussing, 57–8,
      151–2, 170, 205, 327
   early experience of, 153, 158–63
   fantasizing, 163–7
   important, enjoyable, 137, 178–9
   impotence, 177
   marriage problems with (see also
      love affairs), 50, 57–8, 64,
      148–9, 154–5, 170–1, 172–3,
      327
   perversion, 181
   see also homosexuals; porno-
      graphy
sexism, 286
sisters, see brothers and sisters
sons, men as, see childhood; parents
sport, 12, 30, 47–8, 82, 271, 279–80
swearing, 135

telephone, 140
Thatcher, Denis, 9
Thatcher, Margaret, 74, 165, 270
Tupperware parties, 70

unemployment, redundancy, 233–
   45

war, 24–5, 288
wedding rings, 279
weekends, 81–2

wives, 61–75, 323
   annoying habits, 53–5, 62, 250
   and children, 76–80, 217
   as friends, 43–4
   illness, death, of, 52, 255–6
   interests outside home, 46–8,
      59
   mothers as models for, 22–4, 76
   and unemployment, redundancy,
      233, 240–2
   see also cooking; divorce; house-
      work; marriage; and under
      love affairs; work
women
   different from men, 322
   and emotions, 57–9, 131, 139,
      249–50, 269–70
   new freedom of, 152, 292–309,
      328–9
   sense of identity, well-being,
      318–9
   illogical, 141
   good listeners, 139
   men's view of, 131–150, 325–9
   power in, 165
   stereotyped, 305
   strength, 282
   see also mothers; wives; and
      under appearance; work
Women's Lib, see feminism
work, jobs, careers (men), 206–32,
      282, 309
   choice of, 223–4
   and family life, 71–2, 78–83,
      216–7, 222, 301, 311–4, 317–9
   feedback concerning, 229
   motivation, 217–21
   promotion, 227–9, 284
   satisfaction from, 212–8, 225–7
   self-employment, 227
   stressful, 227–9
   wives' support with, 44–5, 71,
      142, 143, 311–4
   see also retirement; unemploy-
      ment
work, jobs, careers (women), 7–8,
      143, 222–3, 230–1, 242, 309,
      311–7, 319–20